LEGAL INTELLECTUALS IN CONVERSATION

Legal Intellectuals in Conversation

Reflections on the Construction of Contemporary American Legal Theory

James R. Hackney, Jr.

NEW YORK UNIVERSITY PRESS
New York and London

NEW YORK UNIVERSITY PRESS
New York and London
www.nyupress.org

References to Internet websites (URLs) were accurate at the time of writing. Neither the author nor New York University Press is responsible for URLs that may have expired or changed since the manuscript was prepared.

Library of Congress Cataloging-in-Publication Data
Hackney, James R., 1964-
Legal intellectuals in conversation : reflections on the construction of contemporary American legal theory / James R. Hackney, Jr.
p. cm.
Includes bibliographical references and index.
ISBN 978-0-8147-3707-1 (cl : alk. paper) — ISBN 978-0-8147-4543-4 (ebook) — ISBN 978-0-8147-6388-9 (ebook)
1. Law—United States—Philosophy. 2. Law—United States—Methodology. 3. Jurisprudence—United States. I. Title.
KF380.H33 2012
349.73—dc23 2012008354

New York University Press books are printed on acid-free paper, and their binding materials are chosen for strength and durability. We strive to use environmentally responsible suppliers and materials to the greatest extent possible in publishing our books.

Manufactured in the United States of America
10 9 8 7 6 5 4 3 2 1

To my colleagues in the academy

CONTENTS

ACKNOWLEDGMENTS

This is a unique project, given the interview format, and relies on support not generally required in the normal course of academic writing. I first thank the interview participants who were enormously gracious in giving their time and energy to the project. It was a personal and professional privilege for me to be able to get to know this collection of academic stars. Institutionally, this project benefited from the support of my dean, Emily Spieler, at the Northeastern University School of Law. Her generosity with research funding for a project that does not yield the traditional "law review article" is very much appreciated. I am also indebted to the comments and insights provided by participants in the Northeastern University School of Law faculty lunch discussion series. In addition, my colleagues Peter Enrich, Karl Klare, and Dan Schaffer were particularly helpful in commenting on drafts. Thanks to my editor, Deborah Gershenowitz, for her guidance and for sticking with me through this project. Also, thanks to the anonymous peer reviewers for their thoughtful suggestions. The most tedious part of getting this project completed was transcribing the tapes for the printed page. I was helped enormously by the able transcription of my research assistant, Josina Raisler-Cohn. Elsie Chan, my assistant, spent many hours helping me finalize this project, and I very much appreciate her diligence and hard work. Inevitably, this sort of project requires a lot of "away from home" time, so I am particularly grateful to my wife, Ann McCarthy Hackney, for being such a stalwart while I traveled the country in search of "interview gold," and to my son, Adrian Hackney, for not being too upset about my lack of presence and for the big hug that always awaited me upon my return.

INTRODUCTION

Some Thoughts on Biography

A bit of personal background is necessary to fully understand the motivation behind this project. I attended Yale Law School between 1986 and 1989. It was truly an exciting time to be at Yale, which had more of the feel of a think tank than a law school. There were ideas flying around from every direction, but the big idea that captivated my imagination was law and economics. This was a predictable outcome given my undergraduate training in economics. But law and economics was only one of an array of theoretical positions being bandied about, which included law and literature, feminist theory, liberal political theory, and philosophy of law. After a brief stint as a corporate lawyer, I eventually made my way into academia as a law professor at my current institution, Northeastern University. It was not until I arrived in Boston that I was introduced to critical legal studies through my colleague Karl Klare, and Duncan Kennedy and Morton Horwitz at Harvard Law School. It was principally through my exposure to Duncan and "Mort" that I became interested in intellectual history. My first major foray into intellectual history came in the form of *Under Cover of Science: American Legal-Economic Theory and the Quest for Objectivity*. I wrote that book very much under the influence of Michel Foucault's *Archaeology of Knowledge*. The focus was on the structural relationship between disciplines. Methodologically, I expressly underplayed the notion of influence, the extent to which individual authors exercised agency, and how their personal background fed into their work. I considered myself a structuralist. While I still do believe that there is much to be gleaned from a structuralist perspective on intellectual history, I found myself to be increasingly interested in the ways that the lives and social contexts of individuals shaped the movements in which they found themselves—a decidedly anti-structuralist inquiry. It was that impulse that acted as the catalyst for this project.

This collection of interviews is an attempt to provide a firsthand account of the movements, personalities, and ideas that so animated my time at Yale Law School and the legal academy in general during the 1980s through the lens of some of the era's major figures. Aside from my personal interest, why the 1980s? This decade was an extraordinary period in American legal theory. There were movements formed and intellectual battles waged. There were not only paradigm shifts, but also paradigm proliferation and disintegration—real battles. Importantly, this is the period that set the stage for the current, and to my mind future, terrain of the legal academy. It marked the shift in the legal academy from a largely doctrinally focused enterprise, to an arena in which high-level theoretical and interdisciplinary work thrives. The theoretical tracks we navigate today and will traverse into the future were laid down during this critical period in the 1980s. Also, as illustrated in these interviews, the developments in the 1980s were in many ways an extension of the sometimes-tumultuous social forces and legal developments that marked the 1960s. This is reflected in the profound demographic shift within the legal academy during the 1980s. During this period, for the first time in the legal academy, there was a critical mass of non-white-male voices. Issues of difference in the composition of the legal academy and the impact that law had on socially marginalized communities first began to surface in a serious way during this period. There was an incredibly high degree of intellectual, social, and cultural vibrancy in the legal academy and profession. This is why it is so vital that we understand this era.

The academics interviewed in this book represent several of the movements or schools of thought that ascended in the legal academy through the 1980s: law and economics, feminist legal theory, law and society, contemporary liberal constitutional theory, conservative/libertarian constitutional theory, critical legal studies, critical race theory, law and literature, law and philosophy, critical legal history, and postmodern theory. This is an admittedly partial list, but it does reflect a broad and representative range of contemporary legal theory. In laying out the plans for this project, I purposefully limited myself to one interview per movement (although some participants straddle multiple subject areas), and there were difficult choices to be made regarding who should be interviewed. Of course, no one individual can fully represent a movement, and I am not making the claim that any one of the interviewees is *the* representative. The final list of interviewees resulted from a combination of choice and fortuitousness. In the end, I was privileged to talk with an extraordinary collection of legal academics: Bruce Ackerman, Jules Coleman, Drucilla Cornell, Charles Fried, Morton Horwitz, Duncan Kennedy, Catharine MacKinnon, Richard Posner, Austin Sarat, and Patricia Williams. All of them entered the academy between the 1960s and 1980s. My interest in this group is no doubt, as Duncan Kennedy makes the point in our interview, the product of my being part of a transitional generation—old enough to have been a student at the tail end of some of the clamorous debates, but too young to have been involved in the initial formations or amid the more raucous disputes.

Why interview? The format is motivated by my earlier expressed interest in getting to know the lives and inspiration of the people engaged in these movements. The most prevalent application of the "interview" is, of course, in journalism. It may strike one as a strange undertaking in the academic setting, but there is a rich history of the interview as a mode of discourse in philosophy.[1] I first became fascinated by this format while viewing a grainy black-and-white movie featuring an interview with Jean-Paul Sartre and other French intellectuals associated with him (most prominently Simone de Beauvoir).[2] I had not been trained as a philosopher, and I knew very little about Sartre. But the interview captivated me because I really began to get a feel for Sartre and his intellectual/social "moment" over the course of the viewing. There is a presentness, spontaneity, and humanity in an interview that cannot be duplicated in exposition—which is one reason I insisted that the interviews be conducted face-to-face. (For accuracy purposes, I did have the interviewees assist in editing the transcripts.) It is a genre that poses unexpected surprises for both the interviewer and the interviewee, and, ideally, those who read the interviews.

There were many surprises during the course of these interviews. They ranged from the sublime, such as Jules Coleman's theory that "most of the people [he] knew who got into analytic philosophy began with existentialism," to the peculiarly personal, such as Drucilla Cornell's discussion of how as a young woman she "saw that Kant wasn't enough when it came to dating," so she turned to Hegel. And you can imagine my shock in finding out that Duncan Kennedy, a prominent critical legal studies founder and outspoken leftist, worked for the CIA in his youth. These interviews also gave me a better sense of historical events that I had read about but never experienced firsthand. For example, it is common knowledge that there was a lot of criticism of critical legal studies from various segments of the legal academy. But it was not until I made my way through these interviews that it became clear how the attraction, aversion, critique, defense, and reaction to critical legal studies was such a big part of the dynamic during the 1970s through the 1990s. Those who one might expect to be critical of critical legal studies—Jules Coleman, Richard Posner, and Bruce Ackerman—are in fact critical in ways that reveal deep animus that quickly surfaces during the interviews. But even "allies" of the critical legal studies movement—Drucilla Cornell, Austin Sarat, and Patricia Williams—reveal a complicated relationship. There is a similar complicated dynamic concerning law and economics, with even those who are sympathetic toward it—Bruce Ackerman, Jules Coleman, and Charles Fried—offering up a critique or qualifying their relationship with it. Of course, the critics of law and economics also reflect great disdain toward it. The soup is thickened once the play of interpersonal dynamics is added to the mix.

Yes, there is personal drama in the academy. Patricia Williams provides us with a revealing account of the way she and a handful of other faculty of color were uncomfortably put in the position of having to "represent" the views of people of color at a critical legal studies conference. Jules Coleman makes it clear that there is no way to understand the philosophical interchange between Ronald Dworkin and him without coming to grips with the complicated and at times nasty personal relationship between the two. Duncan Kennedy characterizes the critiques from Richard Posner and Ronald Dworkin as personal. Drucilla Cornell is blunt and personal in her criticism of Catharine MacKinnon's stance regarding women sex workers. In a twist of expectations, MacKinnon displays warmth toward Richard Posner and respect for the policy focus of law and economics. Particularly poignant is Morton Horwitz's personal disappointment and recollection of a walk through Harvard Yard with Robert McCloskey, the highly regarded Harvard constitutional law historian and Horwitz's teacher, during which McCloskey suggested, presumptively due to his fidelity to legal process norms as opposed to racial animus, that it would have been better if the U.S. Supreme Court had not overruled *Plessy v. Ferguson* (the case that approved race-based separate but equal laws, which was overruled in *Brown v. Board of Education*). These personal accounts not only are interesting peeks into the lives of prominent figures but also have an impact on their (and by extension the academy's) intellectual development. One theme that seemed to repeat itself, which fits with the general existential position of the academic, is the "outsider" status of many of those interviewed. Charles Fried's family, although economically privileged, had to flee Europe as Jewish émigrés. Morton Horwitz's father was a taxi driver and Horwitz discusses attending City College of New York (now City University of New York), which, while no longer the "poor kid's Harvard" due to Jewish students attending the school in the face of Ivy League anti-Semitism, catered to an underprivileged student body. Other interviewees cite their relatively modest economic background as part of the narrative relevant to their intellectual identity. Patricia Williams discusses the level of hyper-marginalization she endured as an African American woman attending Harvard Law School in the 1970s post-*Bakke* (the famous Unites States Supreme Court case that fueled debate on affirmative action). Being situated as an outsider and feeling the compulsion to "speak truth to power"—or, to frame it in less left-political terms, understand the "way the world works"—resonates with me as an African American who grew up in South Central Los Angeles.

"We Are All Legal Realists Now"

The now famous, or infamous, quote, "we are all legal realists now," has been so ensconced in the lore of the legal academy that it is stated without attribution. I take the essential meaning behind the quote to be that all jurisprudential positions post–legal realism are in someway a response to the central penumbra ascribed to the legal realists: the law/politics distinction. Legal realism has its roots in the late 19th and early 20th century. It was Oliver Wendell Holmes who in his landmark *Common Law* (1881) interrogated the natural law position that law was a preordained phenomenon separated from historical and social context. This was the beachhead both for the legal realist assault on natural law to follow, and the realist insight that law is infused with political interventions. One way to frame the trajectory of legal theory post–legal realism is that it is a site of contestation concerning to what extent politics frames law. I am using the term "politics" in a very broad sense to incorporate not just the notion of economic interest-group politics, but also the politics of culture, identity, and other sites of contestation. The law/politics dichotomy is highlighted in my interview with Duncan Kennedy, and he uses it as a unifying theme in his narrative of how legal theory has evolved. The conflict over the law/politics divide was reflected within legal realism. There were two prominent strands of legal realism. One emphasized examining the context of law. The emphasis was on empirical studies and sociological analysis regarding how legal rules affect society. Another, more controversial branch of legal realism emphasized the malleability of law. The negative implication of the malleability thesis is that not only do judges decide law, but they do so in ways that lack any fundamental principles—law as politics. This strand of legal realism came under heavy assault on several fronts, one of which being that in the aftermath of World War II critics took as legal realism's logical consequence that there was no principled way of ruling out legal and government regimes—including those with a totalitarian or Communist bent.

Limiting Politics through Legal Process

The legal process school, which developed in the 1950s, had as its central tenet the idea that the key to legitimating law (and limiting the incursion of politics) is proper process. This view of the world put a premium on various state actors, particularly judges, playing their proper role within the system. Legal process had as an underlying mission an effort to depoliticize law. This charge was particularly salient given the historical backdrop of World War II and the Cold War. Legal process arose against the background of anti-Communist sentiment and the specter of fascism. While there might not be a "right" substantive outcome for legal decisions, there was a correct, *democratic*, process for reaching those decisions.

For anyone attending an American law school from the 1950s through the 1960s, legal process and the general tilt against leftist thought (given fervent anti-Communist sentiment) pervaded their experience. Morton Horwitz eloquently discusses the hold of legal process and the influence of anti-Communist politics in the post-1950s legal academy. To the extent that legal academics during this period were not legal process adherents, which principally affected public law subjects such as constitutional and administrative law, they were doctrinalists without much of a theoretical view at all. The legal process school's "neutral principles" tenet and the doctrinalists' tacit approval of the status quo repulsed 1960s social movement activists.

In conducting my interviews I was struck by the ways the civil rights movement and the Vietnam War affected the generation that rose to prominence in the 1980s legal academy. For leftist students, the failure (by and large) of their legal process elders to support the judicial architecture of the civil rights movement, and the Warren Court more broadly, was damning. This was only heightened by the perceived paralysis of law school faculty concerning opposition to the Vietnam War. Conservatives attending law school during this same period drew an opposing lesson. The cause for concern was the radicalism and chaos generated by movement leftists as they "paraded through the streets and occupied faculty offices" at a time when the echoes of totalitarian regimes still shaped conservatives' views of political order. Richard Posner recalls that one reason for his moving away from a left-leaning political position as a young lawyer in the 1960s was that he "didn't like all the rioting of the late sixties, you know, the Vietnam stuff. I call that disorder."

The Law and Neoclassical Economics Moment

Law and economics, more precisely labeled law and neoclassical economics to make clear that it represents a particular strand of the economics tradition, adopts the position that the touchstone for analyzing law is the efficiency criterion. In 1960, an unassuming economist at the University of Chicago wrote a relatively slender article that would mark the beginnings of an academic and political revolution. The economist's name was Ronald Coase, and the article is titled "The Problem of Social Cost." "Social Cost" was revolutionary because it called into question the progressive, pro-government-intervention consensus, epitomized in the macroeconomics sphere by the belief in Keynesian economics. In law, it was manifest in the idea, largely attributed to the legal realists, that judicial intervention was necessary to aid the disadvantaged. "Social Cost" is a technical article infused with a larger political ideal. The technical point of the piece, that in a world of non-prohibitive transactions costs, private ordering (the free market) can solve the problem of socially detrimental individual behavior, may well have ended up on the proverbial ash bin of history had it not been for an impending political revolution.

In 1962 a "B actor" and General Electric pitchman by the name of Ronald Reagan switched his political affiliation from Democrat to Republican. It was the initial step in a long journey that would eventually lead him to the U.S. presidency and what has been referred to as the "Reagan revolution." Daniel Yergin has done a masterful job of chronicling the ideas and events that culminated in the demise of what has been labeled the "commanding heights" (referring to social regimes in which the economies are managed from the commanding heights of government).[3] The prevailing pro-government-intervention consensus fueled the ire of Friedrich Hayek in his 1944 tract *The Road to Serfdom*. Post–World War II there was a flood of commentary from conservative economists lauding the virtues of the free market in the spirit (and sometimes under the direct tutelage) of Hayek. A few decades later this would be personified in Milton Friedman's wildly popular *Free to Choose* (1980). Friedman and others from the University of Chicago exemplified the model of technically trained economist as free market proselytizer.

Both the free market ideology and neoclassical economics techniques would eventually make their way into the heart of law schools. In 1972 Richard Posner wrote a comprehensive text applying neoclassical economics techniques to legal issues, *Economic Analysis of Law*. Posner was a Harvard-trained lawyer who had some exposure to economic analysis while working as a government bureaucrat in Washington, D.C. But it was not until Posner encountered Aaron Director, an influential University of Chicago economist, while a law faculty member at Stanford that he began to be immersed in neoclassical economics. He very soon moved to the University of Chicago Law School, which, in affiliation with the University of Chicago business and economics departments, was at the center of the movement to spread conservative ideas. While Posner was a free market adherent, there were also moderate/left-leaning practitioners of law and neoclassical economics. In 1970 Guido Calabresi, a descendent of Yale Law School legal realism, applied neoclassical economics to tort law in his pathbreaking *Costs of Accidents*. Calabresi could best be described as a political progressive with pro-consumer impulses. Neoclassical economics had also been placed at the center of antitrust law with Robert Bork's *Antitrust Paradox* (1978). The touchstone of the legal economists, irrespective of political orientation or doctrinal field, was a belief that legal rules and policy could be examined and prescribed through the lens of economic analysis. The legal economists were clearly on the law-as-nonpolitical end of the law/politics spectrum exposed by the legal realists.

The Birth of Critical Studies and Diversity in the Legal Academy

As law and economics was making its way through the legal academy, establishing a foothold in virtually every area of law, at the same time, ironically (or predictably), the leftist critical legal studies movement was also forming. Three of its founding members (Morton Horwitz, Duncan Kennedy, and Roberto Unger) began teaching at the Harvard Law School in the early 1970s. Subsequently, through the mid-1970s, the critical legal studies movement was formed. The initial critical legal studies meeting featured a conglomeration of leftist legal academics that included David Trubek and others who would become prominent in the law and society movement. While critical legal studies enjoyed a period of organizational momentum (roughly 1977 to 1994), as measured by periodic conferences, the law and society movement became firmly entrenched institutionally through the efforts of leaders such as Austin Sarat and continues to have a significant presence in the academy. Law and society adherents were engaged in a form of scholarship that hewed more closely, but not exclusively, to the empirical strand of legal realism. They were largely social scientists interested in legal phenomena. Critical legal studies scholars were more explicitly leftist and political in their approach, and had an affinity for the cultural wing of legal realism. The "crits" were apt to highlight the political dimensions of law. The tension ultimately resulted in the two groups failing to coalesce.

An intriguing development in critical legal studies is the emphasis on historicism. Morton Horwitz is an exemplar of a critical approach to history, but he is joined by such prominent legal historians as Robert Gordon, Lawrence Friedman, and John Henry Schlegel. Their ascendancy in the legal academy illustrates the growing presence of left-leaning historians in the years following the 1960s. But the influx of historians into the academy also highlights a more general phenomenon—an increasing number of PhDs in the legal academy. The increase in PhDs was truly a supply-demand phenomenon. On the one hand, newly minted PhDs found it increasingly difficult to find positions in humanities and social science departments. On the other hand, law schools (particularly elite schools) were rapidly moving away from the law professor as doctrinalist model to the scholar as prototype.

Along with the increased focus on theory was an unprecedented demographic diversification of law school faculty. Prior to the 1960s, women and people of color were in large part not allowed to join law school faculty. Beginning in the late 1960s, however, things began to change. This phenomenon cannot be appreciated without taking into account its connection to larger social movements. In particular, the women's and civil rights movements helped catalyze diversity in law school admissions and faculty hiring. This shift brought along with it intellectual diversity. Feminist legal theory made its way into law schools through the women's movement and gender studies. Catharine MacKinnon played a major role in reorienting the lens through which the legal academy viewed issues affecting women. For example, MacKinnon argued that rape was part of a continuum of violence against women that was embedded in an inherently sexist culture. Concerning civil rights and race, Derrick Bell argued that law was not neutral, and could be understood only through the prism of race. His was a first foray into the field that would become known as critical race theory. Critical race theory also included among its founders such noted scholars as Richard Delgado, and has mushroomed into a multi-organizational phenomenon—including the highly influential LatCrit movement. Patricia Williams, a student of Bell's, is often identified with critical race theory. While historically Williams is most definitely a key figure in critical race theory, her writing is decidedly eclectic. She is widely noted for being in the vanguard of narrative form in legal scholarship, a technique also utilized by Derrick Bell, and specializes in the essay genre. Feminist and critical race theories are left-oriented movements, and they both have an intriguing theoretical and social connection to critical legal studies.

Critical legal studies, given its origins at the beginning of the diversity period, was at first an overwhelmingly white male movement. As progressive-leaning women and people of color joined the academy, however, many were naturally drawn to political and theoretical positions associated with critical legal studies. Critical feminist theory, critical legal studies, and critical race theory share a belief that society is not regulated by the neutral hand of law, but that law is a socially constituted product dictated by social-power dynamics—be they gender, economic status, or race. While critical legal studies emphasized class dynamics, "fem crits" and "race crits" were more interested in identity politics. This belief in the social situatedness of law led crits to be suspicious about claims of neutral rationality in law given the terrain of unequal power distribution. The political dimensions of law cannot be ignored.

The Law and Economics/Crit Divide and the Construction of Contemporary American Legal Theory

In large part law and economics, at least as originally formulated in the early 1970s, and critical legal theory represent opposite responses to the law/politics debate opened up by the legal realists. The theme of law and economics is that politics can be circumscribed by deploying the scientific techniques of economic analysis as the principal tool for doing legal theory—separating law from politics. The crits argue that there is no way to neatly separate law and politics. Crits do not take the position that the law is all politics. There are agreed-on "rules of the game." And those who actively oppose the crits, including law and economics adherents, for the most part do not argue that law is totally devoid of politics. The argument is over how broadly to draw the lines of demarcation. The different movements represented in this collection draw the lines in various and complex ways. Moreover, the line drawing is not uniform within movements, with individuals and subgroups within movements taking varying positions on the matter. These complexities frequently surfaced in the interviews. As a prelude to the interviews, it is useful to delve more deeply into how the participants and their movements fit into the law/politics narrative—with a particular focus on methodology.

When one drills down deep into the theoretical core of neoclassical economics, the unifying belief is in the individual (be that personal or in the form of a business entity) as the basis for analysis. In addition, there is an overlay that the individual is a rational actor. This assumption allows for models of the economic world to be constructed with mathematical elegance. The norm of economic efficiency justifies constructing legal rules to conform to the model because decisions based on the efficiency criterion inure to the public good. This was the basic position taken by Richard Posner in *Economic Analysis of Law* and defended by him in large part under the guise of wealth maximization (which resembles utilitarianism) through the early 1980s. Post-1980s, Posner has since taken up the mantle of pragmatism—defending free market economic policies as justified because of their practical benefits.

Rights theorists approach the world from the perspective of political philosophy but share with neoclassical economists the view that the individual is the locus of analysis. But the rights theorist imbues the individual with an assortment of rights. What this set of rights entails may differ wildly depending on the particular position of any individual rights theorist. John Rawls established the terms of debate regarding contemporary discourse in political philosophy concerning rights theory with the 1971 publication of his pathbreaking work, *A Theory of Justice*. The leading rights theorist in law over the last few decades is Ronald Dworkin. Dworkin's *Taking Rights Seriously* (1977) articulates his vision of the crucial nature of rights in society, and is a frontal assault on legal positivism and utilitarianism. Bruce Ackerman utilizes the rights approach in conjunction with the ideal of citizenship to argue that each individual in the United States has a right to a certain set of economic goods, linking his rights approach to constitutional jurisprudence. This is a rationalist point of view because it is a claim based on rights as being inalienable (determined as a matter of citizenship), and constitutional jurisprudence logically derived therefrom. Ackerman has come to recognize the significant role that the politics of citizenship can play in our evolving view of the Constitution, but he rejects the crit view of law as politics.

There is a strand of conservative constitutionalism that is also rights based. The lineage in terms of contemporary political theory can be traced to Robert Nozick's *Anarchy, State, and Utopia* (1974). Charles Fried's libertarian constitutionalism is centered on the idea that each individual has a set of liberty interests. The rights to liberty set constitutional constraints on the government's ability to impinge on individual liberties. This form of constitutionalism is conservative because it argues for a limited government role in the economic and social sphere. Its adherents situate rights as being foundationally determined and legal rules flowing logically from them (analogous to the left-liberal formulation), because the liberty interest is taken as the absolute basis for law. There is another form of conservative constitutionalism that is not represented in this set of interviews, one that is more Burkean in nature. An originalist constitutionalist believes that the basis of constitutional decision making has to begin with the original intent of those who produced the document. We can determine appropriate constitutional law by digging up its original meaning.

Of course, there is a rich history of philosophical speculation related to law that is not focused on constitutional jurisprudence. Post–World War

II philosophy is marked by the rise of analytic philosophy (which includes under its rubric logical positivism). One of the chief goals of analytic philosophers is to apply rigor and discipline to the discussion of concepts. The analytic philosopher dissects arguments in order to clarify statements. Ronald Dworkin used this approach in thinking about rights, and Rawls's *Theory of Justice* and Nozick's *Anarchy, State, and Utopia* have a decidedly analytic bent. Jules Coleman comes out of the analytic tradition, and his work in tort law theory is built on careful consideration of what we mean when we talk about justice. Coleman's discussion of corrective justice in tort law demonstrates that the reach of philosophy extends beyond debates regarding constitutional rights. Coleman has also been a central figure in the debates surrounding legal positivism, an approach to conceptualizing law that runs counter to the rights view. Legal philosophers share a belief that the rigors of rational analysis will sharpen our understanding, and they are skeptical of critical claims of law as politics. They provide an analytic counterweight to Posner's ideal (as articulated in the 1970s) of efficiency. Both Coleman and Dworkin criticize core tenets of law and economics. But they have a fundamental disagreement regarding the nature of law—with Dworkin rejecting Coleman's legal positivism. Coleman's evolution toward pragmatism (away from an analytic view) is symptomatic of the shift in Anglo-American philosophy. (A similar shift can be found in Rawls, Nozick, and Dworkin.) But he is careful to formulate his vision of pragmatism in a way that does not pull him too far over the political divide. This is evident in his criticism of both Richard Rorty—perhaps the most popular neopragmatist, and a darling of the left—and what Coleman identifies as "skeptical or cynical" versions of pragmatism.

Law and society adherents are concerned with making discoveries that shed light on legal questions. There are a multitude of approaches taken in this endeavor, but a heavy emphasis is placed on social science research. Austin Sarat's background and scholarship typifies the law and society model. He has a PhD in political science, and attended law school subsequent to establishing himself as a political scientist at Amherst. His scholarship attempts to get at the "truth" of law by performing inquiries (ethnographies) related to legal topics such as the death penalty. The idea is that you cannot really understand how the death penalty works in the United States unless you delve into the details regarding players in the system. Law and society scholars adopt a view of legal theory as a rational enterprise in the sense that they believe that excavating facts is central to the process of revealing the truth regarding the law's operation and impact. But there is also a social constructivist strand of law and society, represented by the "later Sarat" as reflected in our interview, which is more open to taking into account the cultural dimensions of law and has some affinity with critical legal studies.

Post-1960s critical legal studies scholars were in the vanguard of questioning the claim that law is an apolitical enterprise. For crits this often meant uncovering the economic/class dynamics underpinning law. We see this move in Morton Horwitz's critical histories, which have a decidedly economic determinist bent. Horwitz works to discredit both Whig accounts of the common law unfolding without political influence and liberal notions of progress. While crits would by and large reject crude Marxist claims regarding economic determinism, they do focus on the role that economic interests play in constructing legal policy. There is also a strand of critical legal studies that is more attuned to cultural criticism. Duncan Kennedy calls on postmodern theorists such as Michel Foucault in his cultural critique of law as false consciousness.

Feminists reject the idea that one can understand or transform law without keeping track of gender dynamics. Catharine MacKinnon has championed the view that male patriarchy is at the heart of law and the societal infrastructure writ large. In particular, the way the law handles issues related to sex (particularly rape and pornography) underscores that it is a male-centered enterprise. Drucilla Cornell takes a similar view of the world, but is flexible in her analysis of male/female sex dynamics. These differences make themselves present in the two radically divergent approaches that MacKinnon and Cornell take concerning prostitution. Cornell's postmodern view regarding the play of life leads her to reject the position that there is a fixed male/female hierarchy that necessarily renders sex work an act of subordination. MacKinnon views prostitution as part of the sexist continuum. Cornell argues that it can actually be a manifestation of women as "sexuate" beings, and refuses to substitute her vision of the "good life" for those engaged in prostitution. Cornell's solution to the subordination of sex workers is union organization in an effort to empower women. Her sense of play is symptomatic of postmodern theorists who call into question any modernist quest to objectify and render static social relationships (including law). (Duncan Kennedy shares a similar view on the plasticity of law.) The play of social construction is evident in Cornell's work, calling on Frantz Fanon, on the existential dynamics of race. Cornell has not only been influential in utilizing postmodern insights in her own work but also played a historically significant role in introducing Continental philosophers, Jacques Derrida most famously, to the United States.

The civil rights movement and 1960s racial politics both cleared the way for professors of color to become faculty members at law schools in nontrivial numbers, and also provided inspiration for theorizing the impact of race on law. Ironically, the book most recognized as ushering in critical race theory, Derrick Bell's *And We Are Not Saved*, is actually a text that questions the viability of a civil rights–oriented approach to legal reform, a reoccurring theme in critical race theory. Bell interrogates the notion that civil rights laws were enacted for the benefit of black progress. In fact, those laws would not have been placed on the books, according to Bell, unless they served the interests of whites. The activist component, with tinges of black nationalist sentiment, of critical race theory is revealed in the protest movement to have the subject taught at Harvard Law School in 1981. There is also an effort to concretize experiences of people of color and their relationship to law, focusing on existential concerns. Frantz Fanon's *Black Skin, White Masks* comes to mind. This desire to illustrate existential realities is evident in the "storytelling" genre in critical race theory as utilized by Derrick Bell, Richard Delgado, Patricia Williams, and others. Williams utilizes the essay form to explore the deep interior of identity on multiple levels. Kimberlé Crenshaw, another prominent critical race theorist, does the same type of work through her intersectionality analysis. Williams's postmodern inquiry encapsulates race, gender, and cultural insights similar to those of Drucilla Cornell. The very form of her work, the essay (frequently with first-person subject position), presses against apolitical accounts.

21st-Century Legal Academia

All the legal academics interviewed for this project have their roots in the 20th century, but the seeds of the movements and theories they are associated with have blossomed into the 21st century. In the latter part of the 20th century, you could identify the major players and movements in the legal academy. Today the legal academy is much more dispersed and specialized. The specialization trend had its origins in the 1980s. It was then that we began to see a proliferation of PhD-qualified legal academics.

Specialization is a product of the increasingly interdisciplinary and theoretical nature of the legal academy generally. There is also, as evidenced by some of the interviewees, a growing trend toward adopting a neopragmatist position regarding the use and place of theory. This move to pragmatism, which has a tendency to soften the hard edges of theoretical conflict, may be further evidence of what Duncan Kennedy refers to as the death of legal theory. While I appreciate Kennedy's position regarding the decline of "grand" legal theory, and this book may be viewed by some as memorializing the event, I have a slightly different view regarding future developments.

In these interviews, I discuss with the participants my view that, because of increased specialization, the legal academy does not have broad intellectual conversations that cut across disciplines. Of course, this contradicts the trend of scholars occupying interdisciplinary fields. Increasingly, debates are being waged within relatively narrow subdisciplines that are "interdisciplinary" but scarcely affect the larger academic community. While the movements represented by the interviewees for this book began the interdisciplinary trend, their impact was all the more significant because they spoke across the legal academy and beyond. This accounts for the fact that many of the interviewees can fairly be described as public intellectuals. The conversation across perspectives, even if it at times came in the form of angry shouting, helped forge some of the most meaningful ideas produced in the legal academy to date. In the end, this is the true legacy of the era. Today's specialists move forward, within their particular subspecialty, doing (borrowing from Thomas Kuhn) "normal science" in the theoretical fields established by the previous generation. Legal theory is not dead. However, it is increasingly siloed. Will the next generation have such a rich field of theoretical inquiry to till?

We might correctly dub this moment in legal academe the era of neopragmatism. However we label the current intellectual enterprise in the legal academy, its origins are found in, and it is in the end shaped by, the generation represented in this text. It is for this reason that we (speaking as one who is forty-seven years of age at the writing of this essay and straddles this generational fault line) owe such a great debt to the contributors to this book, and can still today learn much from their theoretical, historical, and political musings.

NOTES

1. Peter Osborne, *A Critical Sense: Interviews with Intellectuals* (Routledge 1996); Raoul Mortley, *French Philosophers in Conversation* (Routledge 1991); Theo Pinkus, *Conversations with Lukács* (MIT Press 1975, orig. pub. 1967).
2. *Sartre by Himself* (1979, Alexadre Astruc and Michel Contat directors).
3. Daniel Yergin and Joseph Stanislaw, *The Commanding Heights: The Battle between Government and the Marketplace That Is Remaking the Modern World* (Simon & Schuster 1998).

Duncan Kennedy is the Carter Professor of General Jurisprudence at the Harvard Law School. He is most famously known for helping to found and promote the critical legal studies movement. Professor Kennedy has written several books, including *The Rise and Fall of Classical Legal Thought* (1975), *Legal Education and the Reproduction of Hierarchy* (1983), *Sexy Dressing* (1995), and *A Critique of Adjudication* (1998). Professor Kennedy has made significant contributions to the history of legal theory. In his role as a founder of critical legal studies, he helped to introduce Continental legal theory to the American legal academy. Professor Kennedy has also contributed to policy analysis in a host of legal areas, frequently utilizing economic analysis, while at the same time being highly critical of the dominant Chicago school law and economics approach. His work also explores the role of legal education in society.

1

Critical Legal Studies

DUNCAN KENNEDY

HACKNEY: Why did you make the choice to become a legal academic?

KENNEDY: For me, becoming a legal academic was a third choice—given my druthers I would have been a novelist. And if not a novelist, I would have been a participant in a liberal political reform movement as a wielder of state power. Being a legal academic began to look good to me when I was in law school. When I began law school it never occurred to me to go into legal academics, but both the novelist option and the wielder of state power option suddenly began to look much less plausible. There I was in law school and I discovered that I had the knack for being a law student. It was a period of time when we were all very cocky about our talents and possibilities. I thought that this was something through which I could develop both my literary side and my political activist side, but also that I was better at it than I was at either of those other things.

HACKNEY: And who was the U.S. president when you went to law school?

KENNEDY: Johnson was the president, so the idea of working for the government as a left political activist was at least somewhat plausible when I started, but it was unraveling fast while I was in law school. I worked for the Central Intelligence Agency for two years before I went to law school. During the time I worked for the CIA, and during my first year of law school, there was this dramatic shift going on both in me and, more important, in the country. So this was the moment of polarization in which, between 1966 and 1969, there was the split of the liberal camp into a radical antiwar part and a centrist or you might say loyalist part, with the division suddenly arriving all across the culture. I was completely affected by it. I was radicalized between 1966 and 1969. The liberal option became far less attractive in every way. But also, the liberals began their long slide. The right was coming to power—not instantly, you know, it was slow, but the handwriting was on the wall—the reaction had begun.

HACKNEY: The CIA, that's interesting. What did you do for them?

KENNEDY: I worked in the CIA's National Student Association operation, which was basically part of the Cold War liberalism project. It was government-funded sponsorship of youth and student pro-democracy political activities. I was a Cold War liberal. So I hated Communists above all, and thought that this highly deceptive activity was well worth it in the world of the Communist threat. But another thing that happened to me and a lot of other people between 1966 and 1969 was that we really lost our belief not just in the virtuousness of the U.S. role in the world, but also in the Communist threat. A major reason for that was that the Soviet Union was obviously in sharp and irreversible decline. The Prague Spring was very significant. Not because it showed what a big threat the Soviet Union was, but because it showed that the Soviet Union was basically no longer a threat because it could only maintain itself in Central Europe by violence. Therefore, it was not a plausible threat. The United States began to seem like a much worse threat—both abroad and domestically.

HACKNEY: Now, undergraduate, what did you major in? I know you attended Harvard College.

KENNEDY: I studied development economics.

HACKNEY: Were there professors who particularly influenced you in the economics department?

KENNEDY: The person who was prominently identified with the kind of economics I believed in was John Kenneth Galbraith, but he was at the time the U.S. ambassador to India. He was not there. Of the two professors who had the biggest effect on me, one wasn't an economist. He was

Edward Banfield, a reactionary University of Chicago–trained sociologist, who was allied with James Q. Wilson. However, he was a sharp, politically acute, interesting manipulator and understander of how neoclassical thinking could be combined with sociological thinking. I thought he was great—politically alien but a great teacher and with amazing critical intelligence.

The other person was Richard Caves, who was a liberal. He's still alive, and an emeritus Harvard professor. He was an industrial organizations specialist, but he wasn't an institutionalist. He was a neoclassical industrial organizations person, very well respected at the time, but he taught us all the critiques of simpleminded neoclassical policy prescriptions. So there was Banfield, who had a neoclassical critique of all liberal policies, and Caves who had critiques of all the neoclassical policy prescriptions from an industrial organizations point of view. The other person was Carl Kaysen, who taught both in the economics department and at Harvard Law School, and was one of the early people doing law and economics of antitrust. He was a liberal who taught a graduate economics course in antitrust that I took. His basic message was that the mainstream neoclassical arguments that prescribed deregulation were all wrong. So I was exposed to these three sets of critiques by economists, which had as their message there's a very good reason why an economist, on economic grounds, would reject either simpleminded liberal solutions, or the simpleminded conservative solutions. That was my training.

HACKNEY: That must have been a great background for law school because Guido Calabresi was at Yale, and law and economics, I assume, was in the air, right?

KENNEDY: Calabresi was there. Calabresi was writing *The Costs of Accidents*, but had not published it yet. I think he published it in 1970. Actually, law and economics at Yale was represented by Robert Bork.

HACKNEY: This was based on Bork's work in *The Antitrust Paradox*?

KENNEDY: Yes, Bork wrote his first antitrust article before we got there. Calabresi was rising into prominence but just developing his book, which was much better than the articles that he'd written up till then. The articles were all basically somewhat confused in their encounter with the Coase theorem. *The Costs of Accidents* actually did develop a coherent way of understanding the Coase theorem as a lawyer. Calabresi was not very charismatic. He had a quality that we perhaps unfairly interpreted as preening, and we thought he was condescending to us. The faculty was divided up into different schools, but law and economics was just Calabresi and Bork (and Ward Bowman and Ralph Winter, who was eventually to become a right-wing, Reagan-appointed federal judge).

Bork and Calabresi had nothing to do with one another. Bork was a right-wing University of Chicago law and economics person, and Calabresi was the complete enemy of the Bork approach. Much more characteristic of the general faculty were the Harvard people (Calabresi was allied with them), who were Harry Wellington, Alexander Bickel, and Ronald Dworkin. Wellington, Bickel, and Dworkin were all graduates of Harvard Law School, *Harvard Law Review* editors, and Supreme Court clerks—totally into the deep questions of reasoned elaboration and principled adjudication—the liberal rights people agonizing about what to say about the Warren Court at the very height of its activism. They were much more dominant as a group than law and economics types. In fact, we used to say, we student lefties at Yale, that what had basically happened was that Harvard had become Yale and Yale had become Harvard because these people were so dominant. And then there were the social science people; they were another important faction on the faculty, but they were not economists.

HACKNEY: Did the social scientists represent remnants of legal realism?

KENNEDY: They weren't remnants—they were alive and kicking 1960s law and society types. The three principal players were Abe Goldstein, Joseph Goldstein, and Stanton Wheeler. They were all into psychology and criminology. Joseph Goldstein was into psychoanalysis. So that was a significant subcategory of the senior faculty—the law and social sciences people.

Law and economics, as a dominant force in the legal academy, doesn't begin to come into its own, until, I would say, 1975. When I was on the law teaching market in 1970, the fall of 1970, I interviewed at the University of Chicago, invited by Richard Posner, who was very nice to me. He was just beginning to be what we would call "Richard Posner" because he had just published his article about why the fellow-servant rule was good, laying out the critique of modern tort law as interference with free market functioning. At the time, that was a complete outlier position. Most people who read it and could understand it thought it was an outlandish attack from the right on what every good liberal knew was the rational truth. So it was a scandal rather than an intellectual wave.

HACKNEY: So Ronald Coase had not percolated through the legal academy?

KENNEDY: Calabresi and Posner were percolating Coase. That was how it was percolated. There was no other percolation in mainstream legal academia.

In Chicago, there were antitrust people, so the antitrust people were aware of Coase.

HACKNEY: Yes, applied economics. One other strand prominent in your intellectual thought is the Continental strand. Can you describe how you encountered the wave of Continental theorists?

KENNEDY: I was very influenced from the beginning by two strands of Continental thought: the critical theory, Western Marxist, and post-Marxist strand (which would include Herbert Marcuse and Jean-Paul Sartre—two important parts of that); and the structuralist strand (particularly Claude Levi-Strauss and Jean Piaget). So how did I encounter them? Well, in two ways. First of all, I was just a child of the zeitgeist. These ideas were very much in fashion with the intellectual left beginning in the late sixties through the seventies. They were in fashion in a way that is unimaginable now. Most people who thought of themselves as in some left intellectual space were at least a little interested in studying them. So that was one thing. And that applied both to the critical theory and to the structuralist strand. The other thing is that I was a person who was very open to European influence because I grew up in Cambridge in a milieu where people prided themselves on their cosmopolitanism, and the meaning of cosmopolitanism was basically the other side of the English Channel, the Continent, with "Continental this," and "Continental that." We were the "Continentals"—as in the *Saturday Night Live* parody by Christopher Walken. I spent two years of my life in France as a young man. I spoke French, and I could read French easily. I was in a good position to put together this sort of Continental fashion with my post-realist Yale legal education.

HACKNEY: So what age were you when you actually lived in France?

KENNEDY: The first time I lived in France, after I graduated from Andover, I went by myself at the age of eighteen. I lived in Paris, and worked as a clerk in a bank for the equivalent of $120 a month. It was a formative experience. After college, I worked for the CIA in Paris for a year.

HACKNEY: When you first began teaching at Harvard, what was your first set of courses, and when you sat down to think about your existential position, how did you deal with the common set of questions facing any beginning professor: How am I going to approach teaching law and students? How am I going to approach my scholarship? There's always that moment when you first become a law professor when you ask yourself, "Well, what am I going to do here?"

KENNEDY: Sure. I saw myself as part of a collective generational movement—not an organized movement, but collective. I had a strong sense that there was a "we," who were the student law school generation of the period from 1967 to 1971. We had had a striking and unusual experience in law school of rebellion against law school, but also we had begun to think about law in a way that was significantly to the left of the liberal orthodoxy. The mainstream of the law school world was not conservatism; the mainstream was liberalism. This was a cultural critique as well as a political and intellectual critique. The cultural critique was that law schools were governed by an uptight, straight, white male ethos, which was authoritarian. Not everyone was personally authoritarian, but it was organized around the power of the authoritarians. There were "hard" guys and "soft" guys. The soft guys were nice, but they were powerless in relationship to the hard guys. That was a key idea conveyed through legal training. The world is structured around the hard/soft distinction, and the hard dominates. Hard trumps soft. The system, the professorial system, was then mirrored among the students. It produced a kind of "training for hierarchy," to coin a phrase.

One goal, which I had right from the beginning, from the very first day of class, was to teach the class in ways that would undermine or counteract that culture. This involved figuring out different ways to interact with students in the Socratic classroom because I believed in the Socratic method, and I still do. I like large classes, and I like the drama and excitement of the large class. I didn't like the ethos of the intimate, supportive small group as the alternative to the harsh, cruel world because that was just reproducing the hard/soft dichotomy. So my goal as a beginning law teacher was to find a way to be inside the spectacle, the theatrical spectacle, of the large, 140-person, first-year classroom, and turn it into something whose meaning was as much as possible the opposite of training students to be either nasty, hard-guy authoritarians or nice but powerless soft guys.

The question was how could the classroom experience be changed through teacher-student interaction, and the structuring of events? It involved creating an atmosphere in which students really did talk, and teaching in a way that did not "hide the ball." An important part of the structure of the typical first-year classroom was that the teacher talked to the smart students, and basically gave them a sense that they were part of a quite deep and sort of secret knowledge that you have to be very sophisticated and quick to pick up. Large numbers of first-year students were basically just slogging through, doing their best to survive from day to day, and they never got it. So the idea was to abolish that distinction between the student elite and the student masses, by making some of the basic "secret" stuff available to everybody, making it explicit. It was also important that these "student masses" included a brand-new wave of women students and students of color, as well as white male students who hadn't been that well prepared for law school, or who were culturally out of sync with the particular style of the hard-guy professors. It was an egalitarian agenda inside the elite world of law school.

That was the pedagogical agenda. I also had an intellectual agenda that related to my course offerings. I was interested in private law. Why? Because private law was the elementary material from which lawyers' attitudes toward law were formed. In my generation, almost everybody was obsessed with constitutional law because of the waning Warren Court. The Warren Court, which was being replaced by the Burger Court and was just disappearing, was still the icon and the obsession of all leftists. The idea that the Supreme Court was a profound transformative agent, for most people in the legal culture, was just the "thing."

I was more sympathetic to the radical people who saw the Supreme Court as over and over and again selling out, and not taking sufficiently seriously the more radical demands for justice of groups that were excluded. I also thought that it was a mistake to focus on the Supreme Court. The thing to focus on was the base on which all the attitudes of the Supreme Court were ultimately constructed, which was private law. This is the reason I taught contract law.

Also, I thought that if you wanted to affect legal education, you had to get into the core. Again, another structure of legal education was that soft people taught upper-level courses in regulatory, humanistic, and "feel-good" fields. Tough, strong, hard, and powerful people taught basic first-year courses, and dominated the classroom. So the idea was to get out of the soft-guy pigeonhole, and challenge the hard guys on their own terrain. So I taught contracts and legal history as my two main fields, except for the first year. Al Sacks, dean of Harvard Law School, persuaded me to teach the legal process course, which I did. After that, I taught trusts for a couple years because the idea there was to get inside private law, to the part of private law that was excluded because it was too altruistic and too "goody-goody," and to bring it back in relationship to the property-contracts-torts parts. This had actually been part of the agenda of Harvard Law School up until World War II, when trusts was finally eliminated from the curriculum. So I taught trusts for a few years, but the main things I did were contracts and legal history.

A big aspect of first-year private law teaching for me was to undermine some conservative ideas that were very prevalent even in the (fading) liberal heyday. The most important was that there were deep problems with interference with freedom of contract, whether in contract law, tort law, or property law, because liberal intervention "hurts the people you are trying to help," and is condescending and paternalist to boot. Liberal students were unprepared for these arguments, and I taught them as best I could the standard but too often forgotten responses of earlier generations of legal progressives. I didn't consider this indoctrination, since I presented both liberal and conservative arguments very fully and left the students completely free to choose.

My upper-level course was "The History of Legal Thought." The idea of legal history was that legal history was the place to do the critical, theoretical, and structuralist reconceptualization of legal theory. So legal history and legal theory were, in my view, the same.

HACKNEY: Did you approach it as intellectual history? When we think about legal history, it's normally not constructed as intellectual history.

KENNEDY: I called it the history of legal thought, which was intellectual history, except it was intellectual history of law, and it was loaded with legal doctrine. In this first stage of my legal history work, the thing that I was most interested in was what you might call a "death of reason" narrative. That stream ran parallel to the leftist stream, which for me at the time was about class struggle. The death of reason stream was about how elites work to keep law in the domain of the structured, rational, and necessary. What I liked was that the jurists' own internal critiques of their rivals' efforts to keep law rational were undermining the whole enterprise in a kind of process of mutual destruction.

The American legal elite repeatedly engaged in a process of reform and critique, and then reconstruction. Each time the pretensions to rationality of legal science were reduced, making it more contingent, and more political, but still retaining a sharp law/politics distinction. The original, rational conception of American law was extremely powerful, barely even threatened on any level by politics. But over time the politics part got greater and greater, and the law part shrank and became a small defensive enclave, with very strong fences, razor wire, guard dogs, and electrification of the fence, as it got smaller and smaller.

I stuck to the American legal elite in telling this story, because I didn't know anything about any other system, and I had a pretty strong nativist prejudice against European legal thought. Since then, I've gone in the other direction, and I tend to understand the American legal thought story as part of the general narrative of the history of reason in the West, of which law was a part everywhere, along with the history of religion and the history of science. I think of the history of legal thought, in the context of the histories of religion and science, as part of a general Weberian process of disenchantment or derationalization. Max Weber was to be the first person to write about the history of Western law from that perspective. I didn't realize how many other people actually had done a lot of these things. My purpose was to get way beyond legal realism. The idea was that the realists had been so committed to policy science and policy analysis as the way in which they would preserve the law/politics distinction that they were never able to take their own critique seriously.

People often say that the kind of stuff that I was doing at that point (and that the rest of us were doing, too) was an extension of the realist project, and that's true, but it was a big, big, big extension. The people who were actually the heirs of the realists often hated us because, as you are well aware, the scientistic dimension of realist thought was very powerful and dominant—the engineering metaphor. The realists really didn't think that they were dissolving anything except idiotic formalism. Get rid of that, and we will have something that is "hard" to substitute for it, which is rational policy thinking. We crits were basically doing to policy analysis what the realists had done to formal doctrine. So this is a big difference between critical legal studies and legal realism. We were targeting our critique on legal realism. People constantly say, "Well, isn't it all in legal realism?" No! It's the opposite. Legal realism did to legal doctrine what we did to policy analysis. (And it was very hard to do.) The policy analysts, moreover, were very quick to see the difference. People who were the liberal constitutionalists couldn't see the difference, but the people who did policy analysis saw it immediately.

HACKNEY: The social science folks at Yale that you talked about previously could see it coming a mile away.

KENNEDY: Yes, absolutely.

HACKNEY: You kind of slipped from the "I," Duncan Kennedy, to the "we." Perhaps this is the moment to think about the genesis of critical legal studies [CLS] because, I suppose, that's the "we." You're situated here at Harvard Law School, and have a constellation of thoughts in your mind that definitely seem to be a precursor to what we view as critical legal studies. Whom did you first begin to talk with about that set of ideas? Was it your law school group or people here at Harvard?

KENNEDY: That's fairly easy to answer because we've been around this story quite a few times now. However, this answer may have become ritualized and, therefore, be wrong. So my picture of what happened was that there was one network of people who were Yale Law School students from the period between '67 and '71, including, for example, Mark Tushnet, Rand Rosenblatt, and Ann Freedman, who went into law teaching, and they preserved the critical moment of student activism at Yale Law School, which is amazingly described by Laura Kalman in her book *The Yale Law School and the Sixties*. That was one part of it.

When I got to Harvard Law School, I fell in with Morton Horwitz and Roberto Unger. We were all hired at the same time, and as it very often happens in law faculties, people that are hired in the same year form a kind of cohort. There's a kind of intimacy that comes from arriving at the same time, but it developed very quickly way beyond that into a very deep intellectual alliance. And a number of law students, for example, Karl Klare, Cathy Stone, and Mark Kelman, were attracted to our project. So the nucleus of critical legal studies came from putting together the Yale people with the Harvard people—David Trubek was the other person. David Trubek had been denied tenure at Yale during this period of the early seventies, and had gone to Wisconsin. He represented both the Yale connection and a Wisconsin connection, and there was a SUNY Buffalo connection. David had been connected with the Yale students, and I was connected both to the Yale students and all these Harvard people. The result was a set, a significant set, of people. So when David Trubek and I set out to devise the first critical legal studies meeting in Madison, we were easily able to come up with a list of about sixteen to twenty law professors who were loosely within the "idea," which was a confluence of Marxist and Weberian traditions in legal theory with a left spin. That was the "idea" of the initial critical legal studies event. There were efforts to include law and society and social sciences people of the older generation, but they didn't come or quickly dropped out, because right at the beginning it had this generational spin to it. It is important to understand that aspect of critical legal studies. We tried repeatedly to create complex generational alliances, but, generally, we failed to ever bond or link up with people who were born before 1940. There were three or four exceptions, like David Trubek and Rick Abel—Arthur Leff a little bit. It was very striking—the sharpness of generational division—so at the outset this was a creation, overwhelmingly, of people under forty.

HACKNEY: Now that initial moment, how would you describe the set of ideas that had brought you together as a group? You mentioned Marx and Weber.

KENNEDY: I would say that the themes that united us, in the initial group, were very limited. That is, the differences were many more than the things that were in common. As soon as the group was constituted, it attracted lots of other people, with lots of other basic orientations. I would say that at the beginning, the thing that we had in common was leftism, in the sense of occupying what was then a generational position to the left of the dominant mainstream American liberalism. This was not about fighting Nixon; it was about being against the people in legal academia and in the culture in general who are the dominant intellectual forces and were way to the left of Nixon. The idea is, the word is, radical.

One component was Marxism—but there were very few early crits who were Marxist in any usual or orthodox sense. Marxism was an important influence rather than a dogma to be accepted or rejected. Some of us were more into it than others of us. But Marxism was just one of the strands of American radicalism, rather than being *the* thing. You could get to your radicalism from many, many different places, including democratic socialism, the counterculture, or just bitter disillusionment with mainstream American liberalism. Generic radicalism was the single most important idea: we were in favor of doing more, sooner, at greater cost, with greater potential disruption about race issues, economic justice issues, and then gender issues than the mainstream, the liberal mainstream, would do. This was because we had both a more egalitarian and a more communitarian ideology, and because we believed that it was desirable and permissible to operate at a higher level of confrontation with the culture.

So there were two different things. The first was the rejection of mainstream liberalism, as both too moderate in substance and too moderate in tactics, politics, and ethos. The other thing we shared was a belief that our professional life was loaded with politics, that as teachers, we were participating in an institutional apparatus that was producing people who would participate in the political, economic, social, and cultural systems, already programmed to support the status quo. That's the reproduction-of-hierarchy idea. That was widely shared. So I'm saying that the things that brought us together were political—both at the level of the state, and at the level of the institution.

HACKNEY: This seems to go back to your prior discussion—it was definitely generational. It was a thing of the times.

KENNEDY: Oh absolutely. It was a thing of the "young" of the times. Not a thing of the "old" of the times.

HACKNEY: One of the interesting strands running throughout *Critique of Adjudication*, your text, is this divide between the rationalists and irrationalists within CLS. First of all, can you describe the divide? Second, was it always present, even at the nascent stages of CLS, or was this something that had developed after the initial moment of euphoria and meeting of like minds?

KENNEDY: I would say it was present at the very beginning. It was present among people who were at Yale Law School already. I preferred to call the rationalists "Northerners," and the irrationalists "Southerners." Those names were a little more consistent with my version of the irrationalist position. The division would basically be about how to understand the role of theory, descriptive and normative, in diagnosing what was wrong with the system, and in establishing one's utopian project for the future.

It was a spectrum. At one end of the spectrum were people who believed that in order to understand what was wrong with the system, to understand the system, it was necessary to have a theory. The theory could be American empirical social science, Marxism, classical liberalism, or whatever. It could be Weberian sociology, understood as a systematic approach to the study of society. Then when you figured it out, what you needed was a commitment of some kind to a normative theory. You could believe in rights, or socialism, or in overcoming the subject/object dichotomy, or you could believe in communal life, or democracy. From community, or democracy, or rights, or anarchy, or socialism, or whatever, would flow the program for social transformation. That's the North, the far North. Everything depends on having a theory.

HACKNEY: And it could do something for you.

KENNEDY: Not only that, in the Northern view, unless you have it, you are paralyzed. People who don't have theories are demobilized. That was a basic strand of the New Left and sixties generation thinking, which was passionately into the discovery and adoption of new theories. It was partly a reaction against the antitheoretical character of mainstream education—humanist liberal education—in the fifties and sixties.

We Southerners were, right from the beginning, in many ways, a little postmodernist. We tended to be extremely skeptical about pretensions to universality and truth, and dubious about the rational power Northerners attributed to their theories—both descriptive and normative. We tended to believe that both in the understanding of reality and in deciding what you wanted to do, there would be large areas of indeterminacy, or slippage, or confusion, or vagueness. Categories like intuition, decisionism, intersubjectivity, the aesthetic, and (the Northerners might have said of us) maybe even table tapping, were absolutely essential both in deciding what was going on and in deciding what to do.

HACKNEY: So this is where the Continentals, the aesthetic, come into play.

KENNEDY: But it's also very American. We Southerners partook of a particular kind of American pragmatism—antagonistic to European grand theory. For example, William James and John Dewey—their attitude toward the Germans was that they're insane hyperrationalists—they overdo it. They just don't get what life is like. So this is not Europe versus America. Europe and America are on both sides. Sartre is on both sides of this conflict. The older Sartre got, the more committed he was to theoretical reconstruction. So we, the South, are early Sartre. The North are later Sartre. In American terms, it's the same division. The Southerners took from Europe and the Northerners, too. The Northerners took different things than the Southerners. For example, the Northerners treated structuralism as a determinism, where the Southerners treated structuralism as a semiotics of social life.

HACKNEY: I've been thinking about the distinction between objectivism and skepticism. Do you accept the distinction? Would you consider yourself to be a "skeptic"? Of course, you could ask how I define "skeptic."

KENNEDY: Yes, I would ask that.

HACKNEY: It's hard to define it in the affirmative, as opposed to the negative. And maybe that's just the way it's characterized. But one idea is that the skeptic is always a critic of the objectivist or, perhaps better defined, the rationalist, poking holes in the argument. Tracing your intellectual trajectory, there seems to be a pattern. You get to Yale Law School, you look at the social scientists, and you say, "Well, that's insane—it doesn't quite work." You take a grander view of the progression of American legal theory, and you say, "The whole enterprise just doesn't work." Then you get within the contours of CLS and you encounter folks who have the same political objectives, but they constitute the Northerners, so you say, "Let's take a step back . . . "

KENNEDY: Yes, to the south.

HACKNEY: You take a step south. And then, I want to eventually get to this discussion, you encounter the legal economists, contemporary legal economists, who represent the most recent gasp of rationalism, and level a devastating critique, along with traditional liberals, with respect to that enterprise. So, in my historiography of American legal theory, I place you in the skeptic category. Now, this is your opportunity to embrace it or realign yourself.

KENNEDY: I guess I would have to say that within your frame, I'm a skeptic. However, I wouldn't choose to call the object of my skepticism objectivism. The reason for that is that my own understanding of the history of legal thought is that, as I've said before, it's a process of derationalization, rationalization, derationalization, and critique. It's deconstruction, reconstruction, critique, deconstruction, and reconstruction, on a trajectory that is the death of reason narrative. I would associate the category of objectivity with only a few of the strands that together make up the history of law as reason. Many of the most important rationalizers in the history of legal thought have rejected objectivism. For example, Ronald Dworkin, in a famous and quite excellent article, says, "Please don't talk about objectivity anymore." That's actually the title of his response to Stanley Fish and Walter Benn Michaels.

You can be a rationalist without taking the objectivity/subjectivity distinction as central to your understanding at all. What you need within law is the belief that there is a distinction between law and politics, which puts on the law side many characteristics that you would say are the characteristics of objectivism but may be characteristics of other points of view as well. Aristotelians are not objectivists. Finnis, for example, would be horrified, I suspect, to be characterized as an objectivist. His whole Aristotelian shtick is to completely reject that kind of idea, and to reject the fact/value distinction and the concept of subjectivity. But he's a hyperrationalist, and a deep believer in the law/politics distinction. I would say the important distinction among legal theorists is between the vast majority of rationalists and the small but virtuous minority of nonrationalists, not necessarily irrationalists.

The role of critique in the story is a complex one. Critique is a practice of rationalists. It is wrong to think of critique people or the skeptics as different in that respect from the people building the rational structure over time. My picture of it is that the glory of rationalism is its commitment to critique, and its comedy or tragedy, depending on how you look at it, is that in the generational play, and in the course of historical drift, the oedipal young trash their rationalist elders in order to clear the ground for their own rationalist theories. That's how you succeed in life. You first clear some ground, and then you build your own. The irony of history, the sort of Hegelian trick of history here, is that the critical process has turned out to be more cumulative than the constructive process. This is an irony. The development of critical techniques is preserved generation after generation, and developed as the young critique the old in order to lay waste to their structures so that they can build their own. This has produced a vast repertoire of critical techniques, and the possibility of a kind of critical training within legal discourse, which is just much further along than you would ever have imagined a century ago.

The constructive enterprise, where these young destroyers affirm that they are working for the greater glory of legal reasoning, has had a different fate over time, it seems to me. It turned out that the accomplishments of legal reasoning get smaller over time—they're not cumulative. The preservation of a law/politics divide around a rational/un-rational distinction produces a more and more palliated, shrunken, dwarflike version of rational construction, instead of a bigger and bigger, more glorious one. So critique has prospered within this dialectic at the expense of the constructive. This is the death of reason narrative in the domain of legal discourse, and it's similar to that narrative as it plays out in the history of science, the history of art, the history of economics, the history of Western culture in general, and particularly the history of religion. We can even see this development in law as an extension of the derationalization of religion: one of Max Weber's most striking interpretations was that the search for the "absolute" shifts out of religion to law, and meets a similar fate in its new home.

That's my understanding. I don't think it's an inevitable process, and I think as a matter of fact, reconstruction comes back. It's not right that the death of reason narrative is an inevitable story, and I think Weber was quite wrong in the part of his worldview in which he understood that derationalization was an inevitable and irreversible process—disenchantment, as he called it. I think that the world gets re-enchanted all of the time. I'm not claiming to have identified a universal law of history. I actually see myself as a participant—a little, tiny, minor participant—in the process, with the following role (I wonder whether you'd call it a skeptic's role).

I'm interested, as a participant, in deploying the critical tools on two fronts—on the one hand, the leftist front, and on the other, the modernist/postmodernist front. On the leftist front, I think the critical tools are endlessly necessary to deal with the ways in which moderates and conservatives legitimate their practices and proposals by fronting them with false rational facades. It's not that they're doing it on purpose—they're not lying. They're deceiving themselves. They're in denial about how ideological their positions are, and they believe that they're more grounded in rationally structured argument than, in fact, they are. So there is a critical or skeptic's task, which is to demystify proposals on the center and the right.

My first orientation is a leftist orientation to stand in the way of the center and the right's appropriation of rational techniques to make their ideological preferences sound necessary. However, I think that the techniques also have to be used on the left, in order to clarify for the left what's really at stake. At the same time, I'm enthusiastically in favor of proposals. I'm not at all a skeptic in the sense that I'm against proposals, and I'm not a skeptic in the sense of being against organizations. I've spent a lot of my life organizing things, people, and events, and proposing things of a positive character. I don't know whether that still makes me a skeptic. For me, there's no inconsistency in using the tools of critique developed over this long period of time to get at the ideological mystifications of the center and the right, to clarify things on the left, and (in a completely positive and constructive way) move forward to champion ideas.

HACKNEY: I think that's an interesting point with regard to how the rationalists cannibalize themselves. I don't know if that's endemic in the rationalist enterprise, or a historical fluke, but I think you've really hit on an interesting historical phenomenon. Now, I see your encounter with contemporary law and economics as an application of exactly what you just laid out.

KENNEDY: I'd like to start out by insisting on the strict parallelism in my own work between the critique of law and economics and the critique of liberal rights theory. Furthermore, I'm not critical at all, in any way, of the larger enterprise of bringing economics to bear on law and legal theory. In that larger sense, I consider myself to be a practitioner of law and economics. I write articles with graphs in them, and I make economic policy arguments for particular legal reforms and against other legal reforms, in which I try to deploy economic analysis, within the limits of my capacity. I majored in economics, and I went to graduate school in economics for a semester. I've never been a mathematically oriented person, but I'm not at all numerophobic and I was deeply steeped in the underlying technique of microeconomic analysis and welfare economics as they were done in the early sixties. Now it is the mid-2000s, that was forty years ago, but, I must say, I notice as I look around at others who do law and economics, how often we seem to do the actual legal economic work at about the same technical level. Even if they have PhDs in economics, there's not much they can do that's more technically exciting than what we first-generation tyros can do with our rusting, primitive tools. Of course, old people always say things like that.

That said, I have a critique of mainstream American law and economics, on several different levels. First of all, I would distinguish between conservative mainstream and liberal law and economics. Calabresi was the original representative of the liberal strand. Calabresi seems to me to have pretty much given up quite early on, and was marginalized in the field for almost fifteen years. But eventually PhDs in economics, like Ian Ayres and Christine Jolls, and less technical people like Jon Hanson, began to resuscitate the liberal version. The right-winger Chicago school adherents were not technically sophisticated, but believed quite naively that their project was a "scientific" one. They welcomed the PhDs, for their technical expertise, and seemed surprised when the new recruits turned out, paradoxically, to be quite liberal. The conservatives ended up destroying the internal ideological coherence of law and economics by their recruitment practices. The current situation in law and economics, as I see it, is that it is divided between the more or less old school, relatively technically unsophisticated right-wingers and the moderate liberals who are far more technically advanced, but also tend to be less legally sophisticated and less clear about the underlying political issues.

I have a single critique of both groups, which is that their collective preoccupation with the efficiency norm as the welfare economics gold standard for understanding law is analytically untenable. In terms of social theory, it's so primitive and naive as to be ridiculous. We learned in the welfare economics course that I took at Harvard in 1963, by reading I. M. D. Little's *Critique of Welfare Economics*, to reject arguments that have been the absolute total orthodoxy of law and economics ever since 1973. Again, this was in 1963. So I. M. D Little's book is a critique by a right-winger, attacking left-wing labor economists in Britain. The leftists wanted to justify the British post–World War II nationalizations of the "commanding heights" of the economy, using Kaldor-Hicks, to argue that they increased total welfare. Little attacked them on the ground that such a justification was simultaneously radically indeterminate (offer/asking problems, etcetera) and ethically incoherent. In order to do law and economics in a way that is plausible, you have to take distributional consequences into account, and that destroys the illusion that you are applying a value-neutral criterion. Distributional consequences of policy choices need to be elaborately vetted, and then assessed. A similar point was made by Francis Bator in "Simple Analytics of Welfare Maximization," another thing that we had to practically memorize as economics majors.

HACKNEY: And you're talking about the second generation, or still the first generation?

KENNEDY: This is still the first generation, the conservative ones. The liberal ones seem to me to have basically begun to correct a number of the most obvious mistakes. They are much more technically sophisticated, but they still have a background commitment. The liberals are wedded to a distinction in economics between efficiency and distribution that exactly parallels the law/politics distinction in liberal rights theory.

HACKNEY: Louis Kaplow and Steven Shavell emphasize that theme.

KENNEDY: Yes, they all do. So here my basic idea would be that the law/politics distinction in liberal rights theory is parallel to the efficiency/distribution distinction in law and economics. In mainstream law and economics, the point is that efficiency equals law and distribution equals politics—just as rights equal law, according to Dworkin, and interests equal politics in liberal rights theory. The way to preserve the distinction, in each field, is internal to the disciplines. And I have a critique in each case of the way that is done, arguing that sticking to efficiency or rights doesn't keep politics out of the analysis. Let's begin with efficiency. It turns out that the efficiency category, when it's rendered appropriately complex and contextual, can't be done without exactly the types of "subjective" judgments that efficiency analysis attempts to keep in abeyance.

HACKNEY: Is this the Ed Baker "starting points" critique?

KENNEDY: The Ed Baker "starting points" critique is an important part of it. But the problem of instantiating an efficiency calculus, rendering it concrete, goes beyond just starting points. It also includes, for example, the offer/asking problem, the problem of third-party effects, information asymmetry, unstable equilibria, path dependency, and an array of issues now raised in the cognitive psychology literature. Offer/asking was an early example of that cognitive analysis, an example of the much broader contemporary category of bounded rationality. If you take all those things into account, the efficiency calculus dissolves into a kind of complex set of pragmatic judgments that are not easily distinguished from the so-called value-laden judgments that would be involved in doing distribution.

Moreover, the idea that you could do efficiency as "legal rules" and then do distribution through after-the-fact one-shot transfers, or just through welfare legislation, is not coherent, as I have argued on several different occasions, in several different ways. It's not possible to imagine such a system as a functioning social system for both analytic and concrete institutional reasons, and our system has certainly never borne the slightest resemblance to the model that is routinely idealized and/or presupposed in mainstream law and economics, whether right-wing or liberal.

There are three really distinct criticisms. First of all, efficiency dissolves into a subjective, highly valued-laden, and, therefore, political thing, not easily reconciled with the claim to political neutrality. The distributive calculus will often yield a higher level of both certainty and consensus than efficiency. The second one is that the proposal to leave distribution to the legislature, and have judges stick to efficiency, is neither institutionally nor analytically coherent. And the last is that both the conservatives and the liberals have a very large number of "free market biases" built into their analytics that are economically ungrounded. Let me just give an example.

Virtually all economists will assert that rent control is bad. They, including legal economists, are simply ignorant of the economic arguments in favor of actual modern, functioning rent control. They tend to almost mindless repetition of statements about rent control, which show that they don't understand the economics because they don't understand the way it works. The "new model" legal regimes put into effect in several hundred U.S. jurisdictions in the late 1960s (and most terminated in the 1990s) didn't apply to new construction, and provided landlords a steady income stream corrected for inflation, as opposed to the World War II New York City model economists imagine to have been in effect everywhere. "New model" rent control was an anti-gentrification device, not an attempt to shift surplus from landlords to tenants. Economists learn the critique of the old model early in college and treat it as their collective sacred cow. It's a dogma. The free market presumption pervades. Those are my critiques of mainstream law and economics.

For the rights-theory people I have a very closely parallel kind of critique. When you do rights analysis, looking to specify the right that should govern in a specific situation, taking into account that rights conflict, and that there are powers as well as rights in the system, the devil will be in the details. The actual specification of the right in practice, just like the problem of the specification of efficiency in practice, is not clearly distinct from general political analysis. Rights analysis collapses or dissolves into what we understand as the generally value-laden "subjective" character of our political discourse. Using "rights" as law against politics, or judicially articulated "rights" against the legislature, which is what Dworkin does, has exactly the same first difficulty that we find with mainstream law and economics, which is that the analytic is radically indeterminate, or maybe we could say that it underdetermines in situations with high stakes. Taking the ideas like the public interest, general will, or welfare of society into account, which is what's on the political side for rights analysts, is no more subjective, no vaguer, no more value laden, than what you do when you balance competing rights against each other. So that's the parallel to the first critique.

Second, remember my view is that the efficiency people have a consistent free market bias, which affects, drives, and distorts their efficiency analysis. Often, they're just wrong, propagating their ideology under the cover of technical economic expertise. In many, many important, high-stakes situations, the free market solution is not the efficient solution, according to plausible arguments inside the system, or it isn't possible to determine with any degree of certainty which of a number of solutions is the efficient one. Remember, I'm not just a critic, or a skeptic, I also want to do the argument. My view is that more often than not, efficiency is against the free market solution, overall.

The rights argument suffers from the same flaw. I would describe mainstream American liberal rights analysts as generally moderate-to-left liberals. It is transparent that they have a political agenda, which has nothing to do with rights. Rights are the dress-up language for their particular kind of center-leftism. As center-left people they are opposed to any kind of radical change on the left, and equally opposed to any rolling back of the existing social and economic accomplishments of progressivism. They are basically standpatters who would like to move a little bit forward with a little bit of a liberal agenda. They're Clintonians. Dworkin is a Clintonian, maybe a left-Clintonian. Those are the rights people.

Dworkin operates at the level of high theory, but here I've been talking about the way he, and dozens of law professors who have no interest in his high theory, produce "rights" answers to legal questions that are simply the moderate-left program turned into rights language. Doing the same analysis, someone coming from my more left political position would come up with a more left-wing answer to the question than they do, just as conservatives would come up with a much more right-wing one, but we could all do it in rights language, just as we could all do it in efficiency language. So there's this strong parallel between the rationalization project represented by the efficiency/distribution distinction and the rationalization project represented by the rights/politics distinction.

HACKNEY: So in that regard, what I take to be a principal idea that you deploy—the pervasiveness of ideology—is reflected in the praxis of groups. Your connection between ideology and adjudication is also reflected in ideology and legal theory. You can apply the analysis to the rights theorists and you can apply it to the law and economics types, arguing at bottom, it's an ideological project.

KENNEDY: There's no "at bottom." We PoMos don't believe in "at bottoms." That's the whole point.

HACKNEY: Okay, but can you talk about how ideology plays a role?

KENNEDY: The idea is that there is an internal critique and an ideological critique. They are not quite the same thing. I've just been doing an internal critique, combined with an ideological critique. The internal critique stresses the underdetermined character of the outcomes claimed by the law and economics and the rights theorists. They [law and economics and rights adherents] think the outcomes are determined by the working out of the consequences of their premises. That's not true. To explain where they come out we need something else, which is their ideology. Ideology plays a major explanatory role for me in understanding the way legal reasoning, from the level of the court to the level of Dworkin, works. Without the concept of ideology, it's very hard to understand what's going on.

However, ideology is not the "base," or the "at bottom," any more than the economy is the base. I have never said that, and I don't believe it. It is natural for Americans, relatively unfamiliar with these debates in social theory, to think that if you talk about ideology you must be saying this is what's *really* going on. In the prior generation, the generation of leftists of the late sixties and early seventies, the idea was that the economy was what was really going on. The economy was the "base," and ideology was the "superstructure." Now, people often think that we are saying that ideology is the base, and law is the superstructure. No! People like me, we PoMos, reject base/superstructure distinctions. We don't believe that the economy is the base and ideology is the superstructure, or that law is the superstructure. We don't believe that ideology is the base. We believe that these things mutually affect each other and that each level has its resistance, its impermeability, its opacity, none is simply a transparent reflection of or product of another level. All the levels are interacting in a kind of friction. They constrain, inspire, and disrupt each other. When one is completely open another can fill the gap, but that doesn't mean that because it's open, it's totally open everywhere.

The basic formula is that for questions of law that have very high stakes, there is very often a condition of underdetermination by the legal material. Just focusing on legal materials according to the typical criteria of legal reasoning leaves the results radically underdetermined. Policy analysis is also underdeterminative. Under those circumstances, ideology can be highly influential. However, ideology is also full of gaps, conflicts, and ambiguities. Let's suppose you're a typical American liberal. Your liberal ideology is not going to tell you what your attitude should be toward hate crimes. On the one hand, you're a total multiculturalist, left-liberal, politically correct identity-politics person, and on the other hand, you are a civil libertarian and a free speech fanatic. Which way you come out is not going to be the product of the ideology. It's underdeterminative at that level.

Very often, law fills the gaps of the ideology! Liberal ideology is unhelpful on hate crimes, so instead of explaining to you what it requires, a particular liberal might respond, "Well, that's just illegal. That's against the law. We don't need to discuss that. It's in the Constitution," or something. So I don't believe in a base/superstructure distinction, and I believe that both the law level and the ideology level are full of gaps, conflicts, and ambiguities. Each can supplement or determine the other from time to time.

HACKNEY: Posner and Dworkin are viewed as principal representatives of law and economics, and rights theory, respectively. Can you discuss their specific role in these debates, and the recent neopragmatist shift in their intellectual positions?

KENNEDY: Dworkin and Posner are not that much older than me (Dworkin maybe ten years, Posner less), but they are both members of the previous generation, the pre-sixties generation. Of course, they have plenty of representatives in the sixties generation. It's important that the critical legal studies side doesn't have representatives from their side of the divide. The oldest crits were David Trubek and Rick Abel, both caught in between. Dworkin and Posner were, from the very beginning, objects of attack for critical legal studies. The attacks varied from smart, intelligent, highly cogent, and extremely effective, to wild, windmill, and utterly ineffective. The attacks also varied on the spectrum from respectful and within the rational dialogue mode to quite nasty.

Let's loosely characterize what happened both in law and economics, and in liberal rights theory as a kind of neopragmatist turn, or an interpretive turn for that matter. Why did that happen? One reason was the subtle dialectic between law and economics, rights theory, and critical legal studies. Critical legal studies sometimes allied with rights theory against law and economics, and sometimes allied with law and economics against rights theory. I think that the single best early critique of Posner is not Ed Baker's, which is very good, but it's "Is Wealth a Value?" by Dworkin, which is a really devastating attack on Posner. Conversely, I found, Posner's attacks on liberal rights theory in his Holmes lectures a few years ago very convincing. I think the reason I like these critiques is that they so plainly show, if not the influence of CLS on these guys, then their belated discovery on their own of what we had been saying for a long time.

It's hard to know which, because of the strategy that both most mainstream law and economics people and most rights people adopted with regard to critical legal studies. First, they really and truly ignored us. You could study with these guys for twenty years and never hear critical legal studies mentioned. Second, they certainly gave as good as they got in terms of personal attack. Let me say in passing that for myself I preferred to be ignored, because they were so nasty, when they deigned to pay attention to us, and for some reason, in spite of my own pretty respectful attitude, both Dworkin and Posner were particularly contemptuous of me. The third prong in the strategy was the move to neopragmatism. However, I do believe that it can be said that we flogged and whipped them into neopragmatism. So they did three different things: ignore us, personally attack us, and give in. Dworkin's turn to interpretation is equivalent to Posner's neopragmatism—both, in effect, have given in.

HACKNEY: What's your critique of the neopragmatist/interpretist turn by both Posner and Dworkin?

KENNEDY: It's just mush on top of mush—another chapter in the derationalization narrative, the death of reason narrative. American pragmatism is a part of that. They are no more successful in defending the law/politics distinction, or the judge/legislator distinction, with their neopragmatist technique than they were with their more formalist technique.

HACKNEY: Isn't the response that they've perhaps given up the law/politics distinction?

KENNEDY: I would say absolutely not for one second. So here's a humorous example. Just look at their (strikingly nasty) debate about *Bush vs. Gore*. Dworkin and Posner each claimed legal correctness, denying their own positions had anything to do with politics—while each violently accused the other of being totally political. It's great reading. Each of them is a legalist, denouncing the other as a traitor to legality. My reaction was, "Well, every bad thing each of them says about the other is correct."

I think I should introduce the emotional or psychological dimension here, since it obviously influences my thoughts about all of this. I am in a sense a student of both Dworkin and Posner, and, when I describe my attitudes, that shouldn't be left out of the account. So I'm both their student and in some sense an antagonist. One of my reactions to their exchange around Posner's Holmes lectures was that although they took nasty swipes at me in passing, they really only cared about each other. And then, my second reaction was that I no longer think of myself, as I once did, as at least in part addressing my work to them.

At some point, you have to stop; you have to recognize that the people who are older than you, in this case your teachers, are not that interested in you, and anyway they will quite soon be gone from the scene. By now, they should be less significant to you than the people who are younger than you. There's a moment at which perspective has to shift from the inevitable upward gaze toward your teachers, who have authority behind them in that way, with whom one can have all kinds of oedipal relations, to a different set of oedipal relations, the oedipal relations down the scale, rather than up the scale.

When I shift my attention, as a sixty-four-year-old, very senior professor, to more recent developments and more recent scholarship in the areas that interest me, I'm a little disoriented. The fairly clear definitions of opposing positions and their dialectical relationships that are available to me in understanding critical legal studies, law and economics, liberal rights theory, law and society, law and literature, critical race theory, and feminist legal theory don't seem useful. When I try to understand the legal theoretical lives of people under about forty, I'm puzzled in a way that I'm not for the lives of people born between 1938 and 1968, a thirty-year span.

You, James, are at the end of the generational spectrum, according to my model here, because you were born in 1964. The kinds of stories that I've been going on and on about can't be easily replicated if we ask, "What's gone on since about 1990?" There's a sense in which all these dramatic events were sort of over by the early nineties. Posner's Holmes lectures, with the reactions of Dworkin and other senior rights theorists, were a kind of last gasp, a fascinating reliving or restaging of a drama from the recent past. It seems as though—now this could be wrong—legal theory has lost the fairly central place it held in legal consciousness and legal discourse in the period from the late fifties up to the nineties (meaning the elite "United States–ian" world of legal discourse). It has been eclipsed, in a sense even discredited. It's no longer useful on the career ladder, but even more important, it's no longer crucial in the search for enlightenment. That's a really big change.

HACKNEY: So it's very pluralistic?

KENNEDY: It's a common idea that the world of legal theory has become incredibly pluralistic. I'm saying something a little different, that legal theory is out. At the same time, law profs who aspire to be part of the larger discourse have to show that they know what it is, and that they have an eclectic familiarity with it.

HACKNEY: It is the death of legal theory, but legal theories proliferate. Could one put this under the umbrella of the neopragmatist/interpretist turn? Will this lead to more genuine dialogue among the various legal theories as opposed to the drama of conflict?

KENNEDY: I guess I think the opposite. I think that interest in legal theory has waned dramatically. It used to be worth it for a young law professor to try to find some position to occupy in the pluralistic universe, and to take part in the drama of critique between theories. But that's the past.

Today there's no peer pressure, and there's no authoritarian pressure for people to have positions in legal theory. Most people are just eclectic. That's not pluralism. Moreover, very few people, I think, believe it's worth it to engage in the task of defining, comparing, and critiquing the extant theories. A fortiori, it's not worth engaging in the polemics that made life interesting in what I'd call the good old days. So I'm on the other side of your optimistic prediction of dialogue. It seems more likely that the theory enterprise will be dormant for a while, and then it will come back in one form or another.

HACKNEY: When we have the next grand theory?

KENNEDY: Perhaps it will take another grand theory. I don't really have a strong sense of it. I think the ground is not fallow. I'd say the younger generation seems to experience the ground as over-plowed and barren. So I'd say legal theory is out.

HACKNEY: Let me push back a little. Maybe one way legal theory is in, is as follows. If you are a tort law scholar, you take a job as a tort law professor. However, there's almost no way that you can't at least encounter critical race theory, law and economics, law and society, CLS, etcetera. You have to be relatively conversant in a plethora of legal theories. For example, if you teach torts, you have to know about Richard Delgado's critique of hate speech doctrine. In addition, it's almost a must for a torts professor to know the Coase theorem, and the critiques of law and economics. Is that the death of legal theory, or the death of "grand" legal theory?

KENNEDY: I'd say it was the death of legal theory. I don't think it has much to do with grand theory. Torts teachers have to know bits and pieces of various theories, though I doubt even a third of U.S. torts teachers could recite on Delgado's critique of hate speech. So I agree with your description. However, what it means to me is that the theoretical enterprise as it was understood by the people who produced the bits and pieces isn't happening anymore. Of course, there are exceptions. I think the (to me) amazingly durable interest of a small number of younger profs in the whole Coleman/Epstein commutative justice riff is one. But in general I think there are very few younger profs for whom it's a big part of a life project to integrate a theoretical position with a doctrinal position or a political position.

HACKNEY: It's like a toolkit.

KENNEDY: It's like a toolkit, but it's a toolkit that is very divorced from the context in which the tools were developed, and it's not necessary to be particularly proficient with any of the tools.

HACKNEY: Yes, you have to be conversant.

KENNEDY: "Be conversant" is a very good term to describe it.

HACKNEY: That's exactly right. So it's a very shallow level of understanding. Maybe the description isn't dialogue, but a state of equanimity with respect to multiple theories.

KENNEDY: Equanimity, I couldn't agree more. But remember, I come from the generation of screaming and yelling. So the idea of a state of equanimity sounds like the death of legal theory. The twenty years that separate you and me are the twenty years of grinding conflict. The idea of equanimity is not surprisingly much more plausible to people at your end of the period. But I see you as still part of the same generation, at the young end, that stretches all the way back to Dworkin and Calabresi and Posner. So it's easy to understand what you're doing as the youngest person in the generation talking to the oldest people in the generation. That's a classic enterprise. Imagine that you are a person discovering these debates for the first time today, a person who didn't know of their existence, who had been cut off from them because at some point maybe in the nineties, there stopped being an active intellectual/political/emotional legal theory scene. I imagine that person, maybe frustrated and having trouble finding any progressive collective activity in legal theory, picking up this book, not as a participant or part of the audience back then for the events described, but as a newcomer. The reaction might well be something like, "Wow, I wonder what *that* was like."

Richard Posner is a judge of the United States Court of Appeals for the Seventh Circuit. He was formerly the Lee and Brena Freeman Professor of Law, and is currently a Senior Lecturer at the University of Chicago. Judge Posner is most widely recognized for his leadership and pioneering work in the law and economics field in the 1970s and 1980s. He was a founding editor of the *Journal of Legal Studies* and (with Orley Ashenfelter) the *American Law and Economics Review*. However, his scholarly interests cover a wide range of areas, including jurisprudence, regulation, law and literature, the legislative process, family law, and history of legal thought. Judge Posner is widely recognized as one our most prolific scholars and has written or edited numerous books, including *The Economics of Justice* (1981), *The Problems of Jurisprudence* (1990), *Cardozo* (1990), *The Essential Holmes* (1992), *Sex and Reason* (1992), *Overcoming Law* (1995), *The Federal Courts* (1996), *Law and Legal Theory in England and America* (1996), *The Problematics of Moral and Legal Theory* (1999), *Antitrust Law* (2nd ed. 2001), *Law, Pragmatism, and Democracy* (2003), *Catastrophe* (2004), *Preventing Surprise Attacks* (2005), *Economic Analysis of Law* (7th ed. 2007), *How Judges Think* (2008), *A Failure of Capitalism* (2009), and *Law and Literature* (3rd ed. 2009).

2

Law and Economics

RICHARD POSNER

HACKNEY: So why did you choose to become a legal academic?

POSNER: I just fell into it. I didn't have any plan, but when I was working for the government some law schools expressed interest in my becoming an academic.

HACKNEY: And when you were in government what position did you have?

POSNER: Well, it was in the sixties, and I was right out of law school. I spent six years in the government, first as a law clerk, then with the FTC and the Justice Department, and last working with the presidential task force.

HACKNEY: It seemed like a good route. Now, what did you study undergraduate?

POSNER: I majored in English literature.

HACKNEY: When you were at Harvard Law School, can you give me a description of the intellectual climate? Were there particular professors that either mentored you, or that you looked to them in terms of their approach to law?

POSNER: It was very conservative intellectually, and for the most part the faculty were very emphatically legal professionals, much like practicing lawyers. They were smart and it was good training, but it was very conventional legal training. There was one professor there, Don Turner, who had a PhD in economics. I became friendly with him. He represented a different model of academic law—law conjoined with economics. However, the general climate was narrowly professional.

HACKNEY: This was prior to the proliferation of legal theory?

POSNER: Right, exactly.

HACKNEY: Now, did Don Turner have any relationship with Aaron Director or any of those folks at the University of Chicago?

POSNER: No, Turner was a liberal economist, not radical by any stretch, but somewhat liberal. Aaron represented the type of Chicago school approach that was skeptical about antitrust, and he had no Harvard connection. He taught at the University of Chicago.

HACKNEY: How did you begin to pick up economics? Was it self-directed reading, or were there particular classes at the law school or university?

POSNER: There was very little economics in the law school curriculum, but I knew Turner. I cite-checked on the law review part of an article by Derek Bok, who later became president of Harvard University. It was an article on antitrust, and the section I cite-checked actually dealt with economic analysis. I also worked on a major antitrust case for Justice Brennan when I was a law clerk, and I relied in part on Bok's article. I then went to work for the Federal Trade Commission, Justice Department, and communications task force. I was intrigued with economic issues, and by the time I started teaching I had decided that I wanted to specialize in the application of economics to law.

HACKNEY: And did you arrive at the University of Chicago and immerse yourself?

POSNER: At the start I spent a year at Stanford.

HACKNEY: Was there much in the air at Stanford in regard to economics, or was it really just University of Chicago?

POSNER: Well, there was some. There was an economist on the faculty, and a law professor, Bill Baxter, who was very interested in economics. I received encouragement from him, and from Aaron Director, whom I met there. He had an office at Stanford Law School. Through Aaron I began to meet people at the University of Chicago, which is why I eventually took a position there. However, most of the economics I learned was informal, talking to people, reading, and some of the work I had done in government.

HACKNEY: What year did you actually arrive at the University of Chicago?

POSNER: '69.

HACKNEY: By that time Ronald Coase had written his article—"The Problem of Social Cost."

POSNER: Yes, it was published in 1961 (though the date on the journal is 1960, but it was published late).

HACKNEY: So there was a well-formed law and economics group and Chicago-school economists already in place? I'm thinking about folks like Milton Friedman.

POSNER: Yes, it wasn't large, but there was Coase's work. There was also George Stigler, who wrote about regulation and antitrust. There were law professors—Ken Dam and Ed Kitch—who were very interested in economics. Besides Coase, there was another economist on the faculty, Harold Demsetz, and for a time a third, John Peterman. There was the *Journal of Law and Economics* (that was where Coase's article had been published), so there was a little law and economics school within the law school. At Yale there was Guido Calabresi, who had started writing on law and economics during the sixties. Of course, the field was embryonic compared to what it has become.

HACKNEY: I've read your review of Calabresi's classic text, *The Costs of Accidents*. How did you view Calabresi and what he was doing in economics versus your take on economic analysis of law?

POSNER: Well, I thought he was too interested in the issue of how you should regulate, and he wasn't sufficiently interested in the law. What I thought was very interesting was the extent to which the principles of tort law seemed to track economics.

HACKNEY: How would you describe the major tenets of law and economics?

POSNER: Well, that would be hard to do, but I would say that on the side of positive analysis there is an effort to understand the structure of law. Do the various rules and doctrines have economizing features, and what are the consequences? Calabresi's focus was on how can economics help to improve law.

HACKNEY: In terms of the evolution of law and economics, it's obvious that the economists are a lot more teched up now. It's very difficult to get a position at an elite law school without having a PhD, as well as a JD, if you're going to do law and economics.

POSNER: Unfortunately, yes. Partly it's because economics itself has becomes more specialized, more technical, more mathematical. So it's harder for a noneconomist to understand economics today. Another factor is competition for jobs. People notice if you have an advanced degree, and it has an impact in hiring. One thing that's happening in law that's unrelated to economics, but has this effect on "degree-itis," is that law has become a much more academic discipline. As I said, when I was a student professors were more lawyers than they were academics. They were smart and were very good teachers, but they wrote very little. There were always a few who wrote, but that wasn't the focus of law schools. The focus was on teaching, and on participation in professional activities like the American Law Institute. The situation has changed a great deal, and now law school is much more academic, with much more emphasis on scholarship. A person who has gone through the PhD mill and thus has specialized training and a demonstrated ability to do a large writing project (his PhD thesis) is the safer hire. Law schools are still reluctant to deny tenure because they feel they're competing with law firms, and can't afford to be too tough on tenure. Because they're reluctant to deny tenure, they're very conservative in their hiring. They want good evidence that this person is going to be productive. If he has a PhD, it provides good evidence.

HACKNEY: We've actually lost something since we don't have folks who are really grounded in law and then take the economic prospective.

POSNER: Yes, I think it's a big loss.

HACKNEY: Have you been following the debate sparked by Louis Kaplow and Steven Shavell regarding distributional considerations, and whether or not we should take them into account in common law adjudication? Of course, one critique of the Chicago school of law and economics is that it didn't adequately take into account distributional considerations. This goes back to Ed Baker's criticism with regard to starting points, arguing that efficient outcomes are contingent on the initial distribution of wealth. Kaplow and Shavell, quintessential techno-economists, have made the argument that the proper arena for distributional considerations is through the tax and spending function of the legislature. They argue that it's actually inefficient to take into account distributional concerns in common law because the same set of inefficiencies that exist with respect to doing distribution on the legislative side are also found on the common law side, and two inefficiencies are worse than one. That's the essence of the argument. Does that make sense to you? Have you followed the debate, and do you agree with their position?

POSNER: Yes, I have followed it, but not very closely. I gather Duncan Kennedy was involved in the debate.

HACKNEY: Yes, he's actually taken them on, and he's taken them on for reasons that resonate with your views on pragmatic adjudication. Kennedy argues that legislatures won't keep track of what's going on in the common law regime. Kaplow and Shavell have this idea that there is a properly functioning democracy. Then, if we have distributional consequences on the common law side, the legislature can take that into account on the tax and spend side. Kennedy argues that the legislatures won't keep track of what's going on with regard to the common law. Kaplow and Shavell believe that courts do, or at least should, only focus on efficiency norms. Kennedy makes the point that actually courts don't do that solely. Judges have an array of policy arguments and customs of adjudication—such as stare decisis. So it's just not the case that efficiency is the only thing that judges consider. And finally, Kennedy argues that judges do have ideological positions and they might be inconsistent with efficiency. Kennedy concludes that Kaplow and Shavell's vision of adjudication just doesn't reflect reality, and judges necessarily will be taking into account distributional considerations. Therefore, you can't take those concerns off the table and leave it to the legislature. That's his basic criticism.

POSNER: My view is that it's a factual question whether it's more efficient to redistribute wealth through the tax system or the common law, but my conclusion is that it is rather futile to attempt to redistribute through common law adjudication. The clearest example would be contracts. If you create new defenses to contract enforcement, in order to protect consumers, this will raise the cost to the seller and the seller will raise the price. Some consumers will be better off, others worse off. The same issue arises with torts. Suppose we were more generous in our judgments for tort victims. Then automobile insurance rates would be higher, and that would operate as a regressive tax because while everybody's automobile rates would be higher, for people who had limited resources the higher insurance rates equate to taxes, from the consumer's standpoint, and it would be more painful. So taxation would make it easier to target costs and benefits (you know whom you tax and whom you give the money to through the spending power) than common law adjudication would. But I don't think it appropriate to assume a well-functioning democracy, if by that is meant a system in which the government would be interested in redistribution. There isn't much redistribution because it's not strongly favored by the politically dominant people in society. It would be naive to think that there's effective redistribution in the tax and spend system. But the situation wouldn't be rectified by common law judges, who tend to have the same values as the legislators. So if there isn't much legislative support for redistribution, there wouldn't be much judicial support for it either.

HACKNEY: In tracing the history of your position in legal academia, there is a continuing strand of discourse between you and rights theorists, in particular Ronald Dworkin, as well as critical legal studies types, specifically Duncan Kennedy. Was that because they were natural foils in the sense that they had something to say about what you had written, or did it arise because those were the principal disciplinary groups out there?

POSNER: Dworkin was very critical of the economic approach, and so were the critical legal studies people. Now critical legal studies has petered out. Ronald Dworkin is still influential, but he's getting pretty old. However, there is a rights school of thought, and Dworkin is not the only member of it.

HACKNEY: Have your position on critical legal studies (even though you make the point that the movement has petered out) and your views with regard to rights theory shifted since you adopted your pragmatist stance? When I look at your early writings I don't see much explicit discussion about pragmatic approaches to adjudication.

POSNER: Yes, when I started off I was very dogmatic about the application of economics in a very pure form. I modified my views—partly because I got very good criticisms from Dworkin in his article "Is Wealth a Value?" That was pretty convincing. So I have modified my position. I also think that being a judge, now for twenty-five years, has taken off some of the hard edges of my thinking. However, I never found critical legal studies convincing. It was clearly very political and very left-wing. Some of their skepticism about legal reasoning I think is true, but I believed and believe their academic positions were really driven by politics and also that they had too simplistic an idea of the behavior of judges. They thought the only thing judges did was promote political goals, rather narrowly conceived. I consider myself a legal realist, and the critical legal studies model of judges is insufficiently realistic. The crits are at the opposite extreme from Dworkin. Dworkin has a very elevated view of what judges do. He sees them as moral theoreticians, and that's bunk. However, the opposite extreme is to see them purely as politicians, and that's clearly oversimplified.

HACKNEY: You talk about how your position has softened a bit with regard to the utilization of economic analysis. Were you always a pragmatist? Was your initial attraction to law and economics basically that it made sense, that it worked, that it seemed to give you some interesting results, or was your initial attraction more along the lines that it had an air of certainty about it? What initially attracted you to do law and economics versus law and literature?

POSNER: Well, I think that the most attractive feature was that it seemed to be practical, and to get beneath the verbal surface of legal analysis. One problem with law is the tendency to remain on the semantic surface, and argue about the meaning of fairness and other vague concepts. That has always seemed to me unsatisfactory. Economics can help one identify the real stakes in the case, and the real consequences. That is much more interesting than whether you can conform decisions to precedent. Economics deals more with the real world and is less rhetorical, so that has always been attractive for me.

HACKNEY: I have a theory that the intellectual history of American legal theory reflects a contest between rationalists and skeptics—formalism versus legal realism, for example. You could also take law and economics versus critical legal studies, and rights theory versus critical legal studies as exemplars of this phenomenon. It's clear when we go back to your textbook *Economic Analysis of Law*, the first edition, your position is a rationalist one. So your discussion of economic analysis as scientific is consistent with a rationalist worldview. Now, with the pragmatist approach, if we were to put you on that spectrum, between rationalist and skeptic, you seem to be a lot more on the skeptical side of the divide. How would you describe yourself in relationship to skepticism? I know you reject the extreme skepticism that you view as being represented by critical legal studies, but there seems to be a big chasm between where you originally started out and your current position.

POSNER: Well, I don't think it's that dramatic, because if you take the natural sciences, they often have a highly theoretical basis, but the object is to understand reality. I think that's true of economics, though it is not as strong as natural science. The formal theoretical structure of economics is designed to present a simplified model of reality, which can then be made more complicated and realistic. So if you're doing economics, you do feel that you are engaged with the real world. That's consistent with being skeptical about the kind of semantic or formalistic approach to law in which you're not trying not to produce good consequences in the real world, but instead to maintain consistency with an analytic structure. The example I like to give is this question: Suppose I lose my cat, and I post a reward. You return my cat, but you didn't see the sign on which I posted the reward. Can you claim the reward? A formalist might say no; since you didn't see my offer of an award, you couldn't have accepted it, and without offer and acceptance, there's no contract. My approach would be to ask, if we allow you to claim my reward, will that make it more likely that lost items are returned? It's actually a complicated question, because while you, as someone who didn't see the sign, will be more likely to return it if you know that should there be a posted reward you could claim it, people who see the reward posted may be less energetic in looking for the cat because they know that if someone who didn't see the sign finds it first, that person will get the reward. In my way of looking at it we want to encourage risk, because risk taking leads to the best result. That's an extremely different approach from asking, "What solution to the rescue issue is most consistent with existing contract doctrine?" So that's the basic difference.

HACKNEY: When you discuss pragmatist adjudication you explicitly differentiate your version of pragmatism from that of Richard Rorty. You're a big fan of Oliver Wendell Holmes, and I assume that means your form of pragmatism is much more closely related to, lets say, Charles Sanders Peirce and William James. I think I would categorize you as an "old-line" pragmatist, as opposed to "neopragmatist." Is that a correct formulation, and have you actually read and digested Peirce and James? I know you've read John Dewey because you write about him.

POSNER: Yes, I've read Dewey. I like Peirce. I haven't read much James. I'm not sure what you mean by neopragmatist.

HACKNEY: Neopragmatist is usually the description ascribed to Rorty and other post–World War II pragmatists, versus Peirce, James, and Dewey. Of course, this is a very loose formulation.

POSNER: Yes, of course, it's very, very loose because I would think of Nietzsche, Mill, and Hume as protopragmatists. Of course, Quine qualifies as a pragmatist. So it has vague boundaries. Rorty seems to have a lot of continuity with Dewey.

HACKNEY: Rorty, in effect, rescues Dewey because he was reared in the analytic tradition, and then he turned on that tradition, taking Dewey as his exemplar.

POSNER: Yes, that's right. Dewey's way of expressing himself seems extremely old-fashioned, and Rorty in his book brings Dewey up to date. I like the pragmatists, but I wouldn't want to tie legal pragmatism too tightly to philosophical practices. Philosophical pragmatists are interested in a host of issues that really don't interest me.

HACKNEY: Yes, there is a kind of insider "game" in philosophy. One of the things that's interesting when I read your discussion of pragmatism is that you're very careful to try to cabin it off from consequentialism. Why do you find it so necessary to do so?

POSNER: Oh, because I'm persuaded by the arguments that utilitarianism is flawed.

HACKNEY: You're talking about the Dworkin arguments?

POSNER: Yes.

HACKNEY: That has a long tradition.

POSNER: Yes, questions like, "Do you want to maximize average utility or total utility?" In maximizing average utility, you end up with maybe one person in the world who has all the money, so that maximizes average utility. Maximizing total utility, you end up with trillions of people living at the poverty level. So yes, I don't think utilitarianism is satisfactory. Clearly utility, welfare, and happiness are all important social goods, so you would certainly want to consider them. However, to make utility your lodestar would be real dogmatism. I used to be sympathetic to it, but not anymore.

HACKNEY: How do your conversations go with the law and economics types today? Or do you engage contemporary law and economics scholars?

POSNER: Not really. It's become very, very specialized. Economic analysis of law is now focused on very specific issues. So no, I don't interact too much with its practitioners, with some exceptions.

HACKNEY: One of the things that I find very interesting about your discussion of pragmatism and pragmatic judging is that you explicitly take into account the role that ideology plays in judging. You take the position that everyone has a belief structure, but not in the critical legal studies sense. However, you also articulate in conjunction with your pragmatic defense of economic analysis, libertarianism. In particular you evoke John Stuart Mill. Can you reflect on how your libertarian tilt plays a role in your own adjudication, and the perspective that you take on the law and cases.

POSNER: Well, I like Mill's central idea about leaving people alone unless they're interfering with others. I'm sure that has a role in my adjudication, but I'm not really conscious of that. When a judge is actually dealing with a case, he doesn't usually think about the philosophical background.

HACKNEY: And when did you first read Mill?

POSNER: Not very long ago. The first substantial thing I did on jurisprudence was my *Problems of Jurisprudence*, which was published in 1990.

HACKNEY: Would you say, in terms of your ideological formation, you always had a libertarian streak?

POSNER: No, I don't think so. I was a conventional liberal until the late sixties. My views changed for a couple of reasons. One was that I didn't like all the rioting of the late sixties, you know, the Vietnam stuff. I call that disorder. And also, and more important, when I met the Chicago school economists they had an influence on me.

HACKNEY: Was Frank Knight there at that time?

POSNER: He was, but he was very, very old. He wasn't doing well. The intellectual forces were Ronald Coase, Aaron Director, George Stigler, and Milton Friedman. However, I didn't know Milton too well. It was quite a conservative environment. I'd never known intelligent conservatives, so it was eye-opening.

HACKNEY: Another really interesting aspect to your pragmatic adjudication is that you have an explicit discussion of the role of difference. In particular, you discuss the need to populate the judiciary with folks who have different backgrounds.

POSNER: Yes, judges don't really have a cogent methodology. So the danger is that if everybody is alike, they'll agree because they're alike, not because they have a methodology that can drive people of different backgrounds, etcetera, to agree. This is a very sort of Deweyan thought. The best you can hope for, when you don't have rigorous methodologies, is that if you have diverse people, there will be more information and it will influence the development of law for the good. If we pool diverse perspectives, insights and so on, we'll all be enriched by those different insights. Whereas if we just had people who were all alike, who had the same very narrow professional background, and so on, they'd agree, but they'd agree because they were alike, not because there was some strong intellectual justification for their position.

HACKNEY: That's a very interesting perspective because it is actually analogous to a point raised by those who support affirmative action. There's what is referred to as a "cultural pluralist" defense of affirmative action. Would you extend your analysis of the judiciary, and the need for diversity in the judiciary, to society generally? And do you think that has any implication with regard to affirmative action, not in terms of legal doctrine, but as a broad public policy issue?

POSNER: Well, of course, it depends a lot. There are some situations, for example, in policing and intelligence agencies, in which doing the job properly requires cultural sensitivity. Those would be strong areas for affirmative action. This would be epistemological affirmative action, and it's like epistemological diversity. However, much of affirmative action is about responding to customers. If you have a lot of black customers, you may feel that it's important for you to have black executives, even if you don't think the black executives have greater insight into customer needs. You may just feel that your customers would like to think that their people are in your firm. That's perfectly reasonable. That wouldn't be epistemic affirmative action. So I think a lot of affirmative action is responsive to pressures. I don't find that troublesome. Clearly, there's a real problem of race because the black community in the United States is on average, with obvious exceptions, far behind the white community (disproportionately lower incomes and greater involvement in crime, for example), and that's a real problem. I think that affirmative action is an appropriate tool to address that issue.

The problem is that once you have an institution called affirmative action, everybody else clamors to get on the bandwagon, and I think there have been abuses. I think particularly with respect to Hispanics, because the Hispanic community is incredibly diverse. The former governor of New Mexico, Bill Richardson, who had been the secretary of energy in the Clinton administration, is an example. I guess his mother is Spanish, but with a name like that you'd never guess that he was Hispanic; there doesn't seem to be anything culturally distinctive about him. My mother was born in Austria, but I don't think you'd call me an Austrian. However, Richardson parades his Hispanic identity. I think women too raise issues with regard to affirmative action.

I don't think there's any reason for affirmative action for women generally. On the other hand, I do think there is this kind of epistemological diversity argument for having women on the court, because I've noticed that men and women react very differently to certain types of behavior, particularly sexual harassment. Women are more sensitive to sexual harassment, and men are much more sensitive to false accusations of sexual harassment. It's productive to have men and women on the court dealing with issues of that sort because they're bringing these different perspectives, and so the law ends up as some mixture and is not one-sided.

HACKNEY: I think you've covered this somewhat, but a lot of your recent scholarship is a critique of moral theory, particularly "high moral theory." Why do you find that enterprise troublesome? One of your criticisms is that moral theory is divorced from social context. To the extent that social context matters, how does that play into adjudication?

POSNER: Well, I think what's interesting about moral theory is that it's so weak a mode of reasoning. If you believe that a fetus is ensouled at the moment of conception, and I don't agree, there's not going to be a profitable discussion of that subject between the two of us. A lot of these moral principles are based on religious sensibilities, or they're based on hostility to religion, or they're based on temperament, or life experience. Ronald Dworkin is very smart and can give a patina of fancy moral reasoning to his arguments, but the real nerve of those arguments is political liberalism. Clearly one's moral principles are going to influence decisions, but I don't think they can be made into a discipline. Affirmative action is a good example of the problem. You can ask what the consequences are: Are they good, are they bad, what would happen if we abolished affirmative action? If affirmative action is lawful for private entities, do we want to have stricter rules in certain contexts? We can fruitfully discuss all this. However, if it is framed as, any use of race or religion is forbidden, or there is an absolute duty to rectify historical injustices, it isn't going to be a profitable discussion. When you have a disagreement, you should try to see whether the disagreement depends at all on facts, and if it depends on facts, and you have different factual views, then is there some way of deciding who's right on the facts. If so, then you can make real progress. You can have a productive discussion. However, if a disagreement is not fact based, or the facts can't be found, you're not having a factual dispute, then discussion fails, then it's a matter of votes. So a lot of adjudication, especially at the Supreme Court level, but at my level to a certain extent, ends up in voting because there isn't going to be an analytic method that resolves the dispute.

HACKNEY: Is the purpose of diversity representation?

POSNER: If you're going to have voting, you'd like the courts to be representative to the extent that they're really making political judgments. You want them to be representative. Now, with nine people on the Supreme Court, it's not a large enough sample to have real diversity, but you can have some. The other thing about diversity is that if you have an employment structure that is not meritocratic, then affirmative action can actually get you a better workforce, even if there's no sort of epistemic diversity. Suppose with men and women judges that men are actually much more politically connected than women. Some men who are hired, who are appointed, may only get the appointment because of a political connection in the House, or the Senate, or the administration. However, if you decide that you have to have a certain number of women and they're not politically connected, well, then you'll take the best, so you may get better quality. That's one reason I don't worry much about affirmative action.

HACKNEY: You pay a good deal of attention to a host of legal theories in *Overcoming Law*. You talk about critical race theory, feminist theory, etcetera. I'm interested, aside from law and economics, which you still have a lot of affinity toward, what do you view as the legal theories that are doing the type of work you think is good, in terms of helping promote this pragmatic view of legal theory and adjudication.

POSNER: Well, you know, I'm not really that up on it because *Overcoming Law* was published in 1995, and most of the chapters in it are reworked from book reviews or essays published even earlier. They are reactions to things that I had read or argued over in the early nineties. I don't really know where these fields have gone. I do have some sense of critical legal studies having dwindled. In my later book, *Frontiers of Legal Theory*, it struck me that the interesting approaches to law were increasingly based on cognitive psychology.

HACKNEY: Cognitive psychology is very much part of the "new" law and economics.

POSNER: Yes, that's right. So yes, economists have picked this up and run with it. But I think of it as essentially cognitive psychology. I used to keep tabs on economic analysis of law. Now, I know there is a lot of interest in international law. My son Eric has been specializing in that. He is also a political scientist. You probably have a better sense of fields that have taken off than I do.

HACKNEY: There is definitely a proliferation of fields. It is one of the interesting phenomena that I puzzle over as an intellectual historian. Ironically, there doesn't seen to be much real conflict between schools of thought today. There's no school taking on another school. There's just a proliferation. People do their things in their little pigeonholes. You write a book about pragmatism that one could argue has some definite implications with regard to law and economics, but any law and economics type populating a school today would probably never read it—never think to respond to it. Similarly, they can be next door to a feminist theorist on the faculty, and there's no conflict. The feminist theorists go to the feminist conferences, and the law and economics types go to their conferences. There isn't any interchange.

POSNER: Yes, well that's very interesting because as the field expands, and there are lots more law professors than there used to be, the little subunits become large enough that they can just form their own little worlds.

HACKNEY: Yes, they form their own little worlds.

POSNER: And they have their own journals.

HACKNEY: Yes, they have their own journals. My spin on legal theory today is that it reflects the neopragmatist turn. If you take neopragmatism as standing for the proposition that there is no dominant "Truth" with a capital *T* out there, then the natural conclusion is that you have a proliferation of theoretical movements representing "truth" with a lowercase *t*, and they make advances in their narrow field. No one makes a claim for an overarching theory. The last real claim to an overarching theory in the legal academy was law and economics.

POSNER: It's interesting. The turmoil of the late sixties and early seventies was accompanied by a lot of intellectual excitement. Political disagreement can be vitalizing. People disagreed about politics and were upset and then they started thinking about how to build theoretical weaponry. Today things are much blander. People are very careerist, looking for a nice, comfortable academic career and a high salary. I hesitate to say this because it's an old person's sort of reaction, but I do think academic law is less exciting than it was in the late sixties and early seventies. It was remarkable that within a period of a few years you had law and economics developing, you had critical legal studies, feminist legal theory, critical race theory, law and society, and other areas. Now that's all quieted down.

Morton Horwitz is the Charles Warren Professor of American Legal History at the Harvard Law School. Professor Horwitz has made major contributions in the field of American legal history. His *Transformation of American Law, 1780–1860* (1977, for which he received the prestigious Bancroft Prize) and *Transformation of American Law, 1870–1960* (1992) are canonical texts in the field of legal history. He is also the author of *The Warren Court and the Pursuit of Justice* (1998) and editor (along with William Fisher and Thomas Reed) of *American Legal Realism* (1993). Professor Horwitz's major substantive fields are constitutional law and torts. He is also one of the founding figures in the critical legal studies movement.

3

Legal History

MORTON HORWITZ

HACKNEY: I'm going to begin with some general background questions in terms of academic history and influences. So let's start in college. Can you give me a sense of what it was like being a student at CCNY, now CUNY, in the early sixties?

HORWITZ: It would be the years 1955–1959—the late fifties. So one of the general points is I felt the fifties all around me. In general, there was an incredibly narrow set of conventional wisdom about politics and morality and so on. The only difference was, at City College, there was this small active left—ranging all the way to the pro-Chinese Communist progressive labor organization. So there were various battles around that. A big one in the year 1958 was a group wanting to send a delegation to the Moscow Youth Festival, which had its own symbolism—it was a Soviet event. So I became active in politics there, against sending the delegation, and eventually the left/liberal divide came to the fore. It always makes me wretchedly unhappy because the only way to draw the line was to label people some form of red—doing exactly what Senator McCarthy was doing at the same time. So that made me very unhappy in terms of the politics of it all. In terms of the culture of the place, I guess the first thing to say about CCNY in the period that I was there was that unlike the pre–World War II period when you could honestly say—as *Time* magazine continued to say—that it was the poor kid's Harvard, it was not really true by the time I arrived there. There were poor kids, but the kids who before—especially Jewish kids from New York—couldn't get into the Ivy Leagues due to discrimination were now being admitted into the Ivy League schools in significant numbers. Those people in the thirties and early forties had continued to go to CCNY. So it was not a very intellectually exciting place. However, it had lots of virtues, including small classes where you and the professor could really get to know each other. To highlight the influence there was one teacher who really, really made a difference. Her name was Joan Gadol. At a certain point, after she divorced, she resumed her maiden name, Joan Kelly. She became quite a famous feminist scholar—among the earliest feminist scholars. By then she taught at Sarah Lawrence, where she taught for the rest of her short life. I was in touch with her until she died. She died of cancer. She taught me 19th-century intellectual history and introduced me to books and ideas that I had never heard about before.

In 1959 I set out to apply for a PhD. I wanted to get a PhD in philosophy, and I won a Woodrow Wilson doctoral fellowship to study philosophy, which made it all possible. What I only came to realize almost at the end of my undergraduate education was that professional philosophy in the 1950s offered nothing of what I was interested in. John Rawls's social and political philosophy was still in the future. Virtually all major American philosophy departments ignored the subject.

HACKNEY: It was all in political science I assume.

HORWITZ: Yes, the only place to study political theory was in government or political science departments. Yet it was even becoming rare in political science, as the subject was in the process of becoming more "scientific." The Harvard government department was one of the places where you could still study political theory. So the summer after I won the Wilson I switched from the philosophy to the government department.

HACKNEY: You were originally from New York?

HORWITZ: Yes, from the Bronx, and my father was a taxicab driver. I was an only child. My mother was a homemaker. That was my world—the world of a single child, in a devoted, but overprotective, Jewish household.

I had no idea of how you became a professor. It was Joan Gadol who guided my academic progress, and made it clear what one needed to do. I don't think when I was a sophomore I even knew what a PhD was, and in the world that I occupied no one else did either. There was an earlier stage I didn't mention. I went to Stuyvesant High School. Stuyvesant High School is one of the elite schools that are still thriving today; it continues to admit students based on exams. The only difference between then and now is that it was all boys when I went there. It was my first contact with students from professional or business families. In this sense, it was the best version of New York as a melting pot of class, though not of race. Stuyvesant was very important to me in terms of making friends who were intellectually ambitious. That's where I think I first imagined that I might become an academic, though what one did to bring that about I only learned later.

Joan Gadol introduced me to one of the first intellectual works that influenced me, Karl Manheim's *Essays on the Sociology of Knowledge*. Mannheim argued that where you are placed in a social situation matters to what you think about the social situation. So in an era in which the sociology of knowledge and its contextual historicity was suppressed, it was Manheim, who writing during the thirties, was an important influence in shaping historically oriented, European sociology. He was an incredibly important influence in allowing me to realize that ideas—and truth itself—were historically and situationally contingent.

HACKNEY: The government program at Harvard was broader than we think of it today. What was actually there, and what did you latch on to?

HORWITZ: The political theory was—I suppose the easiest way to describe it—centered on the "great books." Though not like the University of Chicago, you took the ideas of the great political thinkers seriously and you read the texts. You knew the difference between early Plato and late Plato, and between Plato and Aristotle. You studied political theory as a historical subject. There were two people in the department who, but for the accidents of the boundaries of fields, could have been American historians. The first was Louis Hartz. American historians think of him as an American historian. He wrote *The Liberal Tradition in America* and several other really fine books. He is one of the few geniuses I have known or studied with in my life. He died in a very sad way. Though he was not ever an intimate of mine, he had a deep intellectual influence on me. When I lecture sometimes, especially in the college, I actually listen to myself and hear Louis Hartz lecturing. He had that kind of influence on me. Unlike other mentors, like Joan Gadol, he was not somebody I dropped in on. I didn't have that kind of mentor/mentee relationship with him. It was only through watching and listening to him that he served as a mentor. The other person who had a more personal influence on me, and influenced me in a more focused way, was Robert McCloskey, who wrote *The American Supreme Court*. This is another aspect of government departments that hardly exists anymore. If you wanted someone with whom to study constitutional law historically, there was no better person than McCloskey. However, he wasn't a great mind in the way that Hartz was.

HACKNEY: Encyclopedic?

HORWITZ: Yes, but I would also emphasize that he was a distinguished scholar. He was especially proud when he was asked to write the *Harvard Law Review* foreword on the reapportionment cases, the first time that a nonlawyer was chosen for that role.

HACKNEY: And his approach to constitutional history, would you consider it to be a traditional approach, or one in which you focus on a more modernist approach, looking at particular breaks and historical moments, etcetera? How would you situate him along those lines?

HORWITZ: That was a period, the 1950s, when if you learned about constitutional law at Harvard Law School [HLS] it was focused primarily on recent Supreme Court decisions. Indeed, the Warren Court contributed to that. Everyday we learned of another pathbreaking decision. The result was that during the sixties, for example, constitutional criminal law massively expanded and left no room for the older cases. In general, it was the time when constitutional law lost its historical focus in law schools. The historical approach was carried on in graduate schools, particularly in government departments, under professors like McCloskey.

Constitutional history also had a particular content. It continued to focus on the progressive critique of the *Lochner* Court. The reason you studied the history of the Supreme Court was in order not to repeat its errors. That was also the subtext of McCloskey's views. He grew up in Wisconsin and received his undergraduate degree from the University of Wisconsin. He embodied what was then a progressive, Wisconsin view on American history. In his first book, McCloskey portrayed late 19th-century conservatives who helped shaped the *Lochner* era. One of them was Justice Stephen Field, whom McCloskey represented as a tool of big business. Interestingly enough, the last area in which progressivism collapsed in American intellectual life was law. Constitutional historians continued to hold a negative view of the *Lochner* Court for a longer period of time than of any other court. McCloskey, and his predecessor, Benjamin Wright, developed that view. Justice Souter's opinion in *Casey* provides an interesting case history of how the progressive view plays out. The case surprised everybody because it was thought that the final death knell of *Roe v. Wade* had come. However, Kennedy, O'Connor, and Souter separated themselves from the overruling justices. They began by asserting that they wouldn't have agreed to *Roe v. Wade* as an original proposition. But because they believed that the Supreme Court should not lightly agree to overrule prior decisions, this was not an appropriate case for overruling. Then they surveyed the history of prior overrulings.

As I read that history, I knew it must have been written by Justice Souter. The account of the overruling of *Lochner* could only have been learned by having been exposed to Wright and McCloskey at Harvard College in the fifties. It was the same history that I had learned from McCloskey.

Now let us fast-forward to 1977, when *The Transformation of American Law, 1780–1860* [*Transformation I*] was published. Where do we place my work for the purpose of determining how I relate to all of these influences? Eugene Genovese wrote an extremely interesting review of *Transformation I*—declaring that I was not a Marxist but rather an interest group liberal. My purpose in writing history was to demonstrate the external influences on the law. Hadn't the realists been doing that since the 1930s? At the time, I only partly understood that the progressive account of constitutional history had been weakened. But I did understand that such a realist account could still be intellectually subversive within a law school world where "neutral principles" philosophy continued to reign. I didn't fully understand at the time why *Transformation I* had this electric shock effect. What needs to be explained about the reaction to *Transformation I* was why it provoked such an intensely negative and critical reaction.

HACKNEY: Before we get to that point, as part of your explanation you highlighted the reaction within law schools. It would be helpful if you could just take us back to your law school experience at Harvard, because then I think it becomes clearer why what you say in *Transformation I* would be so antithetical to the ethos within the mainstream American legal academy.

HORWITZ: So the question is, how can you generalize about Harvard Law School from the years I was there, 1964–1967? I think the first thing that needs to be said is that it was a very apolitical institution. The norms of legal process and neutral principles dominated the sensibilities of the place. It was also a period in which the Warren Court was issuing revolutionary judicial rulings. There was a disparity between what my professors taught, and my reaction to what was happening around me—both negative (Vietnam) and positive (the Warren Court). I experienced law school as out-of-date, and irrelevant for understanding what really mattered about American society.

HACKNEY: I know you took a class with Henry Hart. Can you explain that experience?

HORWITZ: Henry Hart is a wonderful example of what was wrong with Harvard Law School and one of the most brilliant of its representatives. I took Henry Hart for federal courts in my third year. The year before taking federal courts I had taken the legal process course, with the famous, unpublished Hart and Sacks legal process materials. A large percent of any particular class at Harvard Law School took the legal process course. Nationwide they sold the materials at cost to be reproduced elsewhere. The large number of copies used every year in law schools in the second half of the 1950s through the first half of the 1960s illustrates the dominance of the legal process mentality in law schools. Just as I was entering law school, the influence of the legal process approach began its sharp decline.

While I was in law school, the Vietnam draft was instituted with a lottery system that meant that it was no longer possible to avoid the draft by becoming a professional graduate student. Everybody around me in law school suddenly became more political. It was very painful watching all of that. It resulted in a real sort of student revolt at Harvard Law School. Not like what happened at Yale, later. But I think that for the first time in Harvard Law School's history there was contempt for professors as apolitical pedants, if not worse. The Vietnam War and the civil rights movement produced a major political reaction among the students.

HACKNEY: What was the reaction on the HLS faculty to the civil rights cases?

HORWITZ: First, I'll share an interaction with McCloskey as an example. I remember walking through Harvard Yard with him, talking about *Brown* and his suggesting, as he does at the end of *The American Supreme Court*, that it would have been better if the Supreme Court had not overruled *Plessy* but, instead, tightened up the separate but equal standard. I remember that my jaw dropped when I heard him say that. I was shocked. It was an example of how progressives had become politically disabled after years of opposing *Lochner*.

HACKNEY: Yes, technically sound, but politically bankrupt.

HORWITZ: Exactly. And even going one step further, there were some Harvard Law School professors who held the view that *Brown* was wrongly decided. That was a terrible, amazing shock to me. I couldn't believe it. You could see that liberal legal theorists were becoming more and more disillusioned by the actions of the Warren Court. The Warren Court was actually puncturing a hole in our teachers' view of judicial restraint, almost the academic mirror image of Frankfurter. And it really bothered them.

Here's another example. Owen Fiss was in his first year at Harvard Law School in 1961. He remembers sitting in the Langdell Reading Room studying, and he saw this group of people gathering and then growing more and more intense. He asked somebody what was going on, and they told him that *Baker v. Carr* was just handed down. It overturned Frankfurter's decision that apportionment was nonjusticiable. The next day in class, his torts teacher spent the entire class denouncing the decision in *Baker* as destroying the rule of law. So that really captures how interpenetrated all these ideas were. That is, that the Frankfurter wing of the Supreme Court, and the prevailing ideal of neutral principles at Harvard Law School, were self-reinforcing all the way through. There is no question that the legal and political stances of my teachers had a significant negative influence on me. I think the deep truth of the Harvard Law School experience was that I didn't have one person as a mentor. There was nobody who really looked after me, so to speak. But then, of course, it was Harvard Law School.

HACKNEY: We've previously discussed the fact that Martin Luther King and Walter Reuther were tremendous inspirational influences on you. Can you put those two in relief, and your response to them?

HORWITZ: Walter Reuther was a generation earlier than Martin Luther King. He was the first head of the United Auto Workers. He was very important in labor history, and for forming one of the first CIO unions. He was very egalitarian in organizing, and also active in the very heroic labor battles of 1937 when they finally won recognition as a union. For those like me who saw the Soviet Union as both a tyranny and a failure, there were few role models for democratic socialism. Though he wouldn't have put it this way, Reuther was the best representative of democratic socialism in America. He created a strong, egalitarian union that got incredible benefits for its members.

Now, let's talk about Martin Luther King. He was the greatest orator that I ever experienced in my lifetime. Who to compare to? FDR was only a radio stick figure. As an inspiring orator only President Obama comes close to Dr. King. These flashes of recollection go all the way back to my days at Stuyvesant High School.

HACKNEY: Was Stuyvesant integrated racially?

HORWITZ: There was one black guy in my homeroom class, who later became deputy police commissioner of New York. He went to Dartmouth College—in 1959. He was probably the only African American at Dartmouth College. There were very few black students at Stuyvesant High School when I studied there. I do remember, actually vividly remember, the day *Brown* was decided. I was a sophomore in high school. Then one year later, during my junior high school trip to Washington, D.C., *Brown II* was being argued by some southern attorney. I was really connected, emotionally, to the civil rights movement. I went on a few marches to Washington, though I didn't go to MLK's great Washington rally.

HACKNEY: Now, moving forward to your career as a legal historian. There was a transition from being in the government department, going to law school, and obtaining your position on the Harvard faculty. You were a postdoctoral fellow here before you actually got your appointment. When you first started thinking about what you wanted to write, how did you set your academic agenda? It seems clear from your review of James McClellan's and Gerald Dunne's biographies of Joseph Story that the central focus in the beginning was on the consensus view of history. Your intellectual project could be broadly described as critical history. So you're displacing the consensus view, and the consensus view can be framed as the conservative consensus or the progressive response. There are progressive historians who represent the left but with whom you disagree, going back to your discussion about the reaction to *Brown*. Did you have a conscious moment at which you laid out your intellectual project? Did once you began to write your background (with Gadol and sociology of knowledge) just pour itself out?

HORWITZ: I think you are definitely right that at the top of my agenda was the wish to attack consensus history. What I didn't realize was that it was going to be so controversial. After all, *Transformation I* was published in 1977, when a total attack on consensus history was long underway in history departments. However, in law schools it remained part of conventional wisdom. I did realize that there were subversive possibilities in bursting that bubble. I was particularly critical of the consensus view of why law changed. But I didn't anticipate at the time that there would be a very negative reception among law professors. I think the raw nerve that *Transformation I* touched was in its efforts to undermine claims to the neutrality of law and legal reasoning.

From the perspective of professional legal historians, the great challenge was in explaining private law in terms of its social, political, and economic setting in ways that hadn't often been done before. Constitutional law had already been written about in such sweeping terms, and had more or less absorbed the constitutional law history. I set out to do the same thing in private law areas such as contract and tort. So it turns out, and I think this much I was aware of at the time, I wanted to offer an example of how you do real historical work both in doctrine and in archival work. How do you translate that into something you would call a theory? I think it may also be true that most of the theories that appear in *Transformation I* are way too overbroad and contentious, and the evidence only partly, if at all, proves the theory. Maybe that matters for rigorous social science, but for demonstrating how to do this type of legal history, *Transformation I* still remains a good, provocative example.

HACKNEY: The juxtaposition is interesting. Everything we've talked about up to this point has been related to constitutional law, with no real focus on private law. How did you make the move to focusing your critical project on private law instead of constitutional law? It's an interesting connection because Duncan Kennedy did the same thing when he began his career as an academic. Was it in law school that you thought about this as a project?

HORWITZ: I think it's a multistep project that I can more or less trace. First, was writing my PhD dissertation. At that time Perry Miller's book *Life of the Mind in America* came out, which had a very important influence on me, particularly the intellectual history of the codification movement. Here I was, about to receive my PhD in an American history subject, and I didn't know either that there was a codification movement or that it had an intellectual history. Perry Miller was totally confused about how to theorize about law. He encountered law as if it were English literature, and he thought the paradigms of English literature could be applied to law. It didn't really work, but he did demonstrate the existence of rich source material and a robust rhetorical tradition that had emerged from the codification debate over a hundred years. Next, in my second year of law school, there was a totally unexpected encounter with Mark DeWolfe Howe. He taught legal history here. I was taking corporations, taxation, and accounting, and really didn't like it. I went to him to ask him how do I get through this. I didn't get any advice from my first-year teachers, but I heard that he was a nice professor who would be sympathetic, and that was sufficiently rare (as a stereotype). So he recommended to me a book by C. H. S. Fifoot, *Judges and Jurists in the Reign of Queen Victoria*. It was this really broad-brush, elegantly written history of English 19th-century legal doctrine (including contracts and torts) set in a background of political, economic, and cultural history. I immediately realized that his approach was what I wanted to do. It was very clear to me. His book wasn't the sort of thing that you would ordinarily think of as providing a model, but he showed me that there was an intellectual history of private law that I had never realized existed. That was an incredible clue, which I have never forgotten.

HACKNEY: Can you talk about the differences between *Transformation I* and *Transformation II* [*Transformation of American Law, 1870–1960*, published in 1992]? Regarding *Transformation I*, you already covered a few components: the archival nature, and placing private law in historical relief. However, *Transformation I* and *Transformation II* are methodologically different. In the prologue to *Transformation II* you write about it being a methodological shift. *Transformation II* seems to be more explicitly modernist, some might even say postmodern. It also seems to be more explicitly an intellectual history—history of ideas—so we have these broad concepts being discussed. This again might be the Duncan Kennedy influence. You're not digging into the archival minutia as much in *Transformation II* as talking about ideas on broad theoretical levels. Can you juxtapose the two? What was the mind-set in *Transformation II*?

HORWITZ: I would say the major shift between *Transformation I* and *Transformation II* was in the view of how and why you did history. In 1977 when I published *Transformation I*, history was still mostly viewed as a branch of the social sciences. And though there had been many changes by 1977, it was still true, I think, that most historians viewed themselves as contributing another empirical building block. That was still the sort of "unself-conscious" state that I had when I did *Transformation I*. You know, you go into the archives, you spot all the details, and you spin them into this larger thing as you accumulate more and more information. By the time I did *Transformation II*, I was out of that. And there are specific moments in which I realized that things had changed. So let me just talk about a series of parallel methodological reorientations. The first has to do with a big debate that began almost immediately in the 1970s at the first meeting of critical legal studies, and really sort of became the central debate at our first summer camp. It was a huge methodological debate. It was partially about Marxism and partially about general 19th-century legal theory that supposed that you could have these large covering laws, allowing you to make if-then statements and predictions about the future. That was the debate. There were primary materials, and for a week we really argued it to the death.

HACKNEY: And the "we"? Were there other historians there?

HORWITZ: These were the first generation of critical legal studies theorists.

HACKNEY: Okay, so we're talking about Duncan Kennedy, David Trubek, Mark Tushnet, etcetera. Was Bob Gordon there?

HORWITZ: I think that would have been just a little bit too early for Bob Gordon. He wasn't yet a professor. In any event, Bob Gordon always had a complicated, distant relationship to CLS. He never thought of himself as one of the core people in it. However, the CLS conversations to me were resoundingly important. They surfaced, in a way that I never really realized before, the issue of causal attribution. When my earlier social science view was implanted in me, we had a very simple, uncontested idea about causal statements that nobody really called into question. By the time I was writing *Transformation II*, the question of whether you could make causal attributions when there were multicausal influences was a central issue, which also produces postmodernism. So I arrived in writing *Transformation II* very much aware that methodological assumptions had changed significantly in history and social thought during the fifteen years in between *Transformation I* and *Transformation II*. First the local influences. Bob Gordon's *Critical Legal Histories* was one of those learning jolts in terms of finally clarifying for me the critique of functionalism and historical explanations. He finally helped me place myself within that debate. The preface to *Transformation II* discusses these new insights. Another strand, and perhaps the most important, was the influence of Duncan Kennedy and Roberto Unger. I was lucky enough to arrive at Harvard Law School one year before Duncan and Roberto. There aren't too many people who are that lucky. They were just firing off stuff faster than you could handle, so I learned an incredible amount from Duncan and Roberto in those early years. I attended Roberto's jurisprudence lectures leading up to his publishing *Knowledge and Politics*. He had a profound influence on my approach to social theory.

HACKNEY: Let's talk about another influence—Thomas Kuhn's *Structure of Scientific Revolutions*.

HORWITZ: Kuhn's book appeared at a certain moment in my education. It had a specific function in forming my intellectual perspective. The idea of there being paradigm shifts began for me back with Karl Manheim's *Ideology and Utopia*, which Joan Gadol turned me on to. I was in college when I read it. Kuhn's *Structure of Scientific Revolutions* had a relativistic tone about how paradigms rise and fall. So it had the general cultural influence of, again let me state this simply, stating the position that even science wasn't objective. However, its immediate influence on me was the notion of paradigms and structures. Law seemed to me to be just ready to be thought about in terms of structures of reasoning. That was its influence very early. *Transformation II* applies Kuhn to changes in legal paradigms.

HACKNEY: Yes, formalism versus legal realism—the clash. *The Structure of Scientific Revolutions* obviously is a generally important book because someone to which we might not have thought it to be influential, Richard Posner, in a book review of Guido Calabresi's *Costs of Accidents*, set up Calabresi as the paradigmatic foil for the legal realists. I think he might even cite to Kuhn in framing it as one paradigm displacing another—law and economics displacing legal realism. It's a measure of the pervasiveness. Another train of thought that I want you to reflect on is Marxism. Can you trace through your ideas about Marxism—how they situate intellectually, but also politically, because there was a moment in which you explicitly stated that you rejected the stark Communist political view in favor of a democratic socialist view? And then you get to *Transformation I* and Genovese labels you an interest group liberal. Had you really grappled with Marxism at any particular time?

HORWITZ: Marxism is two things for me. There is a whole family dynamic, and there is Marxism as a political-intellectual theory. The political fault lines within my family extended between my mother and her family, who were either Communists or Communist sympathizers, and my father, who tended to be a liberal democratic, Walter Reuther type. My family was very close and we were together all the time. Though these were not people who were well-read in Marxist theory, simple Marxist theory was part of my world by the time I was fifteen. I spent time with my uncles and aunts who were part of a little left-wing colony in Peekskill, New York, where all sorts of left-wing history was recounted. Do you know about the Paul Robeson riots?

HACKNEY: I have heard of Paul Robeson.

HORWITZ: He was a great African American singer. During the early years of the Cold War he was a Communist fellow traveler and spouted the party line. As a result, he was blacklisted and couldn't get a job. Early in the Cold War, he gave a concert in Peekskill. The people who came to the concert were interracial liberals, and reds. The people who stood guard for Americanism were American Legion types, standing atop the bridges, and throwing down torches to disrupt things. The Paul Robeson concert became part of left-American legendary history. But it was also included in family oral history.

When I was fifteen or sixteen years old, I spent time critically studying Soviet history in order to participate in family political argument. I became quite expert on the break between Stalin and Trotsky and on the Stalin show trials, for example. During graduate school, it turned out, I had the opportunity to study with one of the handful of surviving left scholars in the American academy, Barrington Moore. Moore wrote his first book on Soviet Russia while affiliated with the Russian Research Center. He was a serious, critical historical sociologist who became an outlier in his field as sociology was being transformed into value-free behavioral social science.

He taught a rigorous course on classical social theory, covering Marx, Durkheim, and Weber, and accompanied every page of reading with specific questions about the text. This really was my first opportunity to study Marxism. A decade later, when I was a young faculty member, we formed a Marx study group. It included Duncan Kennedy, Kathy Stone, Karl Klare, Gary Bellow, and Jeanne Charn. (I have failed to mention one or two other members for whom it might still be inconvenient to be identified with such an undertaking.) We read actual texts. The split between consciousness Marxism and scientific Marxism was becoming intense after the publication during the sixties of Marx's 1844 manuscripts on "alienation." I was thirty-two or thirty-three years old at the time. Duncan had begun to emphasize postmodernism, so we read Lukács—it was my first encounter with him and it was a mind-boggling experience.

So, again, if you connect the dots that start with Manheim, go to Kuhn, and then to Lukács—that was my learning trajectory. Lukács's essay "Reification and the Consciousness of the Proletariat," published in 1923, was one of the earliest articulations of consciousness Marxism. We were studying Lukács at a point in the history of Marxist theory when the Italian Communist Party represented a Gramscian, anti-Stalinist way of thinking. During these years, dating from my early years as an assistant professor through the early years of CLS, I really read, studied, and thought about Marxism more then I ever had before. Though I never thought of myself as a Marxist, I was very interested in those debates, especially in terms of what it meant to talk about the relationship between the economic system and society. However, I would say that by the time 1980 rolled around I felt that Marxism didn't have anything more to offer me, even as a theoretical understanding of things. Unlike some of my friends and contemporaries, whose attitude toward Marxism approached that of religious doctrine, I always maintained a critical distance.

HACKNEY: And that's up to the formation of CLS. I know there is a historical tension in CLS, at least at its inception, between the Marxist way of theorizing, versus a social scientific approach. Can you discuss this split, and your personal history with CLS?

HORWITZ: CLS was from day one founded with the goal of separating itself from Marxism—maybe the only example in my own life of an organization distancing itself from Marxism not as a defense against McCarthyism. It was a particular historical moment in which there was less need to apologize for being a Marxist than in any time since the Russian Revolution. What I did feel, because Duncan and I discussed this a lot, was that American Marxism, or Marxism that was brought about by Americans, had basically run out of steam as reductionist and mechanical. In organizational terms there was concern over a Marxist takeover. Now, retrospectively that seems totally ridiculous, but the bulk of activist/leftists in the sixties and seventies had a tendency toward a Marxist direction. In the real left of these groups Marxists did, from time to time, take over an organization. Now, to imagine this happening in CLS was ridiculous. There were some folks from the Lawyers Guild—for example, David Kairys, who was the editor of *The Politics of Law*. He was a Philadelphia left-practicing lawyer. These people thrived on exposing the tension between theory and practice, and in American law schools they tended to favor clinical education over theory. One of the purposes of CLS was to dissolve the theory/practice distinction. That is, we said that clinicians had something to offer. That was a very unusual spin in the professional politics of legal education. The other thing that turned out to be a prominent tendency in my early education in CLS was a critique of Marxism. We had some of our best theoretical debates in CLS around Marxism, focusing on problems of proving causation and on the relationship between big theory and the facts on the ground. That was, it seemed to me, a very productive era in which every year we had summer camps—sometimes attended by as many as one hundred people—in which we spent two weeks engaged in serious discussions of legal and political theory.

I think for my own actual learning curve, the critique of Marxism was very important, and helped me to think through a lot of the stuff that I needed to reflect on. It is also true that, after a few years, there was no hard left to speak of within the organization. That had to do, first, with the growing professional obstacles, during the Reagan years, to identifying with Marxism. Only Karl Klare and Mark Tushnet, among the founding fathers, had birth attachments to Marxism. Each of them had to work through their own growing skepticism of Marxism, not to speak of its embodiment in Soviet tyranny.

By this time, I think, Karl no longer felt that it was a question of loyalty or to the "faith of his fathers." Tushnet actually reviewed *Transformation I* together with Lawrence Friedman's *History of American Law*. Though he has mellowed since, to his contemporaries Tushnet was a burner and slasher in his youth. This was one of his burn and slash reviews of two bourgeois, liberal books from the perspective of a Marxist. So there you would see, actually, how unusual Tushnet was. He had studied with Genovese, and was still captivated by Genovese's rendition of an American version of Marxist stages of historical development.

HACKNEY: So Marxism is one strand. CLS has the quality of a relatively open-ended group, as opposed to, for example, law and economics, which has a standard set of intellectual paradigms and rules that everyone in the group adheres to in the movement. Can you provide some further historical background on the movement?

HORWITZ: Jerry Frug, fairly late in this process, gave a course at Harvard Law School called "What Are Critical Legal Studies?" When I first wrote about legal realism, my realization that legal realists could not be lumped together came from my then lived experience of critical legal studies. I think that the critiques of positivism in both Marxism and the social sciences more generally converged with each other. There was also the postmodernist strand. So my basic instinct in studying legal realism, having lived through CLS, was that one shouldn't look for uniform substantive tenets or methodological premises, and that it is best to view the movements as a sort of alliance of different ways of thinking, even though they all more or less had the same politics.

HACKNEY: Another way to say it is that they were responding against the same phenomena. In the case of legal realists, they were responding against formalism, but approaching it in different ways. The allegiance is the attack on formalism.

HORWITZ: Right, I think that's very true. Again, you could probably set up a stage theory of legal realism and a stage theory of critical legal studies, and see that they more or less unfold in the same general pattern. There were people all along who never thought of themselves as CLS theorists, but when you look back at their work you see that they were influenced by it. However, they were never willing to ally themselves consciously with it. One of the really important facts of CLS that is going to be lost to history is the intentionally anarchic organizational non-structure. Duncan very self-consciously set it up in that way. He was from the beginning determined that we should not be a centralized organization with positions, interests, and so on. The responsibility of organizing the next annual meeting was passed from one school to another, with almost complete local control and no central organizational budget. It went on like this for, I don't know, fifteen years or so, and it was really hand to mouth year by year. The basic premise was to not set up a central structure whose demise would kill it, and it worked. But it also, of course, meant that to talk about a central body of doctrine was preposterous. What you actually have to talk about is the evolution of concerns over fifteen years. At the maximum, there was one year [1982] when seven hundred people came to Harvard Law School for a CLS meeting. Most of the Harvard faculty had no inkling that anything had changed until they witnessed this surge in attendance. That was a big moment, as the Harvard Law faculty realized that the movement was serious, at least in terms of numbers and organizational energy, and that it needed to be confronted.

HACKNEY: Which probably led to the political battles on the HLS faculty?

HORWITZ: It did lead to the political backlash. I don't know the dates. But if we could actually line up the date of that conference and then see how many years it took for the purge to begin, I would say probably no more than two or three. They were directly related.

HACKNEY: We think of CLS as a constellation of fellow travelers. There are obviously feminist theorists who are part of that grouping. Then there's the grouping of critical race theorists. One of the interesting moments in American legal intellectual history is the coming together, then breaking apart, of the alliance between critical legal studies and critical race theory. I guess you could tell a similar narrative with respect to feminist theory, but intellectually I've been more focused on critical race theory, as opposed to feminist theory. The critical race theory fissure gets surfaced around a debate about rights. You have a piece titled "Rights" in which you attempt to either mediate or focus that debate. Can you reflect on the sociological phenomenon, and then the theoretical piece of it in terms of rights theory and the response on both sides with regard to rights theory?

HORWITZ: At the large labeling level we are talking about the emergence of identity politics. I couldn't possibly date when the feminist showdown took place or when the critical race theory fissure developed. But both the feminist theorists and the critical race theorists viewed CLS as a white guys' domain—an old white guys' domain, or a Harvard and Yale white guys' domain. When the feminist challenge emerged, all that I think they wanted was to be let in. They were already professors. All that they really wanted was to universalize the discourse, and to show how partial and male-oriented the practice was. By the time the black and minority scholars arrived, they were in much greater opposition to this white guys' institution. There was much, much greater tension. I do remember the feeling that most of the critical race scholars were very much in opposition to CLS. The rights debate captured the moment. There were those who argued—whether they came from realism, from Marxist theory, or from left European theory—that rights were a bourgeois way of understanding things. They argued that rights always ultimately support the power structure. That threw down the gauntlet because virtually all of the minority scholars still thought that rights were critical. So there definitely was a split. I felt at the time that it was an unnecessary split because it was becoming clear to me that the way that Marxists analyzed rights almost never took account of the context of how rights discourse actually functioned in American history. More and more I come to think, by the way again back to Martin Luther King, that the discourse of rights drew on the discourse of religious history, and that there was actually a distinctively religious resonance in the discourse of rights that some in the critical legal studies community would not have recognized.

HACKNEY: Which also explains, in terms of a gross biography, how someone from the African American community, given the general religious influence on that community, would have been very personally taken aback by that sort of critique, so I can see the cultural divide there.

HORWITZ: To me, the simple message that CLS delivered was the politics of law. It stands as the message to future law students, and to laypeople—that law in American society was and is heavily influenced by politics (broadly defined). Then there was, of course, the boundary between law and society and CLS, which more than anyone, Duncan really obsessed about. For him, if he was drawing any lines, the most important one was between the liberalism of law and society and the radicalism of CLS. In retrospect, how sensible that move was would require a large digression into the work of law and society scholars, but, as it turns out, there was considerable overlap between the work of law and society and CLS. Some of the people who came to the first CLS conference, whom at least I thought of as future leaders, like Marc Galanter or Stewart Macaulay, eventually moved away from CLS and became much more involved in law and society. Those people thought of CLS as being filled with irresponsible political rabble-rousers.

HACKNEY: My conversation with Austin Sarat about the need that those in law and society felt to keep CLS at bay definitely verifies that historical point. I want to talk more specifically about law and economics. You have an interesting footnote to Coase in the introduction to *Transformation I*, which you use to support a proposition that you make in the text about the danger of using an overarching theory, economic theory, to explain history because Coase shows that economic efficiency can be reached using different legal arrangements. Then you go on to critique law and economics in your 1980 piece, "Science or Politics?" Can you reflect on your views on law and economics? You're a torts professor, so obviously it plays a central role in tort law theory post-1960s.

HORWITZ: It really did come to me very, very slowly. This is the difference between Harvard and Yale, and mainly the influence of Guido Calabresi. My torts professor was Louis Jaffe. He was very, very brilliant and had a big influence on me. I remember vividly a symposium on products liability that had just appeared in the *University of Chicago*

Law Review. It was the first recognition that products liability had emerged as a separate subfield of torts. Jaffe called our attention to it in my first-year torts class, but only to say that products liability was not yet a subject that you really learned in torts. In fact, I believe, the products liability area made the Coase theorem so powerful because there you actually have a case in which the parties are in a bargaining relationship and yet the law imposed strict liability in tort. The real conservative spin on Coase's theory is the attempt to recontractualize products liability. So when did I learn about law and economics? When I began teaching torts in 1970/1971, Calabresi visited Harvard Law School and was in the office next to mine. I was still very much oriented toward doctrine. Jaffe spent five weeks on libel and slander—just to show you where things still were in 1964. It was only in beginning to teach that I realized there already existed a body of work in law and economics. Though I already knew about Coase by the time I wrote that weird footnote in my book, I didn't yet really see the connection to Coase's most extreme claim—that if there are no transaction costs, you only need contract law. I was then writing about water law and property law, and the issue of the transfer of entitlements. Just after I circulated the manuscript, I received a question from Bruce Ackerman: if when transaction costs are low, parties will themselves act, why is all this discussion of water law and property law even relevant after the Coase theorem? I needed to explain. Obviously, if I were more into the discourse, I would have piled on the transaction costs to show that in the real-world transactions are never cost-free. It was Duncan who sent me off reading the few things that I cited for the notion that efficiency is defined in terms of the prior existing distribution. Now that definitional insight also made it clear that Coase's view of efficiency was a static view, as opposed to a dynamic view that takes place over time. So the footnote was more or less my flailing about to neutralize Coase, whom I realized suddenly loomed as a threat to my explanation of legal change.

HACKNEY: Okay, that's the footnote, and then there's the culmination in 1980 of "Science or Politics?"

HORWITZ: By this time, I had been teaching tort law for a decade—a decade in which Coase, Calabresi, and others in law and economics dominate the airwaves in torts. My initial reaction was very favorable, in the following sense. It took you beyond doctrine, and I, like Posner, had a predisposition for economics as a real social science, consequentially oriented view of how the real world works. Even in my torts course, all the way through, you will see that student course evaluations criticize me for injecting too much law and economics. Gradually, of course, I learned that if you could teach students to read it seriously and not just shuck it off as something that the reactionaries used, you could get them to actually critique it from within. I can hardly remember why I then thought that law and economics theory was in decline. Did I forecast the impending death of law and economics just to be rhetorical, or did I really think that the end had come. There was a moment around then [1980] when, unlike the upward-learning curve during the first part of the seventies—when I found cost-benefit analyses very illuminating—that much of the current law and economics writing had become routine. It had turned mostly into elaborate demonstrations of the obvious. The surprising, counterintuitive quality of the early scholarship had turned into Kuhnian "normal science." There is also an evolution in Posner himself. I don't think he had arrived at selling babies by then. But there was a point at which even Posner no longer seemed to provide insight, but just began to defend more and more strongly tautological versions of his story. However, I am not quite sure that I can remember when I wrote that whether in fact I was just being rhetorical in predicting the decline and fall, or whether I already had begun to feel that it was in the process of becoming normal science.

HACKNEY: The way I look at 1980, and how I would place your "Science or Politics?" piece within it, was that the critique of distribution agnosticism had been so withering at that point that the position that distribution does not matter was untenable. Posner had made the move from efficiency to wealth maximization to stave off the Dworkins of the world. When he made the move to wealth maximization he had to deal with Duncan Kennedy and Ed Baker—the starting points critique. At that point the political dimensions of law and economics had been revealed. It's obvious that you can have different political views within law and economics. Posner is critical of Calabresi for his contemporary liberal bent. When I read "Science or Politics?," it reads as a rhetorical flourish to the end of an era in terms of the notion of a scientific law and economics. However, it is also a statement of the institutional situation, which we can go into in more detail later. Getting back to Posner, the next move he makes, after the wealth maximization move, is the neopragmatist move. When we get to *Overcoming Law* and his writings about jurisprudence, his end result is to say there is no normative, theoretical, or meta-philosophical claim to be made in favor of his form of law and economics, which is basically a pro–free market approach. However, there's a pragmatic defense of it: would you rather live in the United States or the Soviet Union? Posner might add: by the way, it's no longer the Soviet Union, it's Russia, and free market capitalism prevails. So there's a neopragmatist shift in Posner, which we can talk about. There is also a neopragmatist shift throughout the legal academy. We see it with Jules Coleman in law and philosophy. There is a critique of analytic philosophy and Coleman repackages it into a neopragmatist garb. You see it in constitutional law—Cass Sunstein as the quintessential neopragmatist. All of the progressives reemerge as neopragmatists. Can you speak on the general shift in the legal academy to neopragmatism being this kind of overarching idea that legal theorists latch onto to defend whatever program or theoretical disposition they prefer?

HORWITZ: It's very interesting. As I hear you talk about this, I say I never really got to engage in that debate. I felt deeply that it was the same old, same old. That someone showed me the charm of Posner being a pragmatist, when I had come to learn that almost all pragmatists were on the progressive side of the ledger, I never really got into that. My only actual allusion to it was somewhere in *Transformation II*, where I raise the issue of whether law and economics and Posner can legitimately lay claim to the mantle of legal realism. That raised the issue of whether legal realism is just a methodology or if it's very much also tied to a group of political values. And that's all that I can say about Posner, except that when he tried pragmatism I already knew the move and was tired of it. My general view is that there is almost never an occasion when a methodology that really is powerful and has actual oomph to it doesn't in some way incorporate political values. You're just not going to be saying much otherwise. So that was my feeling about Posner—that it was just a rediscovery of how you could play the pragmatist game and make it spin in a free market direction.

HACKNEY: Okay, so now to expand. You had a general view of neopragmatism. My reading of the contemporary landscape of the legal academy is that we live in a pluralistic universe, with no dominant theoretical framework. Up to 1980, law and economics had filled the void—before that you could plug in legal process, before that you could plug in legal realism, and before that you could plug in formalism as dominant modes of legal discourse. Today I don't think there is anyway to identify a dominant movement. What you have is a proliferation of increasingly technical theoretical voices. The quintessential example is law and economics. I think it would be virtually impossible to be hired as a law and economics person on a top-tier faculty without having a PhD in economics. It's become increasingly difficult to do the same in history and other disciplines. If you want to do political science in a law school, you better have a PhD in political science, etcetera. So the legal academy is increasingly teched up, but also less generally relevant and so there is less general discourse in American law. That's my own perspective, but I'm interested in how you view the contemporary landscape.

HORWITZ: Well, I think we are on the same wavelength, but I experience it very differently. For me it's the fifties all over again. I feel the simple point is that professionalism cushions, protects, and conceals one from politics. You develop all these intermediate methodologies, and you can spend your lifetime floundering around in those arguments—never having to connect them to the political issues that gave birth to them in the first place. Certainly I feel that. I don't know if you follow the work of Christine Jolls. She teaches law and economics here, and clerked for Posner (was one of Posner and Scalia's liberal clerks). She has a PhD in economics. Anyway, to make a long story short, she is someone who falls into behavioral economics because she likes its subversive quality. However, she doesn't experience it as being subversive. She experiences it as being superior science—recognizing the limits of rationality. When you listen to her talk it's totally within the box. Because of her training, she doesn't experience any of these economic moves as having political implications. It's amazing but it's happening more and more. My earlier experience of this was during the crit purges. People actually began to frame their faculty job talks to conceal their politics. If you could view the job talks over time, you would see every time the political heat rises. You can actually see the ways in which both faculties and the applicants collaborate in avoiding the political perspective. The simple point there is that if we actually all appointed on politics it would be a disaster. That insight produces all of these efforts to theorize at an intermediate level of methodology at which you won't have to get to the politics of it.

HACKNEY: You don't get to the politics, and also it's a level where there is no conversation between methodologies. I think one of the most interesting aspects of the seventies, and you can work your way backward to prior eras, is that there are always moments of conversation and controversy. There is absolutely no controversy between, let's say, Christine Jolls and the feminist scholar down the hall who has a PhD in political theory. You could look at the two and say that they can't coexist, but there is absolutely no antagonism and no conversation. It's just separate worlds.

Austin Sarat is William Nelson Cromwell Professor of Jurisprudence and Political Science, and Five College Fortieth Anniversary Professor at Amherst College. He is well recognized as one of the founders of the law and society movement, and has served as president of the Law and Society Association. Professor Sarat is best known for his contributions to how we understand the relationship of the criminal justice system, particularly the death penalty, to society. However, he has a broad interest in the connections between culture, society, and law. He is the author of several books, including *Cultural Analysis, Cultural Studies, and the Law* (ed. with Jonathan Simon, 2000), *The Killing State* (ed. 2001), *When the State Kills* (2001), *Law, Violence, and the Possibility of Justice* (ed. 2001), *Pain, Death, and the Law* (ed. 2001), *Looking Back at Law's Century* (ed. with Robert Kagan and Bryant Garth, 2002), *Something to Believe In* (ed. with Stuart Scheingold, 2004), *The Cultural Lives of Capital Punishment* (ed. with Christian Boulanger, 2005), *Mercy on Trial* (2005), *When Law Fails* (ed. with Charles Ogletree, 2009), and *The Road to Abolition?* (ed. with Charles Ogletree, 2009). He is currently writing a book titled *Hollywood's Law.* He is editor of the journals *Law, Culture, and the Humanities* and *Studies in Law, Politics, and Society*.

4

Law and Society

AUSTIN SARAT

HACKNEY: Your initial training is as a political scientist, and Amherst doesn't have a law school, so how did you become interested in law as a subspecialty in political science, or have you always had that interest?

SARAT: I went to graduate school at the University of Wisconsin, Madison, for political science with the idea of studying and doing urban politics. My interests shifted, and my training as a graduate student and my PhD were focused in the field of political science, which was then called public law. After Wisconsin, I did a postdoctoral fellowship at the Yale Law School in the Russell Sage program. I went on the job market as someone who did American politics and law within political science.

HACKNEY: Any particular field of law at that point?

SARAT: I came from a pretty straightforward political science background, so I was trained to do what political scientists called judicial process. However, I didn't do judicial process in the conventional way that political scientists did it. In my first year at Amherst, that would have been 1974, I taught a course that was called "Law, Politics, and Society." So already, I was doing more than just looking at courts. That was sort of the basis of the trajectory of my teaching.

HACKNEY: And then later you got a JD from Yale. What motivated that? You had already had the Russell Sage experience, so what was the motivation for the JD?

SARAT: I did my dissertation on the subject of why people obey the law. Again, it wasn't a court-focused project. My early research interests were in law and culture kinds of issues, but also legal process issues. In the late 1970s and early 1980s, I participated with other scholars in a project called the Civil Litigation Research Project. This was a project funded by the Department of Justice, and what we were interested in was trying to understand how the civil justice process worked in the United States from the bottom up. I was very interested at that point in the emergence of disputes: why is it that problems become disputes, and disputes become lawsuits? In the course of doing this work, the Civil Litigation Research Project, I finally got more interested in what in political science would be called private law issues. The more I researched, the more interested I became in what lawyers did. When I was in college I had an interest in being a lawyer, and then I got distracted by other things. So in the mid-1980s I thought, given what I know about the law and what my research interests are, I should get a law degree. Now, nothing in my professional life required it. I had no desire to leave Amherst; I had no desire to be a law professor. It was a kind of vocational interest, and it was something that I just felt would enrich my knowledge of the subjects I was studying. I took a year off from teaching at Amherst, and did my first year in residence in New Haven. My second and third years I was teaching full-time here, and I was a full-time student at Yale Law School. So I did it in three years, two of which I was teaching full-time.

HACKNEY: I was actually a student at Yale Law School from '86 to '89. Who did you find most interesting among the faculty?

SARAT: I wanted to be a student, but I didn't want give up my career or my research. So I did a lot of connecting with Stan Wheeler, who was someone with whom I had worked as a Russell Sage fellow. His work reflected my research interests so that made sense. I also got to know and respect, and was influenced by, Geoffrey Hazard. Hazard did civil procedure, as you know, and he was completely unlike me in terms of what he was interested in. But I thought he was very smart and he represented what I wanted to understand, which was a very traditional idea of the law. I worked somewhat closely with Bo Burt, whom I found very interesting. I also worked closely with Steve Wizner on clinical stuff. But the person I was closest to at Yale Law School, which is very surprising to me looking back on it, was Joe Goldstein. Goldstein wasn't doing the kind of research I was doing, but I found him to be just a compelling intellect and a very challenging person.

HACKNEY: His specialty was criminal law.

SARAT: His specialty was criminal law, but at that time that is not what I was interested in. I was working on a project at that time on divorce lawyers and their clients, so I was interested in family law. He and Bo Burt were interested in family law. So those are the people that I hung out with, especially Goldstein.

HACKNEY: Going back to Madison, who were the influences there?

SARAT: I went there to study urban politics with a man named Michael Lipsky, and by the time I arrived Lipsky had left. So then I became what in graduate school they call an "orphan" because I didn't have an adviser. There was a man, a very young man, named Peter Eisinger, who was doing urban politics. Peter generously mentored me, but the person that I worked the most closely with was a political scientist named Joel Grossman, who was also my PhD supervisor. He subsequently left Madison for Johns Hopkins. And I also worked with Stewart Macaulay and Howard Erlanger at the law school at Madison. At that time Macaulay was well established and Erlanger was just getting started.

HACKNEY: In terms of background, what were the moments in history that influenced your worldview? Was there anything that caused you to think you wanted to become an academic because *X* is the major problem in the world? The motivation for a lot of academics comes from external events that channel them toward a life of the mind as opposed to various other things that they could do.

SARAT: I may be the deviant case. I came from a very poor background in terms of my family and socioeconomic status. I was a first-generation college student. When I went to graduate school no one understood why I was doing it. I went to graduate school not largely motivated by a social change project or big events in the world. I went to Providence College because I wanted to be a lawyer. When I was there I fell under the sway of two professors who taught political science. And by "fell under their sway," I mean, I remember sitting in their classroom with my jaw dropped. Not because they were changing the world, but because I would read something and go to class and they would teach the same text and it would be like a movie that changed from black and white to Technicolor. I remember sitting in class and thinking, "I want to do that." I want to take movies and move them from black and white to Technicolor. And I went to graduate school to do urban politics not because I wanted to be engaged by a social change project, but because I read a piece by Michael Lipsky titled "Toward a Theory of Street-Level Bureaucracy," and it was a "wow" moment for me in the same way. I decided that's what I wanted to do. Now, the deeper I got into my professional life, the more I became connected with things beyond my own "oh wow" moments. I've said in print, and it's true, that part of the attraction of the law and society movement for me, which is not why I went to graduate school, was that it was focused on the struggles and the world of people who are not powerful. I was very interested in the social world of suffering and pain that's associated with welfare recipients, that's associated with people being prosecuted for crimes, that's associated with people engaged with the capital punishment system, but that was not my motivation for an academic career. I was a grad student during the mid-sixties and seventies, Vietnam and Cambodia were hot topics and there were demonstrations, but that's not why I was there. I was there for intellectual, almost scholastic, engagement. I was just fascinated by all of it.

HACKNEY: It's interesting that the folks you're interested in studying probably relate more to your background growing up as a kid in a particular way. You focus on "ordinary" people.

SARAT: That's true. I'm much more likely to study down, as the sociologists say, than to study up. However, while that is an important part of what I do, I'm still motivated by curiosity. I don't believe that my work has tremendous significance outside of the academy. I'm not one that thinks that the way to change the world is to write a book on capital punishment. I'm not an advocacy academic. I don't spend a whole lot of time in my career working with advocacy groups to advance values. I'm mostly motivated in my professional work and selecting projects by something that strikes my curiosity, which fascinates me. My work on capital punishment is a good example. As part of doing that work I became interested in the way in which the death penalty is represented in popular culture. I began looking at death penalty films, and became very interested in film. So I'm working on a project on law and film while continuing to do other work. I've been working with Charles Ogletree on a project called *The Road to Abolition?*, and another project called *Making Sense of Miscarriages of Justice*, which have a connection to the social world. But even those projects come out of these moments of intellectual curiosity from my point of view. Ogletree might see them differently. Intellectual curiosity motivates me. For example, everybody's in love with the innocence movement in the United States, so let's think about the innocence movement and put it in historical perspective. Let's think about when does it emerge and why does it emerge. Let's think about the innocence movement from a broader perspective with regard to legal process. I wrote a book called *Mercy on Trial: What It Means to Stop an Execution*. A big part of the book is a criticism of George Ryan's clemency in Illinois. And in talking about the book through lectures and the like, I ran into a lot of abolitionists who were very upset with me for criticizing George Ryan—not on the intellectual ground that I got it wrong, though they might have thought that, but on the political ground that we are in a political "struggle" against the death penalty and you should criticize the "other guys," not "our guys." So I would say that yes, I am interested in studying down in the sociological sense. I am interested in understanding social suffering and violence, but it's more of a scholastic thing for me. I go to conferences and academics are always talking about how their work is going to have an effect. I don't think that way. For example, I have never deluded myself into thinking that my book on clemency is going to change anything. It's a set of intellectual arguments.

HACKNEY: In terms of intellectual arguments, your work is most often associated with the law and society movement. How would you define law and society as an intellectual discipline?

SARAT: Well, to answer that question depends on the particular time frame, because how I define it now wasn't how I would have defined it ten years ago or at the beginning of my career. It's very different. I have always been someone who has been moved by boredom. I tend to get easily bored by things. So some academics devote their whole careers to the study of judicial appointments, "that's what I do." For thirty years they study judicial appointments, maybe a little outside of that, but really it's judicial appointments. Or "I'm going to study certain writings"—that's what they do for thirty years. I've written about civil litigation. I've written about divorce. I've written about the death penalty. I've written about white-collar crime. I've written about the Law Enforcement Assistance Administration. I've written about clemency. I am currently writing about law and film. Part of why I was intrigued by law and society was motivated not by anything in law and society, but by a kind of boredom with political science. In graduate school I'm doing political science and I moved from urban politics to public law, and then between public law and courts, and so already in graduate school I was interested in law and society. However, this was not because there was a law and society movement. I have been to every Law and Society Association meeting that there has been, so from the first moment that there was a law and society meeting I went. And, again, I didn't go because of a paradigm. I went because I was uncomfortable in political science and I was looking for people who had a broader view of studying law. I took a course with Stewart Macaulay and Howie Erlanger and, sure enough, they were talking about all kinds of interesting things. It wasn't just about the courts and the Constitution. In an early stage of my career I thought that I knew what law and society was. And what law and society was for me, largely, was a successor to the legal realists, and largely preoccupied with the gap problem. So what law and society people were interested in doing was exposing the difference between law on the books and law in action. And I believed in that definition for quite a while as an inclusive description of all kinds of impulses of the law and society movement. I had become impatient with that view by the mid-1980s and developed a substantial criticism of it. I felt that what law and society ought to be focused on is what I refer to as constitutive theories of law, how law constitutes social relations. So as opposed to closing the gap between what law says and what law does, I became interested in these constitutive theories and argued that law and society ought to take on constitutive theories as the organizing paradigm. For some period of time, we made a lot of progress in that dimension.

HACKNEY: And how would you define constitutive theory?

SARAT: The gap approach is devoted to showing how little difference the law makes: they passed the Civil Rights Act, and there's still discrimination; they passed consumer protection laws, and sure enough women are getting messed over by automobile dealers; or they passed a housing ordinance, but it doesn't make any difference. That's what Stewart Macaulay illustrated when he showed that business people paid no attention to formal contract doctrine. So that was the paradigm: that law doesn't make any difference. The constitutive view is the opposite view. It says that law constitutes social relations. Law is inescapably implicated in social relations. The gap view is that society is over here, and law is over there, and law occasionally sends some missiles into society and we can look at what happens and whether or not they make any difference. The constitutive view says law is in society. That how we think of ourselves, for example, as rights-bearing beings, is constituted by legal ideas. Or how property is organized is constituted by legal ideas, so when we look at any particular intervention in the regime of property we might think that law doesn't work, but that's not right because law is already there in social relations. The constitutive view I would describe as a kind of neo-Marxist/Foucauldian view. Law's power is diffuse and ideological—that was the constitutive view. I felt that it made a tremendous impact in law and society. It didn't convert everybody, but by the mid-eighties that's what I would say that law and society was about. And saying it was about that was both an empirical and normative statement. Now, I would say law and society is misnamed, and it really is "law and stuff." There is no organizing question; there is no organizing paradigm. Almost any stuff about law has a home in law and society. The one thing that is not at home is the most narrow forms of doctrinal, traditional law school scholarship, but people in law and society work with doctrine. They read doctrine for its rhetoric or they read doctrine for what it exposes. So I am one that believes now that law and society is an empty signifier. I can't tell you what law and society is about.

HACKNEY: So it's whoever self-identifies, goes to the meetings, etcetera?

SARAT: Yes. The old paradigm battles are essentially over. We are in an era of good feelings with two different emphases. One emphasis is that we are a community and we're nice to each other, and that's what makes us law and society. The other emphasis is the return to the "if it moves we can count it" empiricism. But law and society is now fenced in by another movement called the empirical legal studies movement, which does really hard-core empirical legal studies on the one hand, and on the other hand a group called law, culture, and humanities, which really cares about the cultural study of law. So my current view is that it is an empty signifier.

HACKNEY: That actually answers the next question I was going to raise: what are the major tensions in the law and society movement? Your basic answer seems to be that there are none.

SARAT: Well, to understand it you have to understand it historically. In the mid-1980s, law and society was filled with major tensions. There were fights with gloves off, names called, and hurt feelings—largely around the positivist/post-positivist, positivist/interpretist, and constitutive/non-constitutive dimensions. There were a lot of sparks flying, plenary sessions, and hurt feelings. The problem was that some of us were sympathetic to critical legal studies, and wanted to bring in more critical legal studies into law and society. And other people thought it was nihilism and the end of the world. There were real fights. Today, I would say, part of what explains the current state of law and society is that the community backed away from the fights: too many hurt feelings, too much trouble about who was in and who was out, and what was the right way. So there was kind of, I would say, retreat (and I think it's true in a lot of places) from the days in which everyone engaged in high theory. Then in the eighties critical legal studies became mainstream, and then every law school had it so who cared about it anymore anyway. Now the big buzzwords in law and society are "globalization" and "internationalization," but they don't really mean anything other than law and society should pay attention to phenomena in other countries. Theory wars are done. It is not as though the fights are analogous to those between the people who studied Schmidt versus the Freudians. I used to say that you knew a law and society person because he or she is conducting a study: "I am studying sentencing and the death penalty, so I'll go to the law and society meetings." "I am interested in revision of antipornography law, so I'll go to law and society." "I'm interested in studying law and film, so I'll go to law and society." There are no big paradigm fights in the law and society movement today.

HACKNEY: And do you think that explains the institutional resilience. For example, critical legal studies falls apart institutionally, in terms of meetings, organizing, etcetera. Law and society has had a longevity that a lot of these other movements haven't. Do you think the explanation is the idea of "lets end the fighting"?

SARAT: I don't think that law and society has been much of a political movement. Although it had a political edge to it, it was more of a professional thing. Our fights were intellectual fights. We weren't trying to bring down liberal legalism, and "Oh my god, you haven't brought down liberal legalism?," or "Oh my god, you people who want to bring down liberal legalism in the name of equality are all teaching at Harvard and pay no attention to black people or women." So that was the end of critical legal studies. Law and society is composed of more people like me—who are more curious about something and more scholastic in their orientation. The general pull of politics, people who declare, "We would really like it if the world were to change," these are not the type of people drawn to law and society. Of course, there were some, for example, who'd be interested in showing how the story about the McDonald's coffee cup was really a myth and that somehow tort litigation reform would be stopped. However, if you look at what law and society people are doing with their spare time, I would say your average law and society person is not allied with a movement.

HACKNEY: I think your average law and society person has a PhD. That's an interesting development. With more frequency what we have in law schools are lawyers garnering PhDs. In law and society we have people with PhDs who are interested in law but not necessarily based at law schools.

SARAT: Well you have to look beyond that. In a sense that's true, but a lot of the leaders in law and society are people in law schools without PhDs. You could do a count of who is where in the law and society pantheon, a lot of them, especially in the old days, did not hold PhDs.

HACKNEY: Yes, they had JDs. But when you go to meetings today you notice that a lot of the participants are not situated in law schools.

SARAT: Yes, today it is not a law school movement. I think the "resilience" of law and society (that's a nice phrase) had something to do with the fact that it's not a political movement. I think that was actually good for law and society, in terms of its resilience. Now, when the Law and Society Association meets in St. Louis nobody goes—Berlin, two thousand people will be there. So that tells me something. They want to go to a nice place, and they want to see their friends. It's just like the American Political Science Association meetings, only smaller. It's just like the American Historical Association meetings, only smaller. Some of us have organized a new thing, which is regional, called the Northeast Regional Law and Society meeting. We had our first meeting this year in June and had seventy-five people. That's another thing that was characteristic of law and society, that it was small. People knew each other, it was very friendly, and it was very oriented toward support for junior scholars—mentoring—and to me now it is big. Who knows all those people? Who wants to know all of those people? So a lot of us are trying to do other things now to capture a little bit of the intimacy, community, and mentoring that the Law and Society Association meant to me. That's a big part of the early identity of law and society—mentoring. As Lawrence Friedman used to say, if you felt marginal in your own discipline, then you were at home in law and society. You could be appreciated as a political scientist, as a historian, or whatever. There was a self-conscious effort at outreach to different scholars, and that was a very big part of it.

HACKNEY: Can you tease out your methodology?

SARAT: Remember what I said before, a lot of my academic interests are motivated by curiosity and boredom. And I am someone within law and society who has tried to keep the intellectual pot stirred. So as president of the Law and Society Association I made a deep push within law and society to bring humanities and cultural studies in: organizing plenary sessions on cultural studies, bringing Homi Bhabha to speak at Chicago, etcetera. My experience of law and society now is different. I'm not going to Berlin in 2007. It's the first time that I haven't attended, but I'm not going. I'll go next year when it's in Montreal, but I'm not going to Berlin. It's too far and too big. Ten years ago I founded another group, which is called Law, Culture, and the Humanities. We now have had ten annual meetings. It meets in March, and it has a journal now. I expect that in ten years, or twelve years, or forty years, I'll find something else. And my heart will move away from Law, Culture, and the Humanities. Rick Abel used a great phrase about law and society many years ago; he said the law and society movement is in danger of developing a phenomenon called "clack, clack," which is a train rolling down the tracks, "clack, clack." So that's sort of my feeling. But I want to admit that for me some of it is boredom, and if law and society is just interested in "hey, how are you, you are nice," that's not for me.

HACKNEY: So I guess part of the answer to the question is that you aren't motivated by a particular methodological approach, as opposed to finding ways to think about interesting problems. If that leads you to cultural studies or if it leads you to literary studies, etcetera, then so be it.

SARAT: I will tell you the methodological story. I was trained in quantitative, positivist analysis. I was a true believer in it. I was not a practitioner of the most sophisticated quantitative methods, but I was a true believer in it basically until the Civil Litigation Research Project I told you about. We had over $1 million, money was no object. We explained 12 percent of the variation with the high-tech quantitative stuff. The other influence on my methodology was teaching at a liberal arts college. Being at a liberal arts college meant that I was hanging out with historians and philosophers, and that had a big influence. It moved me away from the quantitative. Would I do quantitative work now? Sure I would do it. But it's not where my heart is. And you described it exactly right. I am not guided by methods. I am interested in problems. If I want to understand the cultural life of capital punishment, I am going to figure out what it is I have to do. It means I have to read Supreme Court cases. It means I have to attend capital trials for observation. It means I have to look at films about the death penalty. It means I have to do historical work. So my heart doesn't beat faster when someone says "method."

HACKNEY: Now, an interesting moment in *When the State Kills* is when you make the distinction between you not being interested in what society does in terms of the death penalty, or what the United States does in terms of executing the death penalty, as opposed to what having the death penalty does to us as a society. And you come at this in a multitude of ways: historically, firsthand observation, film study, etcetera. What have you taken away from it in terms of what the death penalty means to us as a society, and it's implications? How does it, to go back to the Foucauldian idea, permeate and shape American culture?

SARAT: I'm not a death penalty academic. There are people who are death penalty academics. The center of their intellectual interest is capital punishment. They study it. They want to end it. They do research, and they pick their research in connection with ending capital punishment. I did a death penalty study in the mid-1970s. Why? Because Thurgood Marshall in *Furman v. Georgia* said if people only knew about capital punishment, they would reject it. I thought, that's an interesting idea. His idea is that support of capital punishment is based on ignorance. So I thought that was interesting, and I did a study on capital punishment to try and test this. I stuck with it because I thought that capital punishment provided a window into American culture. And I was interested in the cultural landscape. If you look at the books that I have written and edited, since 1990, they have in the title "state killing," "killing state," or they have the "cultural life" of something. I was interested in capital punishment as a window onto American culture—onto issues of race, onto issues of violence, onto issues of victimization, and onto issues of retribution and what that meant. I wanted to understand this cultural impact. I think that what capital punishment does is it offers simple solutions to complex problems, so it kind of has a reductive component when you think about it. I think it distracts us from largely systemic problems. We get the bad person and we kill them so we don't have to think about different structures. I think capital punishment panders to a belief in violence to solve problems. As I say in *When the State Kills*, capital punishment signifies the fragility of sovereignty in the United States, and reassures us that there really is sovereign power in the United States. It's a democracy—how do we know that we have real sovereignty? We kill people. So those are the things that I think capital punishment does for me.

HACKNEY: This may depend on jurisdiction, but how do you think the average U.S. citizen views capital punishment? Is it really in the forethought of individual consciousness, outside of the spectacular cases such as Timothy McVeigh, or the local context of, for example, a county in Texas where there is a decision that the death penalty is going to be rendered in a local case?

SARAT: I'm not interested in attitudes. I'm interested in culture—what I would call the cultural surround in which American citizens operate. I'm not saying that people are consciously saying, "I like capital punishment because I am worried about sovereignty"—give me a break. My methods are interpretive. I am trying to understand the meaning of capital punishment as a practice. I am reading capital punishment as a practice. I'm not back where I was in the seventies, looking at the influence of capital punishment by drawing arrows and saying people are less worried about sovereignty or people are anxious about sovereignty. That's not my method. So yes, you're right, I don't think that most Americans would recognize that because of capital punishment we tend to deploy simple solutions to complex problems. My argument is not empirical in that sense. I am interested in the cultural surround. I'm interested in reading the practice to try to understand its cultural meaning.

HACKNEY: Now one policy that you focus on that I do think has a lot of resonance in popular culture is the use of victim impact statements. And I was struck by your ability to really be constructive in terms of their meaning, because if you were to do an empirical study of attitudes I think you would get the vast majority of U.S. citizens saying, "Oh, that's a great thing, the family should be able to come forward and give testimony," etcetera. Can you flesh out how you came to this really contrarian view with regard to victim impact statements?

SARAT: Right, well, I like the word you just used. I said a little while ago it captures why I was attracted to law and society and it captures my work, which is "contrarian." Remember what I said to you about George Ryan? I mean, everybody loves George Ryan. I'm not drawn to it because everybody loves it, and I have to find a flaw. It's my intellectual temperament—a friend said I am a better counterpuncher than I am a puncher. So I'm interested in examining theories, and taking a look at them and seeing what's wrong. The victim's impact statement research is sort of based on reading and thinking about what's going on in the case. Everybody says that this is the return of revenge. And I say, I see some of that, but that's not all that I see. Again, my work, now especially, is largely interpretive. It's based on the reading of practices. What's going on with George Ryan? He stands up and says, "I'm going to grant clemency to these folks." It's not positivism. It's not like I wonder, "What do people think about what George Ryan is doing?" It's about what's going on there. So I am reading legal and social practices the way that literary critics read novels. I'm giving you a reading of what that novel means. Then you can read it and think, "Oh, I don't think he's right. I actually think this or that, and the other thing." So I've given you a reading, not necessarily representing what others would think when they read the novel. That's the work that I am doing. Now, to jump back to our earlier discussion, that's much more like what people were doing in the early stages of critical legal studies. They would read contract doctrine to try to understand how contract doctrine encodes certain assumptions about individuals. It's not going out and asking people what they think of contracts, or do they use them, or do they even know about contracts. I'm not studying the impact of the Uniform Commercial Code [UCC] on the practices of business people. I'm sitting there with texts reading. I'm looking at the Wagner Act and trying to think about labor law. That's more the kind of thing that I do in my work now. In the late nineties I did work with jurors. I was part of the Capital Jury Project, which was a large-scale empirical study of jurors. I was interviewing jurors, finding out why they decided the cases that they did. I did a small project that's part of a study called *Just Schools*—people interested in multiculturalism, and its impact on schools. So I did a study in Amherst, Massachusetts, with a tape recorder, talking to school administrators and teachers and parents, asking them to tell me about multiculturalism in the schools, tell me about the way it works, tell me about how you think about it. So that's still a strain of my work. I still do that.

HACKNEY: I want to talk about the critical legal studies movement in a bit, but just to get back to your point—the analogy between your reading and the classic CLS reading. One distinction that could be made, you can clarify this, is that the classic CLS reading generally has a background, a structure that's influencing the reading. Of course, that structure is not uniform across CLS scholarship. It could be structuralist and have a neo-Marxist bent, or it could take a class view of the world. But there is a way in which one can say, "Okay, I know when CLS person *X* approaches a problem I can kind of figure out where it's going because of their interpretation." Getting back to your eclectic methodological persona, we wouldn't necessarily expect the same from you. Would you draw that as a distinction?

SARAT: Absolutely. Again, I respect people who did that kind of work, but it became very predictable. It was classic deconstruction, showing how the doctrine was contradictory, and they would show you a lot of its contradictions. So, again, my work is analogous, in the sense of doing reading. It's not analogous in the sense of calling on an apparatus and applying it everywhere. That makes life easier, but I don't want that. I'm not saying that all CLS people did that. However, it's not the way in which I proceed. My readings are largely bottom-up and top-down. I read from the text, informed by a set of theoretical questions. But I'm reading from the text. And in that sense, I like to think my readings are less predictable. Someone reading my book about George Ryan is going to say, "I won't know until I read the book," as opposed to "I know what he is going to say in this book, he said it in the prior book and the book before that." That's not to say that the readings are completely random. They are informed by theory, but I tend to try to bring to bear the theory that is most relevant to the reading.

HACKNEY: Let's talk about the discipline that takes that total opposite view of what you just articulated, which is law and neoclassical economics. One narrative that you could spin out in terms of the history of American legal theory is that there is legal realism, and post–World War II (fifties/sixties) law and social science branching into law, extending legal realism, and filling the gap in a particular political moment where there is a progressive ideal. Generally law and social science scholars and law and society scholars are progressive, pro-government supporters of the administrative state. Then we get to the 1980s. As Daniel Yergin in his book *The Commanding Heights* chronicles, there is the rise of Thatcher and Reagan, and a withering attack on the regulatory state. It's at that point law and neoclassical economics becomes the dominant intellectual movement in law schools. The quintessential paradigm represented by Richard Posner is the idea that neoclassical economics can explain everything in law. Do you agree with that as a sort of historical chronicle of the rise of law and neoclassical economics and its political backdrop? It also fits very well with a particular vision of the scientific enterprise, because what neoclassical economics can do is to provide you with a single technical solution to problems, and then, by the way, produce generally conservative (or moderate to conservative) policy prescriptions, which are supported in the post-eighties political environment.

SARAT: Well, I haven't studied the history of the rise of law and economics, and what I have to say to you is really impressionistic. I think your basic story is right, but you left out of the story some of the post-realist reconstruction in legal thought, of which the legal process school was important. And that's important because I think that law and economics in law schools doesn't just serve a political purpose. It also does something in law schools that Langdell and Hohfeld sought to do, which is to provide a perspective that organizes legal doctrine. It tells you what cases are about. And that's very powerful in law schools. Law and society could never tell you what cases are about. We don't read them. We are more interested in criticizing the people who write the decisions because they don't make any difference in the world, or we are interested in criticizing their decisions because they are not progressive, or they are ideological in some sense. Early law and economics, especially, was a kind of universalizing system. It was a methodology that allowed you to read law, whether it was in property, corporations, or securities law, etcetera, and tell what the law was about. And that's an important part of the story. I think the power of law and economics scholars in the legal academy wasn't just that they were conservative. They could tell you that actually what the law ought to be was market-oriented. They delivered something that is very powerful in the American legal academy, which was, "We can give you the Rosetta stone to these judicial opinions; we can tell you how doctrine operates, and what rationalizes doctrine." And then, of course, what happens is that law and economics moves from the positive, in the sense of this is how the doctrine operates, to the normative. And the other part of the story is that then the graduates of law schools who go on to be the clerks of these judges, and later on the judges themselves, are then saying this is how to decide these cases, because you ought to decide the case in a way that minimizes the transaction costs, or produces some greater optimal result. But I think the story of law and economics that isn't often told is this other one, which is powerful in law schools—its "my God, someone has brought back the Rosetta stone."

HACKNEY: Yes. It represents a simple, universal theory to explain law.

SARAT: Yes. It's a tool to organize doctrine. It doesn't mean I am going to sit there and read these cases and I really don't know what's going on. I've got a paradigm that's going to help me explain how the doctrine operates.

HACKNEY: Let's talk a bit more about CLS and its relationship to law and society. There are historical linkages. The first CLS meeting was in Madison; David Trubek is part of that. Going back to those moments, how did you view the relationship? I know earlier you said there was the idea in law and society that the last thing the group would want is to have an incursion of CLS folks because they were politicizing, etcetera. So was there any spillover?

SARAT: Well, I think law and society had almost no impact on CLS. You know, Mark Kelman wrote a piece called "Trashing," saying that law and society is no good while saying it is good. People in law and society mostly disliked CLS, and disliked what CLS stood for because it wasn't empirical. It was just the old critique all over again: Law professors will never leave their law libraries. They are these elite people, "wine tasters," and they're just tasting their wine, and we are out there in the hot sun picking the grapes. Sure enough, it's law professors all over again. It's back to law in the books and law in action. They're not in the police station, not riding around in cop cars, not sitting in welfare offices, and not sitting in court rooms. So, in terms of the impact of law and society on CLS, I think that for most of the people in CLS law and society wasn't very important, and they could flick it off their shoulders because it wasn't that important. For people in law and society, CLS was to law and society what the evil empire was to Ronald Reagan. It was just another law school–based movement, saturated with privilege, which was conceptualist rather than empirical—crazy lefties. There were people who tried to bring CLS stuff into law and society. However, beyond David Trubek, and people who knew him and liked him, I don't think you'd even know their names. There were people in law and society who did important criticisms of the CLS movement from the law and society perspective. There were some of us who were sympathetic to the deconstructive, neo-Marxist, Foucauldian influences, and picked up from CLS, in part, this interest in what I call the constitutive theory of law. Some of us here at Amherst participated in the "Amherst Seminar." We met and we had a study group, and out of that group, I would say there were a dozen people (most of whom were associated with law and society, but not all of them were), in a very short period of time came three presidents of the Law and Society Association. So the influence of CLS in the law and society community is mostly as the evil other. Some of us were sympathetic to it, and tried to take this paradigm of, again, what we called the constitutive theory, which Bob Gordon also called the constitutive theory in a *Stanford Law Review* article, and apply it to law and society. I can be in a welfare office and be thinking about the constitutive theory of law. I did a piece published in 1990 called "The Law Is All Over," which is about the welfare office. I can be in divorce lawyers' offices and be thinking about the constitutive theory of law. The problem that I ran up against was the empirical. The debate in law and society in the eighties was, is it empirical and what makes it empirical? There was a large conversation about what makes something empirical? Is it generalizable, is it verifiable? So I think the most important role of CLS, and I think CLS was very important to law and society, was in largely negative ways. Like the Russian military works for the American defense department. Well, they're our enemy, but thank God for them because we can have higher spending. And, again, I don't think there was any intent, but looking back, I think it was very important for people, for the law and society movement, to have to confront, or if not confront at least imagine this enemy. It was mostly understood as the enemy, not David Trubek's miraculous synthesis of law and society, and critical legal studies.

HACKNEY: I want to go back to the wing that was sympathetic toward CLS in a moment. I find it striking that CLS was considered the enemy. I didn't get the same response from you with regard to law and economics, which seems at odds with law and society on both political and methodological grounds. It is the dominant law and social science idea out there, generally isn't empirical, and for the most part has moderate to right-wing political implications. But it wasn't considered the enemy.

SARAT: Richard Posner came to a law and society meeting and basically said to law and society scholars you ought to be doing the right kind of work. And people in law and society were offended by that. There were really no entrepreneurs for law and economics within the law and society movement. There weren't any law and economics scholars who played positive roles in law and society in the way in which some people who were marketing constitutive theory played prominent roles. No one played that role for law and economics. A president of the Law and Society Association, named Lauren Edelman, in her presidential address in 2004 talked about the need to reconcile with law and economics. It was a very interesting talk, but I don't see it having any impact at all. It wasn't like the next year there were panels organized at law and society about how to do law and economics. If you look at the program of the Law and Society Association, or at articles published in *Law and Society Review*, there are very few economists represented. So a major reason that CLS assumed the role that it did in a way that law and economics didn't is that some people who felt included were marketing what would seem to be an approach that sounds like critical legal studies. Nobody was doing it for law and economics. And that group signaling CLS was very visible and very prominent in the law and society community. People thought it was something like a coup d'état—that these crazy lefties were in their midst. Again, this is very important in the eighties and the early nineties in the law and society movement. Remember I discussed my scholastic impulse, but if you talked to people in the late eighties and early nineties about me in law and society, I think they saw me as a crazy Communist talking about constitutive theories of law—that's communism, that's crazy lefty CLS talk, and we are empirical and he's not empirical, he wants to infiltrate. There is nobody doing that from law and economics. There were law and economics scholars like Lewis Kornhauser, who wrote this great piece on bargaining and the law, but Kornhauser didn't come to most of the meetings.

HACKNEY: He didn't try to organize.

SARAT: And the other thing is, which is what you said, law and society, to the extent that it has a political identification, it identifies left. So law and economics, they're righties. They're not occupying our territory. Even moderate law and economics scholars were perceived as quite conservative. But the real answer is that it's idiosyncratic, not intellectual in the sense of any kind of paradigm or people looking at what competing paradigms posed a real threat. This had to do with a group of folks who happened to be at a certain stage of their career and a set of intellectual influences. I don't think many in the law and society movement would talk about CLS the way I did. I was the most CLS-interested. They were very empirical. They didn't want to read doctrine. If you focused on doctrine you were labeled an interpretist—"Those are the interpreters." You didn't go out and count things. On the other hand, Posner said you should be doing what I am doing, and people were offended with respect to that. But there weren't any entrepreneurs from the economic analysis movement, so people in law and society didn't feel threatened by it. People didn't like it, but it wasn't a threat.

HACKNEY: I read your piece with Susan Silbey, "The Pull of the Policy Audience" ["Policy Audience"], and thought to myself this is CLS.

SARAT: A lot of people in law and society thought that.

HACKNEY: Okay, so I'm not alone.

SARAT: However, it wasn't CLS. It was perceived to be CLS. It was two pieces. You see part of the reading of "Policy Audience" depended on another piece Susan and I worked on together, titled "Critical Traditions in Law and Society Research" ["Critical Traditions"], which was published in 1987. "Policy Audience" was published in 1988. The "Critical Traditions" piece was very short. In addition, "Policy Audience" was also informed by "Legal Effectiveness and Social Studies of Law," a piece that I published in 1985 in a journal called *Legal Studies Forum*. So the reception of "Policy Audience" in law and society was led by these other things. From my point of view, "Policy Audience" was really an attack on legal realism. The basic idea was that we ought to not be liberal reformists—not because we ought to be radical crazies, but because we ought to be less interested in the policy world. What "Policy Audience" argued was that the fact that law and society people were interested in and had an influence on policy diluted the ability of law and society scholarship to be critical. Wanting to influence existing policy had a normalizing effect, a mainstreaming effect, on law and society scholarship. That's the part that got painted with the CLS brush. But I think that the major thing that we were trying to do was take on the legal reformist/legal realist influence, and that for me was the energy of the piece. Yes, it made an argument for being more critical in a way that people thought of as being CLS. However, it was really a counterpunch, remember I'm a counterpuncher, to the continuing legal realist belief that "we've got to find out what is going to happen if we pass fair housing laws, so lets do studies that the people in the department of housing and urban whatever will read." The article was also very controversial in law and society because it did something that violated some norms in law and society—it named names. It criticized some prominent people in law and society, including some of my teachers. It did readings of these classic law and society articles. It's not the typical law and society move. The typical law and society move is kind of gap filling—"So and so did this study and it's a really good study, but it left this out so I'm now going to put it in," or "This was the wrong method to use, let's try a different method." "Policy Audience" did readings of people's articles, and tried to pull out from the reading of those articles the telltale influences of the policy audience. Some people just thought it was the equivalent of intellectual terrorism. I'll tell you another story that reflects this. Long before I was president of the Law and Society Association, I was a pretty young pup. I was invited to give a major address at the association meeting. And I gave this speech criticizing gap studies. I stood up and I criticized gap studies, kind of a precursor to "Policy Audience," sprinkled with lots of references to Foucault. I'm at this raised dais up in the front of the room, and I finish the speech and I sit down. The person sitting next to me, who was very prominent in law and society and had been president or was on his way to be president, said to me, "You will never be president of the Law and Society Association." He didn't say, "That was a terrible speech," or "Gee, I'm bored." He said, "You will never be president of the Law and Society Association." And the reason why that was said was because I had been critical, and law and society was a space where if you feel marginal in your discipline you would feel welcomed. In the law and society community people didn't have big fights, it was more along the lines of "I think your way of studying this thing isn't right and I am going to correct your mistakes." However, there wasn't a lot of the meta-critique. I'm not saying that I was the first one to do it, or the only one to do it. But, that era, of the eighties, and the culmination of the "Policy Audience" piece, people were sick of the meta-critique. They had had it, and they were ready to strike. David Trubek had published his piece on critical legal studies and empiricism, and it was meta-critique. People complained that that was all we were doing—meta-critique. That's part of the way in which, during that period, the Law and Society Association received "Policy Audience." It was just more meta-critique: "You're doing a reading of my article, and you're suggesting that my article has some meta-level problem, not that I got data wrong but that it is complicit in the liberal state." I think that the law and society movement hasn't fully recovered from that late eighties, early nineties period. Maybe it had something to do with, as I said, the university at large—"The big theorists are old, who cares." But some of it was, "That's not why we're here. We're going to network, and contribute to our community, and mentor new scholars. We don't want to have those fights anymore."

HACKNEY: I think there is some of that within legal academia generally, which I want to flesh out, but before getting to that point, there is another counterpunch moment in that piece where you and Susan Silbey discuss the collapse of analytic philosophy. The result is more interest in philosophical neopragmatism. You talk about Rorty and others in philosophy. Part and parcel with the public policy establishment, there was a particular scientific belief—scientism. You and Silbey attack scientism, and demonstrate the ways in which a similar critique has been leveled in the philosophical realm. Therefore, law and society scholars should not bow to scientism. This is interesting because neopragmatism is very much in vogue in the legal academy today. So you see various legal academics who take up the neopragmatist mantle—Richard Posner is now a neopragmatist. Do you consider yourself to be a philosophical pragmatist? What do you make of this wave of neopragmatists in the legal academy?

SARAT: Well, good questions. I'll answer the first question in a slightly different way. And the question is a good one because it allows me to say something that I think is very important to what I understand about the law and society community, and what has held it together. What we did in that part of "Policy Audience" was to call into question the philosophical assumptions of positivism. And that was a strike at the heart of the law and society enterprise (which was social science). It goes back to what you said earlier about a lot of PhDs. But even law professors who were there—Lawrence Friedman, Marc Galanter, etcetera—believed in social science, and they had a very sophisticated, but not very critical, approach to social science. Neither Galanter nor Friedman, just to mention two people whom I have enormous respect for and who do great work, were quantitative data crunchers. However, they believed that what was produced as scientific evidence was, in some sense, the truth. So here are Silbey and Sarat saying all you're able to do is pay attention to policy. Why should you be paying attention to policy? In order to pay attention to policy you have to present your work in a positivist mode. If we actually look at the pragmatists, we would have a very different view of the scientific enterprise. Remember I said I can't tell you what law and society is about. Well, it shouldn't be called law and stuff. It should be called law and social science. It's an eclectic version of social science. What held the law and society community together is a set of commitments to believe in and accept the reliability of social science evidence. So the answer to the first question is yes, I do consider myself to be a pragmatist. Incrementally—because of a certain type of eclecticism, a certain kind of methodological eclecticism—I've become interested in and attracted to a kind of philosophical pragmatist position. How did that come forward in the legal academy? I think the legal academy in general, and the law and society movement as part of that, in a sense, hasn't gotten over the fall of communism. And by that I mean there's nothing left for any good leftie to believe in. You can't use socialism. So, for a lot of progressive academics (and here again some are coming from totally different places) pragmatism, minimalism, and consequentialism are the only places to be. Grand solutions produce bad results. I'm interested in Cass Sunstein and his kind of pragmatism more than I'm interested in Posner's. I have not traced Sunstein's intellectual biography, so I could have this completely wrong. However, for someone like Sunstein pragmatism is a terrific place to be when your guys are not in charge. So if the right is going to run the Supreme Court, well, I could tell them that they are just wrong, I could just write more stuff about their interpretation of this or that. I could promote liberal doctrinal arguments, or I could say that actually what the judicial role requires is minimalism. Now, again, I'm not attributing to Sunstein some kind of political motive. I'm just reading its meaning. If your guys are not in charge, then advocate minimalism. I also think there's this other side. Even if we were in charge, it doesn't seem that we are going to get universal health care, so it is better to advocate for things like better health programs for children. We're not going to end poverty through the Great Society, so we better think about the Earned Income Tax Credit. I think those two things go together—pragmatism and the metaphor of the "end of socialism." Robert Martinson wrote a piece about rehabilitation. He's not a progressive scholar. He published it in *The Public Interest*. It was called "What Works?"—and the answer was nothing. There are a lot of skeptical progressive academics who had in a sense learned that lesson—not Martinson's lesson that nothing works—but small steps are better then big steps, latent consequences, etcetera. You know, we advocate for desegregation in schools, and then it turns out that fifty years later schools are more segregated in the United States. Again, you've asked me to speculate way beyond my academic confidence, but I think that those two things help explain the comfort with pragmatism.

HACKNEY: I want to explore some other aspects of your work. Let's discuss *When the State Kills* and your perspective on race and the death penalty in the American context.

SARAT: There are a few things that I want to say before we move on to that question. Though I advocated distance from the policy audience, like every other academic, or many other academics, I have an ambivalent relationship to it, so some of my work ends up being devoted to policy concerns. I write op-ed pieces, go on the radio, and do that stuff, too. The reason that I interrupted you is that I am thinking about the end of *When the State Kills*. The end of *When the State Kills* is a description and embrace of the new abolitionism. Well, and I hadn't even thought about this before, you could describe the end of *When the State Kills* as minimalist, or pragmatic. In other words, I am criticizing people, the old abolitionists, for being non-minimalist, for being comprehensive: we are going to get rid of the death penalty, and convince people that the death penalty is evil. And I say that that has never changed anyone's mind, no one has ever been persuaded by that criticism. If you want to end the death penalty, you better think about the new abolitionism. Some of that is situational. I'm looking at what's going on in the United States, and saying the only chance of ending the death penalty is this way. But some of it is that I'm like everybody else. In the eighties I felt one way about things, and in the nineties and 2000s I'm feeling somewhat different. But that's some way in which you could say, if you're a textualist, to answer the question about my sympathy for pragmatism, you could say there is some pragmatist influence at the end of *When the State Kills*. That's one thing. The other thing I wanted to say to you because you haven't picked up on it, and I hope you will pick up on it, is this other thing called law, culture, and humanities. You see, in addition to law and economics, and critical legal studies, there were people who were interested in law and literature. I'm not a law and literature guy, but I established this group, in part, because I've been reading law and literature as well as reading cultural studies scholarship. And I saw no place for that in law and society. I saw no place for it. I saw a lot of places for it at workshops at law schools. Law schools had all of these workshops, and all of these law and literature people came through, but where did they come together, where did they meet? And so more than ten years ago I approached Robin West, Jack Balkin, Michael Perry, Robin Chandler, and Anita Allen, among others, and said let's try to bring together people under this rubric called law, culture, and humanities because those people are really marginal. They didn't stay in the legal academy. And now we have 200 or 250 people a year show up to the meetings, and the journal is in its third volume. I don't know whether it is as significant as law and economics, or law and society, and it's not the same as law and literature because we don't say we are only interested in literature. It says we are interested in law, culture, and the humanities, so it can be literature, it can be film, it can be philosophy, and it can be history. And I hope that in some of your reading you'll pay attention to this law, culture, and humanities movement.

HACKNEY: It actually leads to another area for exploration. There seems to be two strands of critical race theory in *When the State Kills*. One is the idea of the permanence of race. That it's here, and it permeates throughout. The other is the utilization of narrative (in your instance, narrative with regard to your observations) as literary critique (or using literary tools). I relate it to Patricia Williams's *The Alchemy of Race and Rights*. It reads like that to me. So the question I have is whether or not you have been influenced by, or interested in, critical race theory—particularly when you came to law, culture, and humanities?

SARAT: The answer is yes, depending on how you define critical race theory. I think *The Alchemy of Race and Rights* is a great book. It's a tremendous breakthrough book. I've read a lot of critical race theory. I don't go to the conferences, and I don't imagine myself as a contributor to critical race theory. I did do some work with Charles Ogletree. We edited a book together on lynching and state killing titled *From Lynch Mobs to the Killing State*. The essential insight of critical race theory for me is to move away from race as a variable, to race as a social fact. Social sciences often treat race as a variable. There's race, there's education, etcetera. Critical race theory has taught me that in the United States race is a social fact. And by social fact, I mean the equivalent in society of air. I mean we don't think of air as a variable, we think of air as a fact. So yes, that influenced me when I wrote *When the State Kills*. The narrative issue is a little trickier. I don't want to make too fine a distinction, but there are two different ways that narrative scholarship has been used by critical race theorists. The first way is not particular to critical race theory, which is their interest in law as narrative. They're interested in stories that law tells. And I think that is an important part of critical race theory, and it's important for law and literature. It's an important part of qualitative sociology. If you look at qualitative sociology, they do narrative analysis and participant observation—look at ethnography. My interest in narrative scholarship was influenced by all of them, not particularly by critical race theory. The kind of narrative work that Patricia Williams does, the autobiographical part, I wish I could do. I tried while giving a talk at a plenary session of law and society that was about autobiography. After hearing me talk about my autobiography and how it influenced my scholarship, a colleague said, "When Patricia Williams talks about her life it's poetry, when you talk about your life it's a bellyache." So the kind of skill in what's called the use of autobiographical narrative to break with convention of legal scholarship, which I think is tremendously important and I admire it a lot whether it's Derrick Bell doing it or whether it Mari Matsuda doing it or whether its Patricia Williams doing it, I have tried it on a couple of occasions, but it's not where I am. But you're right, the turn to an interest in law as narrative is partially critical race theory, but it's also politics, sociology, ethnography, and law and literature that have pushed that. There is another name if you're interested in understanding *When the State Kills*, which you haven't mentioned and that I would be at fault not mentioning, and that's Robert Cover. Robert Cover's "Violence and the Word," a piece he published in 1986, was for me a seminal piece in reorienting my scholarship. And much of my scholarship since the mid-eighties, for example, a piece I wrote with Tom Kearns called "A Journey through Forgetting: Toward a Jurisprudence of Violence," had been influenced by Cover's piece. In my teaching and my work, I'm interested in what I call law's violence. So that's the cultural part. I'm interested in culture, but I'm also interested in the practices of law's violence. That's what state killing is about for me. It's a window not only into American society but into the practices of law as violence. And Cover's piece, "Violence and the Word," in which he says (and he says a lot of things), but he says law combines words and violence, and seeks to master violence in language. It's the most important influence on my work since the mid-eighties, and I'm still in conversation with Cover's interest in exploring the violence in law and the violence that law does. "Violence and the Word" is a tremendously influential piece throughout the legal academy, along with Cover's "Nomos and Narrative"—"Nomos and Narrative" less so for me. For lot of people in the legal academy—not so much in law and society—those were key pieces that people read and knew about.

HACKNEY: I want to wrap up with a couple of thoughts about the general state of the legal academy, and I think it relates nicely to your historical accounting of law and society. You recounted that there were big fights occurring in the eighties, but post-eighties there was "fight fatigue" and a sense that we should get on with the business of producing scholarship. I think we see the same phenomenon in the legal academy generally. In the late eighties there were big conflicts between schools of thought—CLS versus law and economics, for example. There were lots of fights. Today there isn't much conflict in the legal academy. Everyone's a pragmatist and people are teched up, so we have economists who are teched-up economists—everyone is teched up. And they just do their own thing, churn out their work, and meet at the watercooler together. So you can generalize from the law and society phenomenon to the legal academy generally. Do you see the same thing?

SARAT: I think you can generalize beyond the legal academy. It's the death of meta-theory. It's the exhaustion of meta-theory. There are no more Foucaults and Derridas, who everybody's reading, everybody's thinking about. "What are the fads?" Well, again, in the worlds I travel in, the fads are Agamben and Schmitt. But they're not organizing the world. So I think in the social sciences communities writ large, and I would put law school in there, there's meta-fatigue. My institutional location is not a law school. In terms of what you said, I accept that, and I think that's true. I'm going to add another possible piece of the puzzle. I think the political battles over appointments at Harvard Law School are part of the cultural surround—Harvard has big roots. Others in the legal academy look at Harvard and say, "We don't want to be that." Again, it's cultural, not necessarily a product of conscious individual thought. I think Harvard is an example of the perils of politics that is weighing on a lot of people's minds. Everybody knew that Harvard couldn't make appointments. But I think you're right. I think the general thing I was describing about law and society is not particular to law and society.

Patricia Williams is James L. Dohr Professor of Law at the Columbia University School of Law. Professor Williams uses literary and legal theory to investigate a host of contemporary concerns, particularly with regard to race and gender. Her interest in the role of race in the United States has led her to be associated with the critical race theory movement, which began its ascendancy in the legal academy as Professor Williams was rising to prominence. Her books include *The Alchemy of Race and Rights (1992), The Rooster's Egg (1997), Seeing a Color-Blind Future (1998), and Open House (2005)*. Professor Williams writes a column for *The Nation* titled "Diary of a Mad Law Professor." She was named a MacArthur Fellow in 2000.

5

Critical Race Theory/Law and Literature

PATRICIA WILLIAMS

HACKNEY: Can you give an account of your undergraduate educational experience? What was the academic and political environment?

WILLIAMS: Actually I was cross-registered at Wellesley and MIT; that is to say, while I matriculated from Wellesley I spent nearly half of my undergraduate years at MIT. My major was urban studies and city planning, which wasn't exactly a strength at Wellesley, with its leafy green environs, at least not back then. However, MIT had an outstanding urban studies program so I took most of my major classes there. It was an extremely interdisciplinary curriculum, and that had a big impact on my intellectual life to this day. It included courses ranging from sociology, psychology, and anthropology, to early semiotics and linguistics. MIT has a very strong linguistics department, and although that is not something I would lay claim to as an area of my own expertise, my study in that department got me very interested in framing and syntax and theories of language. Nor was it just the neuroscience of language (for which MIT is perhaps best known); I was fascinated by the art of rhetoric and persuasion and metaphor, and how different languages convey an idea or craft a narrative. I took a course called psychohistory, for example, which looked at how individual states of mind and broad social movements are intertwined and how ideas are formulated, or go viral, or can be decoded by clues in expressive styles. For me that notion was very provocative. Until then, I was intending to go on in urban planning, even had a fellowship to study for a master's degree at MIT; but at the last minute I decided to go to law school instead. In retrospect, I think I wasn't so much committed to becoming a lawyer as I was to studying the intricacies of advocacy.

HACKNEY: What was the political climate at Wellesley and MIT?

WILLIAMS: These were the years of student rebellion throughout the nation; these were the times of Kent State, Jackson State, and great political foment. However, Wellesley and MIT were peculiar in terms of their intersection with the larger world. Wellesley, at that time at least, was quite sheltered, quite the "young ladies" environment. I think I wrote an essay once describing how political devotion at Wellesley came in the form of silk-screening protest banners for boyfriends in Cambridge. But more seriously, this is not to say that there was not lively critical debate; Wellesley was a very studious environment and there was a lot of introspection about the Vietnam War and the civil rights movement, and, of course, women's liberation.

My time at MIT, on the other hand, was lively in a different way. My dorm was filled with eccentric prodigies of one sort or another. I remember the guys downstairs had had a squirrel come into their room and chew up a physics book, so they spent the rest of the semester building a squirrel electrocution chair. Whatever I got from MIT—it was different.

HACKNEY: Then you made the transition to Harvard Law School, which must have been culture shock.

WILLIAMS: Well, it was culture shock because I had gone to all-girls' schools since the time I was in seventh grade. I had gone to Boston's Girls' Latin School, and of course Wellesley was all women. And even though I was one of only two women in a dorm of five hundred at MIT, prankish quirkiness ruled the day more than any other human quality. It wasn't the same thing as going to the law school where there was a clear sense that "you are a woman"—and not only that, but that "you are a black woman." I got to law school a couple of years after the *Bakke* decision, so affirmative action was being debated noisily, and it was very uncomfortable. People would come up to you and ask, “What are your LSAT scores?” (For today’s students, I think it’s only gotten worse.)

Yet it was still close enough in time to the civil rights movement that many of my classmates were idealistic, were still riding high from the euphoria of the legal successes. A generation of us came to law school hoping to do public interest work. But there was work to be done. Law schools everywhere focused nearly exclusively on corporate practice. This was before law schools recognized much in the way of clinics. Gary Bellow’s curricular influence was still nascent, and Michael Meltzer was experimenting with the idea of cooperative legal education—this when he was at Columbia, before he implemented his ideas as dean of Northeastern.

It’s hard to believe now, but I never had a female teacher the entire time I was in law school. Although Harvard had officially done away with “ladies’ days,” there were still professors who unofficially adhered to the old ways, and would only call on women one day a month or week. Of five hundred students in my class, there were only 8 percent women, and to this day we are still all good friends. We e-mail each other and chat about our lives and our children. This enduring friendship is indicative of how bonded and apart women felt back then.

Moreover, there were only nine women of color—all of us African American, and I can recall no Latina or Asian women. It was so uniformly white/black. There were two Latino men in the class, maybe one or two Asian men. There were also quite a few international students, but they seemed to clump apart, in an invisible world unto themselves. All this was uncomfortably overlaid by viciously competitive circles of those deemed “on the inside” and those who were not—the books *The Paper Chase* and *One L* were written in this era—oh, and then the social cliques based on legacy, and, of course, the secret clubs. So there was everything you can imagine to make everyone feel different, self-conscious, and apart.

HACKNEY: Were there professors who you gravitated toward?

WILLIAMS: Derrick Bell was and is still my mentor. If it weren’t for Derrick I would have dropped out. I was miserable in law school. Derrick Bell and his then wife, Jewel, were incredible resources. I worked as his research assistant. They were so generous: I was at their house all the time, and they would cook me meals, give me advice and pep talks. I walked their dogs and babysat all three of their children. Derrick not only kept me in law school, but convinced me that persevering would be worth it. I found my niche thanks to him, and years later it was Derrick who pushed me into teaching.

HACKNEY: Was he experimenting with narrative form at that time?

WILLIAMS: No, this was well before the *Harvard Law Review* foreword and *Faces at the Bottom of the Well.* He was considered experimental enough just teaching a course on race and the Constitution. It wasn't till later that Derrick started using almost a black preacher format for his Geneva Crenshaw books.

HACKNEY: When you began thinking about alternative formats for how we write about and conceptualize law, why did you choose literature or the essay format as opposed to some other form, such as philosophy, linguistics, or urban planning?

WILLIAMS: I published my essay "On Being the Object of Property," which I wrote in 1988, not for a law review but for *Signs*, which is a journal devoted to women and history. And that generated a lot of controversy; I guess because it was so unconventional for a lawyer to play with language at all, or to use the first person. But even before that I did a very short piece for the *Harvard Black Letter Law Journal* in which I mocked the formal conventions of law reviews. The piece had three lines of text at the top of each page and all the rest was footnotes, so all of the important discussion was in the footnotes. It was a parody, a reversal of text and subtext. I was experimenting and really just having fun in those days. I don't really consider myself having gone into literature per se. Law has its own symbolic system and the defined boundaries of genre. Its language is a type of architecture. Take the rules of evidence—the rules really act as a screening device allowing you to see certain things or keep certain things back. Or consider how modes of address are used in law; or when you can use the first person and when you can't. The theater and ritual of the courtroom is endlessly fascinating. It's like a trompe l'oeil painting where you can see depth or not depending on how you view it.

Persuasion is about giving an argument dimension, and sometimes that operates at as basic a level as the grammatical. For example, using the subjunctive creates a sense of conditionality and tentativeness; but if we eliminate it, as we often do in modern English, then you go into a mode of almost instant wish fulfillment. And that has subtle ideological implications.

HACKNEY: Can you talk about the transition from practicing law to the academy?

WILLIAMS: I did trials and I liked it, but I burnt out. I was doing health law and consumer protection that had to do with finance. Then, when Ronald Reagan became president, I was working for Legal Services and as I recall he signed an executive order prohibiting Legal Services from either representing undocumented persons or taking on class actions. This had very constraining implications for the type of litigation I was doing, so the future didn't look promising. I went into teaching with the support of Derrick Bell, and I never looked back.

HACKNEY: How did you decide what direction to initially take your scholarship? Would you describe yourself as an essayist or literary theorist?

WILLIAMS: Well, my first years of writing are now lost to history, thank God! I was writing things like "A Refinancing by Any Other Name." Nobody knows me for that, but I started out teaching contracts, Uniform Commercial Code, personal property broker laws, and consumer protection. I also taught "The Jurisprudence of Food," which was all about poultry and ovine and bovine breeding contracts. My writing from that era is just about as uninteresting as it sounds. I was determined to be a traditional scholar. I wore little suits every day and pumps with gold buckles. But I was not really happy in my job. Then I came across an ad in the *Chronicle of Higher Education* for CUNY law school, which had taken Michael Meltsner's idea to a whole new level—patterning the law school experience on the law firm—students were writing memos, and treating their professors like senior partners at a law firm. They were interested in group dynamics. Charlie Halpern, former head of the Nathan Cummins Foundation and founder of Demos, was the dean at the time.

Before CUNY, I had never done team teaching before. I co-taught a course called "Law in a Modern Economy" with Dinesh Khosla, a wonderful colleague who held both a law degree as well as a PhD in sociology. His specialty was property rights in south India. It was an amazing experience. Everyone spent twelve hours a day working, and working together. It was also a very new school, which meant that the students were largely risk takers, for it wasn't even accredited at the time. But they were extraordinary students, many of whom were already accomplished in other fields of endeavor—professors from Queens College (the law school was located on the Queens College campus), local politicians, senior people in the police and fire departments, elderly and retired men and women, veterans, ex-convicts, poets, and the working homeless. It was certainly the opposite of Columbia, where I teach now, and where everyone is pretty much young and quite privileged. My time at CUNY was an experience that stretched me, gave me greater perspective.

CUNY had also rearranged the curriculum so that you just didn't teach contracts—you taught contracts and property together, because anytime you have a contracts case it's probably going to involve some property issues. And you didn't teach torts separate from criminal law. You taught "Accountability and Responsibility for Injurious Conduct," which combined criminal law and torts. That whole thought process that went into thinking about how to reassemble a curriculum around the practical dimensions of real problems was fascinating.

HACKNEY: Did it have any impact on your scholarship?

WILLIAMS: CUNY's environment of innovation was enhanced by the technology of the large, primitive Wang computer in our office. It was before split screen or all the other bells and whistles of today's laptops. It was hard to footnote; you had to set up a separate file to keep your footnotes, and I always thought of it as my "garbage file." So I was doing all of this writing about contracts and began to notice how thin it was in the main text and how all of the interesting stuff was in the garbage file. That's when I really began to play with form.

I also was doing some freelance writing, just because I like writing. But it was not about law. I started out with children's books. By 1986 or 1987 I thought about going back for a PhD in English. I attended a program called the School of Criticism and Theory, which is a summer program that was then at Dartmouth, now it's at Cornell. It brings together all types of theorists. Jacques Derrida and Barbara Johnson and Sacvan Bercovitch were there that summer—really wonderful people in literary theory. I spent the whole summer writing like mad, and they found my work really interesting even though I had no formal background in literature. That's where I wrote "On Being the Object of Property," which is the last chapter of my book *The Alchemy of Race and Rights*. I let myself be creative without the constraints of writing about law. I think it's the best thing I've ever written, and after that, I took everything out of my garbage file and put it back in the foreground. Nothing has been the same since.

In a weird way, that shift dragged me back into law school teaching because suddenly I was controversial, suddenly I was critical, and suddenly I was a theorist. People don't remember that I teach contracts and Uniform Commercial Code, and that in essence I am very boring.

HACKNEY: At the end of the "On Being the Object of Property" essay you have the encounter with the Dartmouth basketball players. There's a discussion of their symbolism. From that essay, and the connection with Harvard you began to compile the pieces for the book. Aside from the issue of form and removing everything from the "garbage file," integrating it into the center, did you set out to articulate a particular set of themes in the text? Did you take it as an opportunity to tackle the issue of race?

WILLIAMS: I know that people view *Alchemy* as being exclusively about race. For me it wasn't, and I didn't set out to write solely about race. I'm not a civil rights lawyer; I've never taught constitutional law. "On Being the Object of Property" was about placing me in a law school environment. When I started teaching I was one of six women in the entire United States teaching in law school. So it was about negotiating my own story in my own mind, not writing to a particular audience or trying to persuade anybody. It was more of a reflection piece about my place in the profession. When I set out to structure the book I was thinking about *Pilgrim's Progress*, of all things. In *Pilgrim's Progress* there is the "house of the interpreter" in which Christian, the pilgrim, describes a home, each room of which is set staged for the reenactment of a biblical lesson or morality tale. So my books are arranged around a very particular kind of epic form. I don't mean that I styled *Alchemy* as a religious epic, but I did riff off classic political rhetorical models like the Puritan jeremiads. And I like the essay form. I like Emerson.

The reason I called my first book *The Alchemy of Race and Rights* is that it's literally formulated like an alchemical process. Every chapter is a step, all the titles have mirrors or reflections, some reference to what you can see through or what you can't see through. The first chapter mirrors the last chapter and so forth, and then in the middle there is a hinge in which things switch and there's a little story about my sister in which my sister, who is logical and rational, starts speaking in magic terms. It is very carefully organized in a way that probably no one else is ever going to pay attention to, but that's how the book was organized.

There are also a lot of imbedded alchemical images because alchemy is a process that purportedly turned lead into gold. For me the image encompassed identity in the broadest sense; it's about transformation of the self. That's why you also find these tropes of polar bears and rabbits in there. Polar bears are obviously about polarity, and they also have black skin and white fur. Everything has a double meaning in the book. Alchemy wasn't real science, but it was a practice very grounded in mythological images, philosophy; it had teleological coherence, and many psychological and psychoanalytic images were borrowed from its symbology.

Alchemy was also a process that experimented with sequencing. I employed some of its ritualized, step-by-step theatricality when, in the last chapter, I told a horrific story about a little boy who was mauled and eaten by polar bears at the Brooklyn Zoo [Prospect Park Zoo]. Every part of that telling was very carefully structured. The tale ends with a series of paragraphs all of which begin with "In the": "In the newspapers"; "In the public debate"; "In the egalitarianism of exile"; and "In the plenary session." Then, kind of like a musical break, the very last paragraph switches to "At the funeral . . . " And that's the point at which the "Hispanic-welfare-black-widow-of-an-alcoholic mother" comes out of the background and is made manifest through the stringing together of all her varied and contradictory descriptors. That's what I was trying to do throughout *Alchemy*. If you read the book just straightforwardly it has one meaning; if you read it another way it has another meaning.

But you can't read it too literally or you end up locked within a very counterproductive kind of fundamentalism. Some people have read it and said, "She clearly needs psychological help because she channels bears." But I don't. They're missing the point. And I'm not crazy. At least not that crazy.

HACKNEY: A lot of folks attach different meaning to the polar bears, and your use of them does stir controversy. Can you talk a bit more about their meaning?

WILLIAMS: I did not want it to be the type of signifier that people translate exactly. I wanted the reader to struggle a bit with the mystery of its meaning, to think to themselves, "What the . . . ??!!" It was my hope that suddenly you are aware that you are attaching a meaning—assigning a meaning. It's literally to stop you in the middle of a sentence and have you say, "What does this mean?" That's what I was trying to accomplish, so that in reading that text you become aware that meanings are constructed, and that you're participating in it. I was trying to create a text in which you're aware of your own struggle for understanding. Tropes that are carefully placed can prompt the reader to figure out what they are feeling and what meaning they attach to the text.

HACKNEY: It also forces an engagement in dialogue with others.

WILLIAMS: Yes. I try to do it in a way that has people question, "Is this really as black-and-white as it seems?" It takes that cliché and interrogates the use of words. I start out with one use of a word in one chapter and hopefully it will be turned upside down and inside out in subsequent chapters, and in ways that will make you think.

HACKNEY: You've written three other books—*The Rooster's Egg*, *Seeing a Color-Blind Future*, and *Open House*. *Seeing a Color-Blind Future* has a distinct format. Can you expand on the differences?

WILLIAMS: Only that *Seeing a Color-Blind Future* is the transcript of a series of lectures I gave in Britain for the BBC Reith lectures. So that book was specifically tailored for a British audience. The BBC has its own requirements as to form, so each essay is tailored in a way that's a bit less layered, or maybe just more straightforward. There were six chapters because there were six programs, each thematically tied together, but each dealing with a separate issue.

The other books are written so that the themes flow through all chapters, and an ongoing problem is revisited over and over, through to the end. So *The Rooster's Egg* has discrete chapters but there's a thematic flow throughout it. And *Open House* is, as I mentioned, explicitly predicated on "The House of the Interpreter," an early chapter in Bunyan's *Pilgrim's Progress*. In that chapter, the pilgrim is guided through each room of the house and the story unfolds. And so, in *Open House*, I used the metaphor of my family's house when we were moving out and selling the place after literally a hundred years there. Each chapter of the book focuses on a different room of the house, its contents, its memories. Each has some ongoing parabolic meaning.

HACKNEY: From the beginning it sounds like family history has played a significant role in your writing. One can look at *Open House* as being explicitly so. How do you situate the significance of storytelling in your writing?

WILLIAMS: My writing has sometimes been dismissed as "just storytelling," and I don't think it's an entirely correct label. I do use lots of literary devices and I have employed the first person even in law reviews, but I've done it for very specific effect and in a very calculated way. People sometimes forget that a lot of my writing is not in the first person; that it's not stream of consciousness; or that I would never do it in a courtroom or a brief. It's not for any and all purposes, and it's not done because I write stream of consciousness. I only do it when I'm trying to make a point, such as stretching the limits of a given genre. What happens when you use the first person in a law review that never uses the first person? It's like using polar bears. It's play, and it's intended to make you think about the context and ask what new information this might be imparting. If you write exclusively for any and all purposes in the first person it does risk becoming solipsistic; but in an unexpected forum it can be startling in a good way.

Sometimes I've also styled essays that are a bit like fairy tales—playful, but with a purpose. I'm doing work now about genetics, and it's not in the first person, but I'm still doing it in a fairly unconventional form, not necessarily the style of writing you commonly find in social science magazines.

HACKNEY: Regarding the Reith lectures, did they ask you to write about that particular topic?

WILLIAMS: I presented the Reith lectures in 1997. Named after the founder of the BBC, it is the highest honor that the BBC gives, and I become somewhat controversial because I'm an American, and I was also the first black woman to deliver the series. The lecturer is awarded six half-hour slots on Radio 4, over a month and half time period. It's a big deal. Everyone is listening. It was the year the European Union had dedicated to the eradication of racism, sexism, homophobia, anti-Semitism, and the whole list of other isms. I was chosen because I had done a few programs for the BBC before, and the board of governors had read *Alchemy*. It was appreciated in a different kind of way in Britain. They have race problems, but they hear it differently. They read *Alchemy* as much about class as about race, which is interesting.

HACKNEY: Do you actually see a color-blind future?

WILLIAMS: No, I need to remind people that the full title is *Seeing a Color-Blind Future: The Paradox of Race*. It is about paradox, about seeing blindly. It's the same paradox that arises when people talk about "post-Obama" or "post-racial moment." It's like those proverbial three blind monkeys: see no evil, hear no evil, and speak no evil. Everybody knows that racism and class division are still big problems in the world. So simply labeling our society "color-blind" is more aspiration than reality. Taken to an ideological extreme, it becomes a kind of willful blindness. And there's a difference. So much of the lecture series was an analysis of how race operates as a kind of taboo topic, or as a public secret. We squirm and get embarrassed or offended. We don't allow ourselves the rational vocabulary with which to deal with it.

HACKNEY: You talked about your work and your connection with Derrick Bell. Did you play any part in the institutional development of critical race theory?

WILLIAMS: There were several institutional moments—including a conference. But it wasn't critical race theory at that point. It was critical legal studies. Critical legal studies was an ongoing conversation among people interested in all types of issues—Roberto Unger, Duncan Kennedy, Peter

Gabel, David Kennedy, Mark Tushnet, Jerry Frug, etcetera. So initially the conversation wasn't about race at all. I went to CLS conferences because I was generally interested in jurisprudence.

This was the time when Mark Tushnet was writing his critique of rights. I felt that there was a symbolic power to rights. And even though Tushnet was correct that rights weren't doing everything they were supposed to do, I thought they were mobilizing in a different type of way. There was a different hermeneutic going on that shouldn't be underestimated. Other scholars of color felt this way but a lot of us were very shy about making the point because the "big boys" had a great deal of authority and luster. They were interesting people, but it was very hard to get a word in edgewise. This was also a time when Martha Fineman, Mary Joe Frug, Frances Olsen, Clare Dalton, and others were writing on feminism. They were also trying to be heard, or carve a niche in what was still very much a male-dominated academic fraternity. Remember, this was a time when there were few women or people of color in the legal academy, so we were trying to figure out how to make ourselves heard.

HACKNEY: So how did the issue of race surface?

WILLIAMS: At one critical legal studies conference in the mid-1980s, some of the organizers were wondering why they were having such difficulty recruiting minority attendees. So they asked the few of us who were in attendance to give a session on how critical legal studies might be more attractive to people of color. I was there, along with Mari Matsuda, Neil Gotanda, Chuck Lawrence as I recall, maybe Richard Delgado, maybe Gerald López. I've forgotten precisely who, but it was a very small handful of us. We each gave presentations, and critical race theory was born.

HACKNEY: Were Lani Guinier and Derrick Bell there?

WILLIAMS: No, for all the grief they gave her during the Clinton years, Lani wasn't a part of that phase of the critical movement, and neither was Derrick. Derrick did work related to race, but never through critical theory, at least not in the early days. Later, of course, everyone who happened to be black—and whether or not they worked on race—got lumped under the umbrella critical race theory and then disparaged for it.

HACKNEY: What happened at the conference?

WILLIAMS: I remember one funny encounter. The group of us gathered on the lawn to figure out what we were going to say. While we talked, a succession of people kept asking us why we were "segregating" ourselves. There we were, trying to put together a session on how they can have more of us, and they're asking us, "Why are you segregating yourselves?"

It was this odd situation in which we were minuscule in number relative to the entire congregation, yet hyper-visible, and mixed in with the sense that if we were all together we must be doing something hostile (like "shunning the rest of us"). So we used that example to begin our discussion about why they were having so much difficulty attracting people of color. Not long after that, there was another conference where women and minority scholars discussed how race, feminism, immigration, and other issues could be analyzed within a critical legal studies framework. Organizationally we were still getting together under the CLS umbrella. After that, however, and as the numbers of "others" in legal academia began to grow, the feminist legal theory movement came into its own, and, when Kimberlé Crenshaw began teaching a few years later, she played a large role in organizing specifically critical race theory meetings.

Later, a series of informal dinner meetings developed into the Northeast Corridor Collective—less focused on jurisprudence than in supporting each others' writing. Then that really mushroomed, encompassing everyone east of the Mississippi and becoming much more organized. From that, there developed a West Coast support group, then LatCrit, and all of the rest. But that was much later. So the critical race groups evolved from these disparate networks and were very free-flowing as opposed to developing out of a particular ideological or jurisprudential position. These days, I think the groups are very general. They involve people from different disciplines and methodological perspectives. It's a networking vehicle. This is consistent with my view that neither critical race theory, nor critical legal studies, has a particularly coherent ideological underpinning. I don't mean that as a negative; I just think it's too diverse for that. If you look at Mari Matsuda's work, it's very different from my work or Richard Delgado's work or Roberto Unger's work, etcetera. We have a common interest and a common antidiscrimination paradigm, but there's no unifying label like "Frankfurt school" or "postmodern."

HACKNEY: Would you consider yourself postmodern?

WILLIAMS: Some of my writing falls under that. "Object of Property" incorporates postmodern devices and postmodernism playfulness. Self-consciousness about the process of writing is very much built into the way I structure some of my work. But let me be clear: I do have problems with the way in which postmodernism has been bastardized as mere relativism. That's a really careless understanding. I am not a relativist. I consider myself an advocate with a grounded political sense. And while I could and often do express that advocacy or advance my political commitment in perfectly straightforward prose, my academic interest is in the construction of rhetoric and narrative—the way in which the form of a declaration can persuade or not persuade. So I toy with syntax and vocabulary. I do not have a fundamentalist's sense of language; I believe that there is always a degree of play in the word we use and the thing it represents. There's always some play. The issue is how you understand it, who translates, translation, what transitions are in operation, what's tucked away in that subordinate clause, what tense you are using, and does it shift.

HACKNEY: One notable critic of yours has been Richard Posner, who has a discussion in *Overcoming Law* where he's actually quite complimentary of you as a writer but critical with regard to what he views as your loose understanding of truth and use of facts, because Posner views law and legal writing as based on the telling of "truth." However, he is careful to note, given his pragmatist bent, that he is referring to truth with a lowercase *t* as opposed to any universal "Truth." Do you have any reflections on his criticism, which is a standard critique of your work and some others placed under the storytelling rubric?

WILLIAMS: I think that one of our major ideological disagreements is that he seems to believe that truth is constructed in a much more fundamentalist way than I do. I believe in the standard definition of scientifically reproducible truth. But much of law is not about the science of truth; rather, it is a verbal negotiation that depends on the appearance of truth, to wit due process. In trials, we adhere to an ethic of avoiding double jeopardy. We deal in singular cases and controversies, and thus resist the notion that there ought to be endlessly testable or reproducible results; we insist on "closure." In deciding outcomes, we rely on demeanor and probability, analogy and metaphor. We adhere so fervently to this model that even when there is reliable scientific evidence—like DNA testing in the post-conviction setting—many are inclined to forbid its consideration if it threatens the appearance of justice having been done. In recent years, the consideration of writs of habeas corpus has been constrained by technical rules about deadlines, as well as the institutional efficiencies of considering a case "closed"! So my goal is in no way an attempt to play fast and loose with truth; my purpose is to make clear when we are in the realm of appearances. I try to illuminate how appearances are inflected by context, rhetoric, belief.

Furthermore, I think Posner's sense of truth is highly dependent on a kind of social science that, while grounded in useful probabilistic correlations, he mistakes for proof or truth. When you put everything into very narrow econometric models, which he tends to do, you can shield yourself from considering certain transactions costs, human costs, incalculable costs. If you think about his ideas in "The Economics of the Baby Shortage," he packs complex lives into reductive equations, pie charts, axes, and it looks so terrific, but there's just so much that he leaves out. Please understand me—I'm not inherently distrustful of the kind of models or data he uses—rather, I think that you need to use very sophisticated stochastic models to be able to back up your assertions. And he doesn't. What Posner does instead is repeatedly take a really simpleminded social notion and put it into a model so that it looks inevitable because of its elegance. From behind the facade of his supply and demand curves he can assert that everything from rape to race is mere consumption preference, just requires some tweaking of pecuniary or behavioral incentives. But this short-circuits all kinds of other important data, factors, disciplinary insights. Consumption preferences are formed within a context of consumerism; if that's your only or chief measure, you've removed it from the forensic realm, the healing realm, the psychological realm, much of the moral realm, the sociological realm, the constitutive realm, the constitutional realm, etcetera.

HACKNEY: Posner has taken on the mantle of pragmatism so he actually emphasizes his belief in truth with a lowercase *t* as opposed to "Truth." His response would be that he used to expound metaphysical beliefs about truth when initially advocating for economic analysis in law, but today, as a judge and even in his scholarship, actually would agree with you that the truth is contingent and contextual.

WILLIAMS: I understand the move, but I still find his particular deployment of economic analysis objectionable. To go back to "The Economics of the Baby Shortage," it would be one thing if he were merely describing what actually happens in the adoption market, for it is true that there is a market for babies, and it's raced and eugenic, and it's generally not very pretty. There are indeed different price tags attached to different children, and that's the truth. But what I find specifically troubling about his analysis is that ultimately the piece is prescriptive. And, bottom line, what he prescribes is the reduced "production" of what he calls "second quality" babies, whom he goes on to define as "older, black, and other handicapped" kids. That's what gets me. This is not some summary of patterns of consumerist behavior. What he affirmatively advocates is the reduced numbers of certain babies, and I can't see that as anything other than eugenic. I don't think that he's necessarily a bad person; I think that the incredible fundamentalism with which he is secured within the neat, succinct, firm boundaries of his own framework does not allow him to take into account all of the ramifications of his positions.

HACKNEY: Can you reflect on the current state of the legal academy? Economic analysis has broadened out to include behavioral economics. There's a lot of discussion of neopragmatism as a framework, and all other sorts of developments. There's more technical expertise—a proliferation of PhDs, etcetera. How do you view the legal academy today as opposed to when you began your career?

WILLIAMS: I do like the fact that things are much more informed by multiple disciplines. I think that was missing when I started out. Certain boundaries of calcified doctrine are crumbling. The first-year courses are being reorganized. But I also think that things are closing up again so there's an emphasis not just on economics, but econometrics; not just sociology, but very narrow pools of data. Some of these academic conversations are breaking off into their own little worlds with not as much exchange across disciplines as I would like to see. As always, I suppose, one has to follow the money. A lot of this is being underwritten by specific interests, like the Olin Foundation's adventures with law and economics, so that's where a lot of this is going to end up. It worries me because there's not always the most comprehensive discussion of ethics. The currently favored economic models are self-contained, with very little sense of social implications and the kinds of ethics that you have to have for a sense of ultimate justice. For example, in contract law, the expectation interest is being unbalanced by an outsized regard for efficiency interest. And efficiency interest is not the same as expectation. Expectation involves an examination of parties' representations and what people undertook or agreed on. Efficiency is what's best for business or the movement of goods. The private-agreement nature of contract law becomes infused with or supplanted by the interests of industry. Perhaps efficiency-as-king will translate into the larger social good or a moral good—maybe, maybe not—but without a careful consideration of expectation as well, you tend to end up favoring a normative merchant class rather than individual transactors.

Catharine MacKinnon is Elizabeth A. Long Professor of Law at the University of Michigan and James Barr Ames Visiting Professor of Law at Harvard Law School. She is a leading feminist scholar, activist, and theorist on sex equality issues, both domestically and on the international stage. Professor MacKinnon has done pioneering work establishing the framework for sex harassment claims and legal challenges to pornography. She was cocounsel in a suit that led to a $745 million damage award to Bosnian women who were victims of Serbian genocidal sexual atrocities. She is currently serving as United Nations Special Adviser on Gender Crimes. Professor MacKinnon has written several books, including *Sexual Harassment of Working Women* (1979), *Feminism Unmodified* (1988), *Toward a Feminist Theory of the State* (1991), *Only Words* (1996), *Are Women Human?* (2007), and *Sex Equality* (2007).

6

Feminist Legal Theory

CATHARINE MACKINNON

HACKNEY: Please give an account of your undergraduate training prior to law school and graduate school.

MACKINNON: At Smith College, I was a government major but took courses in many other fields, taking advantage of its being a liberal arts college. My plan was to take everything but government the first two years, and then major intensively the last two. Political theory and constitutional law were my primary interests.

HACKNEY: Were there any professors there who you studied with more closely?

MACKINNON: Yes, Leo Weinstein, who is acknowledged in some of my books. I learned an immense amount from him. He was a phenomenal teacher and a brilliant mind and a wonderful man.

HACKNEY: What was the interest, in terms of Weinstein's ideas?

MACKINNON: He taught classical political theory and constitutional law at the same time, so it was clear what each had to do with the other.

HACKNEY: At Yale Law School, did you continue with a focus on constitutional law?

MACKINNON: I first went to graduate school for political science at Yale and continued with political theory. More or less overlapping you could say, but not in the joint degree program, I went to law school. I took the regular first year, and then many other courses, including constitutional law.

HACKNEY: You received your JD from Yale Law School in 1977. Did anyone there have any particular impact?

MACKINNON: I'm not sure that we will find much looking for impact. But I very much liked and learned a lot from Tom Emerson. Also Barbara Underwood, Guido Calabresi, and Owen Fiss. I learned from everyone I studied with, but probably more from the other students, especially Kent Harvey and Anne Simon, and more from all the women in New Haven Women's Liberation. As I was leaving law school, Burke Marshall and I connected strongly. Burke, Tom, and I stayed close until their deaths.

HACKNEY: You got your PhD in political science.

MACKINNON: Right. I studied with Robert Dahl, who pretty much saved my life. And also with others there, from whom I learned a good deal. But again, influence—not really.

HACKNEY: Did you begin teaching in law schools or graduate schools?

MACKINNON: I started out teaching Yale undergraduates to put myself through law school and graduate school. I taught political science as a teaching assistant and designed my own seminars in the College Seminar Program at Yale. Then I was hired to create the first women's studies course, and to help design the program at Yale. Most of the time I was in law school, I was teaching Yale undergraduates.

HACKNEY: At that point did you have any particular theoretical focus in terms of the way you thought about the direction of your own scholarship?

MACKINNON: What I was thinking about wasn't scholarship per se but what work we should be doing. Maybe it was 1971 or 1972, I first taught a seminar called "The Personal as Political," on feminism, and after that one called "Feminism and/or Marxism," which focused on the central issue of my dissertation and became the *Signs* articles. I wrote that material in 1972/73, but it was not published for another decade. The thesis, as published, became *Toward a Feminist Theory of the State*.

HACKNEY: In terms of external forces, did anything in particular, historically, shape your worldview?

MACKINNON: The Black civil rights movement and the women's movement did. Those most powerfully—even more than other things that were happening at the time.

HACKNEY: New Haven was a crucible for that type of activity.

MACKINNON: Exactly. I worked with some of the lawyers who were defending the Black Panthers, sleeping on their lawn when police raids were anticipated, although I wasn't in law school at the time, but graduate school. We had demonstrations. We shut down Yale the year I got there.

HACKNEY: When you began to consider what you wanted to think about, particularly regarding feminist theory, what was the intellectual landscape, in the 1970s, that you were faced with?

MACKINNON: I don't think I ever considered what I wanted to think about, certainly not regarding feminist theory. There was not much intellectual landscape for feminist theory as such, because it hardly existed. There was a little bit in French. What there was, were women in a vibrant movement of women speaking and talking and writing about the situation of women as part of actions we all participated in. That was the intellectual landscape. What I decided to do for my dissertation was to write about the theory of the relationship between consciousness and social change that was embodied in that movement. I researched everything I could get my hands on, all ephemera. There began to be a few books as well. There was Andrea Dworkin's first book in 1974, Juliet Mitchell's book on Marxism, Germaine Greer's *The Female Eunuch*, that came early on, and Kate Millett's *Sexual Politics*. I think Kate Millett's book had as big an impact on me as anything. I saw parts of it in mimeograph before it came out. And Robin Morgan's liberated issue of the magazine *Rat*, and her poetry book, *Monster*. There was really nothing on law. At a certain point in the mid-1970s there was the casebook, *Sex Discrimination and the Law* by Babcock, Norton, Friedman, and Ross, which was a real start. It collected materials and cases on the subject.

HACKNEY: So it was essentially the women's movement, writings related thereto, and some beginnings of the sketches of theoretical interventions, but nothing particular to law except for the casebook.

MACKINNON: The reason I wrote what became *Toward a Feminist Theory of the State* for my dissertation was that I thought that the women's movement should have a first-rate theory of its own, a real political theory that addressed women's issues philosophically from the ground up. And it seemed to me we didn't have that. There had been Mary Wollstonecraft, Christine de Pizan, John Stuart Mill, Engels, and others. It's not like there was nothing. But in terms of a contemporary theory that grasped the insights of the movement of which I was a part, I thought we needed a theory that articulated that.

HACKNEY: Can you describe your encounter with Marxist theory, how you viewed it as germane, and how you used it as a starting point? A lot of your work begins with pointing out distinctions with respect to how Marxist theory operates, and how feminist theory would operate.

MACKINNON: It seemed to me that, methodologically, Marxism started with reality, or what it took to be reality. It was material first. For a people whose reality had never been the ground of a theory, that seemed an important place to start. It also talked about class, which the liberal theories avoided, at least in any collective sense. Marxism did not understand the status of women, although some had tried in the past, and it seemed to me that there was something there to work with, as well as against. I was aware of the Continental philosophical tradition, and affected by it, and of the British analytic tradition, and for the most part reacted against it. But, while I learned a tremendous amount working through the approaches of the existing schools of thought, it was obvious that Marxist theory grappled more directly with the reality of oppressed people's lives in a way that tried to change them. That was the closest to what we were attempting that I had seen anyone try.

HACKNEY: Marxism is a starting-off point, but then there is a decided break. So when you frame a feminist theory, and characterize it as feminism unmodified, you explicitly take on the mantle of post-Marxism. Can you explain your definition of post-Marxism, and is there a particular strand?

MACKINNON: Actually, I created my own theory. To say I had a decided break from Marxism sounds like I was all in it and then broke from it. That isn't what happened at all. I saw Marxist theory, in particular its way of approaching the reality it saw, as instructive. I decided to do for women what Marxist theory did for the working class, which required figuring out how to approach the reality and what the reality was, both at once. It had to do with the reality first, though, rather than building on other theories. There was no theory of the reality I wanted to theorize. My theory came from this reality, rather than from some other theory. What I thought was useful about Marxism was that it was a theory that came from a reality. I learned, in part, how to do what I needed to do by seeing how Marxism had done what it needed to do, including where it had fallen short.

HACKNEY: Let's focus on the theory itself. A central concept is the role of power, and gender subordination. There is juxtaposition between sex, sexuality, power, and gender subordination. Can you lay out how they all fit within your theoretical framework?

MACKINNON: It theorizes gender hierarchy, which analyzes and describes the distribution of power between women and men in terms of how it is structured and implemented. Subordination means men dominate, substantively. When men are dominant and women are subordinated, you have gender hierarchy. Sexuality is a central site for it, even the key dynamic in it, in my view.

HACKNEY: One of the aspects of this is the role of the state. How do you see the state underpinning this reality, fostering this reality?

MACKINNON: The state is one institution of social power that reflects and reinforces other forms of social power that exist and also can at times be used to counter them. So, for example, in a white supremacist society the state largely enforces and reflects white supremacy and, at the same time, can be used to attempt to counter that, through, say, civil rights law. In a male-dominant society, the state is a male institution in its behavior, ideology, and activities. And the two combine. At the same time, some of its concepts—I have worked with the idea of equality—can be, and have to be, worked on and worked with to counter those inequalities.

HACKNEY: We do have moments of liberation—discrete moments in which we have the civil rights movement, we have the women's movement, etcetera.

MACKINNON: These movements decided to use the state as a means of getting legal equality to get social equality. They were under no illusions about its character or qualities, or in whose hands the power lay, or in whose interests it tended to operate. They work to make the state true to its purported ideals, as opposed to being the instrument for white supremacy and male dominance that it has, in general, been. Sometimes we win. Sometimes we have gotten it to respond, this being a supposedly democratic state.

HACKNEY: One of the ideas that grows out of the concept of gender subordination is the role of consent in legal doctrine with respect to rape. What are your views on consent, and how it plays out in sexual politics?

MACKINNON: Consent is a degraded term that usually refers to the acquiescence of a person with less power in something pressed on them by a person with more power. Yet the word is used to stand in for her freedom, even her desire. How one can be free under conditions of inequality is what needs to be addressed here, and is not.

HACKNEY: This idea is principally deployed with regard to heterosexual sex. Does it spill over into homosexual sex as well?

MACKINNON: Sure. The paradigm of sexuality, which is the heterosexual one, eroticizes hierarchy—domination and subordination of which gender is the substantive form. But under heteronormativity, sexuality and roles of domination and subordination are not limited to what are understood as heterosexual encounters, that is, between women and men, by any means.

HACKNEY: The other theoretical approach that is discussed in the two *Signs* articles is liberal theory and the deficiencies of liberal feminist theory, which is the dominant paradigm, at least in the United States. What do you find to be the deficiencies in liberal theory vis-à-vis feminist theory, and the general shortcomings of the liberal theoretical approach?

MACKINNON: You know, it is kind of wild to be asked to recapitulate work that it took years and volumes to properly articulate. If it could be explained right in a few sentences, I would have done that in the first place. Anyway, one basic problem is liberal theory's individualized, rather than group-based, approach to issues. And also in law its "let's pretend" methodology, as if we can get where we are going by pretending we are already there and making rules accordingly. A lot of the problems can be traced to Aristotle. Social change was not on his agenda.

HACKNEY: So it's a critique of Rawls and his liberal political theory?

MACKINNON: That is in general what *Toward a Feminist Theory of the State* did, although Rawls is not a central focus of it textually.

HACKNEY: Related to the concept of focusing on the group as opposed to individual, you discuss the way in which consciousness-raising is the principal epistemic tool—in terms of a feminist theory of politics. How does it serve as a tool for on-the-ground politics?

MACKINNON: It did not begin as a concept. It was happening. My project was to find out how it worked and what it was doing. Its primary dynamic involves changing how one sees one's own position within a collective framework. Other groups had done something similar before. With all women's particular difficulties, this is how women did it.

HACKNEY: I understand the distinction between observation and conceptualization. But there is a way in which, for those who aren't involved in a movement, the conceptualization can lead them to think about how they might operationalize. So I understand your point in terms of where it came from, but how does that effect the reader in terms of taking an idea and thinking about the world differently?

MACKINNON: That's one of the points of writing—to accomplish on paper what, in this case, was being accomplished by interpersonal interactions. Once the insights are taken in—and it's a continuing and ongoing process—once grasped as real, the insights can be treated by diverse methodologies. They can form hypotheses for social science investigation, be documented by statistical studies, analyzed in history, literature, case law, or media, or by talking to your mother. Once you see how you have been taught to see yourself, and document that that is how women have been taught who they are, then anybody can learn the way this process reproduces inequality on a daily basis. At that point, you don't have to have experienced it firsthand, or talked to other people about it, or see it happen to people around you even. It becomes information.

HACKNEY: One of the substantive areas that you focus on and utilize this idea of group analysis and consciousness-raising is pornography, and the way in which the theorizing about pornography is limited to individual qua individual action or depiction really misses the point. I know that you have written a lot on this, but can you link up that basic theoretical approach and how it came to be with respect to pornography as a particular point of reference in terms of applying that approach, and also the way in which you locate pornography as a vortex, with respect to a lot of what happens regarding consent and domination in sex politics in the United States and worldwide.

MACKINNON: It is certainly a vortex of these forces. One of the ways that pornography works is by being a huge ideological engine for generating a sexual experience of women as a subordinated class. It isn't just talking about this or stating opinions about this; it is actualizing this experience in the consumer. The consumer believes it in their minds because they have experienced it in actuality in their bodies. As I understand it, the way that it does that is by producing a sexual experience of women being accessed and used, fundamentally, and often being violated or hurt or tortured. That is experienced as sexual pleasure, sexual arousal, sexual fun, sexual fulfillment. It is a very powerful conditioning device. It uses all kinds of women and any inequalities that exist among women in the world. It also uses men—particularly men of color in a racist way. It sexualizes this experience in a way that can circumvent your value constructs. It operates on an unconscious conditioning level. That doesn't mean it's incapable of being overridden, particularly when it comes to action. But it has a very deep effect. As societies become increasingly media-dominated, and increasingly capitalist, pornography grows worldwide, spreading this effect.

HACKNEY: It's Madison Avenues meeting sexual exploitation. In parts of your writing you interestingly make the connection between different forms of pornography, and how they effectively reinforce different tropes in society. For example, there's the white supremacist trope, and there is pornography directed specifically to that. There is an interesting cause and effect dynamic. The pornographer is actually targeting markets, and also creating markets.

MACKINNON: They are in the business of creating demand. Their demand-creation strategy is, yes, to respond to what is going on in society—sexism, racism, the interlinking of the two. Class politics are sexualized in pornography. When they do this, they are making it stronger, entrenching it, not only pandering to it, but increasing, deepening, and spreading it. Anyone they can reach with this dynamic, which the rest of society already tacitly supports, is another buck in their bank account.

HACKNEY: This idea of reinforcing stereotypes is intriguing to me because I had an interesting moment at a recent LatCrit conference where there was a presenter discussing an empirical study of the treatment of Latinos and Latinas in a television show called *CSI: Miami*. It's a show where Latinos and Latinas are prominent. In her study, she revealed different tropes essentializing Latinos and Latinas. There was the over-sexualized Latina, the violent Latino, and then the different ways that sex politics play out in terms of white characters versus Latino/a characters. So that idea of media depiction is obviously not limited to pornography. It's pervasive in terms of the media industry?

MACKINNON: Inequality in media is definitely pervasive, and it has a powerful impact. But within that, pornography is distinguishable in its degree, immediacy, and the long-lastingness of its effects, when and because it combines sexual explicitness with subordination. When you have the sexually explicit alone or just the subordination, you still have effects—I don't think anyone thinks you don't. The reason that we have groups like the Anti-Defamation League is because people are well aware that the media has a powerful effect on how people are seen and treated. But pornography has distinguishable effects in being extreme, immediate, largely unconscious, and hard to get rid of. If your bottom line is, "Will this get women raped?," pornography occupies a distinct position in the answer from these other materials. That doesn't mean these other materials have no relationship to it, but it is more conventionally ideological and ideational. Materials that we know will get women raped with a fairly precise degree of predictive accuracy is something that we ought to be able to do something about, particularly when we can prove that the harm has, in fact, taken place.

HACKNEY: Pornography and rape stand at the pinnacle in terms of violence against women. But you also look at them as part of a continuum in terms of sex harassment and other sex acts. How do you view that continuum, and are there distinct lines of demarcation, or do these things spill out onto each other?

MACKINNON: There is a continuum, or several of them, depending on how you delineate it. There is more or less explicit violence. Greater and lesser aggression or severity. There are forms of force that are not violent (for example, employer/employee, teacher/student, etcetera), relied upon for sexual harassment, but it can be extremely severe. There are not necessarily sharp lines of demarcation here. So it depends on what continuum you are talking about.

HACKNEY: And they also do explicitly spill into each other. So, there are sexual harassment cases in which the harasser utilizes porno in the workplace.

MACKINNON: Absolutely. A woman may be sexually forced because she doesn't want to lose her job. There can be rape there in reality even if there is no rape case. The case of Mechelle Vinson, the first sexual harassment case the Supreme Court of the United States reached, illustrates this point.

HACKNEY: You have explicitly intervened in this debate by promoting anti-pornography statutes. These statutes would give a woman the ability to bring a claim for herself based on the subordinating effects of a particular piece of pornography.

MACKINNON: Andrea Dworkin and I conceived that statute, yes.

HACKNEY: That statute represents a distinct break with the liberal feminist perspective. It breaks from the notion of individual harm and connects to the idea of consciousness-raising and thinking in terms of the group harm as opposed to individual harm.

MACKINNON: Well, yes, although individuals are harmed by it. Sex discrimination is frequently viewed as being an individual harm, but it's done on the basis of group membership, like other kinds of discrimination. Each person who is hurt by it is hurt in her own life, just not because of anything individual to her. It's group based. Nevertheless, although courts have not denied that the pornography ordinance addresses a form of sex discrimination, they have struck the statute down, although it passed in various legislatures.

HACKNEY: Do you think the reason for judicial resistance is the power of liberal doctrine and thought in American legal culture?

MACKINNON: Partly, combined with the power of the pornographers in getting liberals and libertarians, who are also classic liberals, to support them. That is exactly how it happened given those who challenged those laws the people passed.

HACKNEY: Can you discuss the connection between your statutory initiatives and the work you've done with Linda Boreman, who was called Linda Lovelace (who starred in *Deep Throat*)?

MACKINNON: Yes. In large part the statutory initiatives happened because of the work with Linda. Linda didn't sue because there was no appropriate or effective legal claim for her to sue under, which was a major reason we became involved in creating the civil rights ordinances that you referred to. There was nothing for her to use to address the pornography she had been coerced into making.

HACKNEY: Are there any other policy directions that you have been at the forefront of in terms of the anti-subordination movement?

MACKINNON: Yes, there have been many—some I can talk about, some I can't. My theory of equality was adopted by the Supreme Court of Canada through litigation that I was involved in for many years, with the organization LEAF (Women's Legal Education and Action Fund). That approach went from Canada to South Africa and is now being used in a variety of international settings. The Violence Against Women Act was basically my idea, although it was spearheaded and drafted and supported by others, including a large coalition. My international work includes conceiving and bringing a lawsuit for Bosnian and Croatian women for rape in the genocide by Serbian forces in Bosnia. We brought the civil suit against Radovan Karadžić under the Alien Tort Claims Act in 1993 for rape in genocide, as well as for rape in war and rape as torture. We established the legal claim for genocidal rape, and won at trial in 2000. I have also worked with international tribunals on rape jurisprudence. There are a lot of other things that are confidential.

HACKNEY: I am interested in knowing what the concept of the Violence Against Women Act is. But, before that, when I went over your CV I did find interesting an initial focus, even early on, with respect to Canada. Politically it seems to be a less hostile legal and political environment for the approach that you believe would actually further women's interests, as opposed to the United States.

MACKINNON: I worked in Canada because they asked me to. But yes, all cultures are hostile to women's equality in their own ways, and the United States is certainly very trying in ways Canada has proven not to be.

HACKNEY: Can you give me the basics of the Violence Against Women Act?

MACKINNON: The VAWA made gender-motivated violence civilly actionable as sex discrimination in federal court. The Supreme Court in the *Morrison* case said that Congress didn't have the power to pass this law, which I think is not correct.

HACKNEY: One of your interests currently is on human rights as a tool to fight gender subordination generally. Earlier we discussed the obsession in the United States with the individual in the legal and political realms. When I read your human rights work there seems to be a more hopeful sentiment. One gets the sense there is actually a set of tools that, while not perfect, seem to fit the issue and can be deployed in a way that actually moves the ball forward to a greater extent than possible given internal U.S. politics.

MACKINNON: There is something to that. The international order has been more responsive and faster than the United States has been to looking at the reality of what women need.

HACKNEY: Is there a way in which women's focus on nongovernmental organizations internationally plays a role similar to the women's groups domestically in the 1970s?

MACKINNON: Yes, there are connections, although in both instances we also work both in and against governmental organizations. There is also something else that involves objectivity and what men mean by it that connects to that earlier work. Apparently what men in power mean by being objective is that they don't identify with that man: he doesn't look like them, talk like them, worship the same god. If we say the man right next to him has violated the woman right next to him, he can't see that because he identifies with him and sees him as like him so buys into the other excuses, whether cultural divisions or "boys will be boys." The international lens gives spatial distance that increases epistemic clarity, so they can see what he is doing for what it is. It probably helps that the man can't retaliate, too, because he is a long ways away.

HACKNEY: So, one way to look at it is that the state represents the individual male ideal, and international law is a way of puncturing the veneer of statehood in a way that actually, to go back to our earlier discussion about the state, works against subordination.

MACKINNON: International law doesn't puncture the veneer of statehood all that much, but maybe some. A lot of times the men are just identifying with each other, and what they're identifying most with each other is that they are all states. And that doesn't help much. But there remains a possibility at the international level, a small but significant one, of seeing what is really going on because it's at a distance.

HACKNEY: But then there's an interesting convergence. The same public/private distinction that is used domestically is utilized internationally to draw the borders of what is private and public. It's the point of sovereignty. You want to protect your own sovereignty and private sphere.

MACKINNON: Yes, it is the same problem. And it is becoming clear on the international level, even to men, that there are real problems with that. It didn't work on September 11. The attackers were not a nation. They were non-state actors. So now suddenly the door is open to look at the power of non-state actors, who are the people who have been violating women all along. And the door is open to look at state borders as not necessarily being the line that will protect people from outside attacks or that distinguishes the severity of attacks within, just as those borders have always been largely irrelevant to women's violation. September 11 and what's happened since has thrown a lot of this business about the state into question in a way that may be beneficial to women, although initially it may appear that men are off being more distracted than they ever were.

HACKNEY: In the long run, making problematic the concept of the state, even though it has the short-run consequence of adding credence to warmongering, might have beneficial effects.

MACKINNON: There can be many detrimental effects for sure, but I think it also, as is often the case when things are really problematic, has opportunities. Make lemonade.

HACKNEY: And that's a piece of the human rights equation that differentiates it from domestic U.S. politics. There is at least a nod toward economic justice and rights that is totally off the table in terms of U.S. constitutional politics. You make an interesting point, that a women's perspective on human rights really changes the order from private-political-economic-group to group-economic-private-political-civil. The linchpin of economic rights is the point at which there is absolutely no discourse in the United States, but it definitely comes into play in the human rights arena.

MACKINNON: Some of my colleagues are interested in freedom from want and have observed the way that has been built into the international legal structure. So there is some discussion about it, but you are right there is very little.

HACKNEY: Let's take a moment to think about some other legal theories that are out there, and situate them. Critical race feminism seems to be growing in influence. There have been at least two anthologies.

MACKINNON: It's a brilliant literature, consistently original and illuminating.

HACKNEY: Do you see any connections or tensions between your work and critical race feminism?

MACKINNON: The connections are profound. We are doing the same work in the same way and always have been. Tensions, none, where the work is accurate.

HACKNEY: Law and economics, or, as I've framed it, law and neoclassical economics, has taken up considerable space on the legal theory scene. Taking a cue from Gary Becker, there have been legal-economic interventions in areas that at one point we may not have envisioned as having economic dimensions—such as family, adoption, and sex. It obviously has the pitfalls you note with regard to classical liberal theoretical approaches generally, but in an interesting way it reveals the pervasiveness of the economic sphere (which had all too often been submersed).

MACKINNON: I learn a lot from law and economics. I find it often revealing and get a lot out of interacting with it and with the people who do it. Many of its assumptions and theoretical underpinnings and standards I don't agree with at all, but I still get a lot out of it. I especially identify with their wanting to figure out what's really going on out there. Sometimes they get too caught up in their models to do so, but they do want to know. And also, as you say, they are onto the material and economic dimension of much that has previously been analyzed in sentimental terms.

HACKNEY: Have you ever had exchanges with Richard Posner?

MACKINNON: Oh yes. On my long-term visit at Chicago for about seven years, I saw him quite often. I've had lots of exchanges with him and with other people who apply law and economics to issues we are mutually interested in.

HACKNEY: An interesting component of law and economics that I don't think people focus on consistently is that the second generation of law and economics scholars are actually more methodologically open than the first generation, so it's not all rational expectations. There is a lot of cognitive behavior work out there.

MACKINNON: The cognitive behavior work done by Cass Sunstein recently and some others is extremely interesting. It does go rational choice one better.

HACKNEY: Yes, if the purpose is to figure out what is going on in reality, then the cognitive behavior literature actually really does the work to a better extent than a rational choice model, and even economists acknowledge this. There is an interesting recurrent theme in your work, critiquing pretensions in science—be they pretensions with respect to a certain strand of Marxism, or pretensions with respect to liberal theory. I would assume the same criticism would apply to certain assumptions in law and neoclassical economics. They are all tied to this notion of objectivity, which, as you earlier pointed out, frequently is at the service of ratifying some status quo distribution. The idea is that you really can't do anything scientific using methodology that is characterized as subjective, the traditional notion of science being objective and removed from subjectivity. There is a very male-centric view with respect to observation and objectivity. One can make the point that science is one of the central tools for subordination. Cornel West when he talks about the creation of racial categories and racism goes back to the initial scientific conceptualization of race and the fixation on racial categorization. In terms of Western intellectual history, there is a melding of subordination and science. Interspersed throughout your writing are references to these scientific notions, and how they are actually deployed.

MACKINNON: *Toward a Feminist Theory of the State* was a direct and systematic attack on that. People do tend to assume they are standing nowhere when they recommend or argue something, but what comes across to me is where they're standing. Point-of-viewless-ness is a legitimating device. Covering up your determinants elevates your position.

HACKNEY: It's the classic Cartesian idea, "I think, therefore I am." I am removed. One of the things that I observed as part of this project is that there was a renaissance of legal theory post-legal realism, 1970s/80s legal theory, in which there was a generation of scholars who had really big ideas that were accessible to others broadly in the academy and beyond. From my perspective, as an intellectual historian, that period can be counterposed to what I view as law schools currently moving toward the university model through increasing specialization. We see this in hiring decisions. It's almost impossible to gain a position at elite law schools without having a PhD. There is increasing specialization.

MACKINNON: Most of the people I've studied with didn't have one. I don't think any of them did.

HACKNEY: Exactly. So if you look at the Posners, the Calabresis, etcetera, they don't have PhDs. But now, it seems to be a requirement. Arguably, it has stunted the ability of scholars to actually interact among each other because they are so heavily specialized that there is no point of connection.

MACKINNON: It used to be that they would have specialized in law. These people in a way are less specialized because they know something other than law. Law and economics, as narrow as it can be, has broadened law. Even though the people who do it are fairly specialized, it has brought a lot into law that wasn't there before that pulls in the opposite direction from specialization.

HACKNEY: There is an issue as to whether the generalists within law have the same access to this generation of specialists that they had to the first generation. Everyone could read Posner and Calabresi with respect to law and economics. It seems to be more problematic with increased specialization because legal academics are using increasingly sophisticated techniques that allow them to communicate with other specialists, but query whether the torts professor down the hall, who has no economics background but might have a background in critical theory, would have access to the teched-up work of her economist colleague and vice versa.

MACKINNON: That's true, and it also means only other specialists may be qualified to assess the work. But that raises the question of what the vocation of legal scholarship should be. What is the purpose of the legal academy?

HACKNEY: What do you think it should be?

MACKINNON: It used to have a direct relation to practice. A lot of the people who had that commitment in their lives and as a major part of their focus are mostly the older scholars now. In our generation, a number of us—women, people of color, international lawyers in particular—have that same commitment. The generations following seem to have less of a commitment to the real practice of law and more of an attachment to other academic fields. What may be getting lost or is decreasing as people's scholarly qualifications have increased, is their relationship to the real world and the practice of law.

HACKNEY: You're thinking about the practice of law broadly, including policy implications as well.

MACKINNON: Yes. I mean doing it on a level other than by writing op-eds or declaiming from your tower. I mean actually getting involved in doing real legal work and valuing what practitioners do, and seeing your teaching as preparing your students for that work, which is what most of them are going to be doing. The work that people do in the legal academy has tended to have less connection to legal practice, and the practitioners have returned the favor. They want even less to do with the legal academy.

HACKNEY: It's interesting because if we look at the rest of the university, the catchphrase is this idea of translational research. So they are moving toward practice, and we are moving away from practice. Maybe there can be some kind of congruence at some point.

MACKINNON: All these older people who think they could never get a job in the legal academy today because they don't have the qualifications called for today are the real leaders—Burke Marshall or Tom Emerson. What I really learned from them was, I saw them doing law. Their teaching was made better by that, and so was the part of the world that they interacted with. Most people who teach law today don't also practice. You would never get away with that in medical school.

HACKNEY: Practice can actually be a disqualifier.

MACKINNON: In some places, although some places value it, like Michigan at times. But a lot of the elite schools don't. There are also people, like Elena Kagan [dean of the Harvard Law School] for instance, who respect it, and who have a feel for the real world, who see law as a vocation of reality.

Drucilla Cornell is Professor of Political Science, Women's Studies, and Comparative Literature at Rutgers University and National Research Foundation Professor in Customary Law, Indigenous Ideals, and the Dignity Jurisprudence at the University of Cape Town in South Africa. Professor Cornell is a leading postmodern and feminist theorist who has made major contributions to modern legal theory. She played a major role in introducing prominent Continental theorists, particularly Jacques Derrida, to the American academy. Professor Cornell has also engaged deeply with John Rawls's Kantian constructivist project. She has published several books, including *Beyond Accommodation* (1991, new ed. 1999), *The Philosophy of the Limit* (1992), *Transformations* (1993), *The Imaginary Domain* (1995), *At the Heart of Freedom* (1998), *Just Cause* (2000), *Between Women and Generations* (2002), *Defending Ideals* (2004), *Moral Images of Freedom* (2008), and *Clint Eastwood and Issues of American Masculinity* (2009). Her most recent book is *Symbolic Forms for a New Humanity* (2010, with Kenneth Panfillo). In addition to her academic work, political activism plays a major role in Professor Cornell's life, and she has a background as a union organizer.

7

Postmodern Legal Theory

DRUCILLA CORNELL

HACKNEY: First, if you could just give a brief account of your undergraduate training. I think it was philosophy and math.

CORNELL: I went to undergraduate school starting in 1968. By that time I'd already been a political radical, and had been involved in the civil rights movement from the time I was in high school. In fact, I volunteered to go to a black high school when I was fifteen. My first college was Scripps College and there was a struggle at that time to have a black studies program, so I quickly became involved in that. I became unhappy in what I saw as a very privileged white environment at Scripps, so I transferred to Berkeley that summer. At that time I had also been reading, very seriously, the texts of German idealists (Kant, Hegel, and Marx), so I decided that I would go study in Germany and travel in Europe during the fall semester. I ultimately ended up attending the lectures of probably one of the greatest Hegelians of the 20th century, Michael Theunissen. After that I transferred to Stanford, where I again became very involved in the student movement. Nineteen seventy was the year the U.S. government entered Cambodia, and basically that entire spring all the students were on strike. From there, I became involved with an organization called Venceremos. Venceremos was very much involved with the Black Panthers. So again the antiwar direction of my politics became combined with that of black power, and what it meant to be a white person supporting black power. I was, with many other students, suspended from Stanford in an illegal search warrant that was challenged by Tony Amsterdam, who at that time was a professor of NYU Law School. I returned to college six years later, to Antioch College, studying philosophy and mathematics. Prior to entering Antioch, I remained a member of Venceremos, went to work in a factory, and got more involved in organizing the electronics industry. When my husband moved to New York to go to graduate school, I continued as a union organizer. So throughout that time, I continued my work in unions, in community groups, and in the left generally. The reason I am going through this history is that I had a very unusual undergraduate career, in the sense that most of it was devoted not only to studying Kant, Hegel, and mathematics, but also to my attempt to realize Marx's fundamental proposition, that the point of philosophy was not to study the world but to change it.

HACKNEY: To what extent did your study of philosophy affect the way you interacted in the realms of union activism, politics, etcetera, and then to what extent did your activism affect your study, or the way that you approach ideas?

CORNELL: Philosophy influenced my union activism and political activism more generally in two ways. First, because of my commitment to German idealism, starting with Kant, I had become convinced that we could claim our freedom, and we could aspire collectively to something like socialism, even as understood as a regulative ideal. My Kantianism allowed me to have the reasonable faith that human beings could act morally. Of course, even in radical politics many activists put themselves on moral holidays. Even on the left, many activists were still horrific racists. But Kant taught us that even horrific racists, and Kant was a racist himself, could potentially overcome it, and aspire to work with others toward the Kingdom of Ends. If you and I can together act morally, and if I can recognize your dignity as you recognize mine, together we can lay down a law unto ourselves and aspire to live together in harmony in the Kingdom of Ends. If one understands Kant broadly construed so as to protect the possibility of moral action, then there is every reason to think that it is possible to change the world in a just direction. And you are responsible for it—nobody but you. My commitment to the possibility of justice still points to the hold of one reading of Kant on my life and my work. Kant argues that if there is one person acting in accordance with the idea of justice and that one person does not give up, then the moral law is not dead and the possibility that we can aspire to regulate ourselves in accordance with the Kingdom of Ends is also not dead. Given a certain Kantianism, I did not feel that it was an option not to join the civil rights movement, because there were human beings who were not being treated with respect for their dignity. The movement was something that any morally responsible person had to become a part of, and that was how I got involved in it. I initially turned to Hegel because of early heterosexual encounters, and trying to negotiate men. So I read the early Hegel to my dates to try to convince them that the "me that is I" and the "I that is me" is a much more worthy way of being a human being ethically than making ridiculous passes in movie theaters. And my grandmother was a printer so she made me this beautifully bound edition of the early manuscripts of Hegel. So if a man misbehaved on a date what he got in return was a lovely bound edition of Hegel's manuscripts. I turned to Hegel because I saw in Kant not individualism, but an abstract notion of the moral self that didn't take into account my life as a woman. So Hegel became the basis of my feminism, and of my early dating life. I wasn't a German idealist who was thinking of becoming a professional philosopher. German idealism profoundly influenced how I lived my day-to-day life. I didn't know anyone who was reading Kant or Hegel. Charles Dickens was not allowed in my library at my high school because he was too subversive. So I didn't know that these were famous German philosophers. These were, as the wonderful feminist Sara Ruddick calls them, "my brothers." These were the people that I turned to when there was a life problem and I had difficulty solving it.

HACKNEY: Well, how did you initially encounter them?

CORNELL: When my brother went to college, he took "Humanities 101" at Stanford and came back with a reading list, and I said to my grandmother I would like to get these books. I fell in love with them. I saw that Kant wasn't enough when it came to dating. I needed some help. I tried a couple of times with Kant, you can imagine: "But Joe, the moral law!" I needed a little more depth and understanding of the ethical to get to why Joe was not rising to the ethical occasion. I thought, okay, I need Hegel, so then I read the early manuscripts and the *Phenomenology*, and I was completely hooked by it.

HACKNEY: You eventually ended up at UCLA School of Law. What was the connection there? Was it union organizing and labor law?

CORNELL: Yes, very much so. I had started out my life as a poet. I actually published some poetry when I was very young, eight or nine years old. And I thought I would be a poet. But poets don't make money. And then I thought I would be a translator of women's revolutionary Polish poetry. That was one of the more practical moves of my life. So I took intensive Polish. But I never really saw myself as someone who would be outside the active left, which shows you how powerful it was at the time when I was young. I could only aspire to be something like an academic in a conventional sense by imagining myself teaching at a workers college or an institution like that. However, I went to law school after a huge defeat in union organizing. In 1976, I was working for the United Electrical Workers, and all of our union efforts were met with the Teamsters disrupting the union drive by making sweetheart agreements with the employer. This, of course, is all dated now because our industrial working class has been so politically weakened and has diminished in numbers. So the Teamsters were making these sweetheart deals, and I convinced the UEW to stand up to the Teamsters. Now the Teamsters in Hackensack, New Jersey, were the Mafia, and nobody thought it was a good idea to stand up to the Teamsters in Hackensack except me. If you're a Kantian/Hegelian idealist, there's no reason why a Mafia thug can't get in touch with the moral law and so you never give up. Indeed, my tires were slashed, the windows of my car were broken, and I was bombarded by death threats. One day I walked up to two Teamster thugs and said, "You don't get who you are as a human being. However, I believe in you, and I believe you can get in touch with the moral aspect of yourself and truly be free." I think if they hadn't been stunned, or if I had been a man, I probably would have been dead. Instead, this guy says to me, and I hate to even quote this now because it's a popular book, "Are you from Venus, little missy?" Ultimately, I hung in there and hung in there and hung in there, with very little support from the United Electrical Workers, and we couldn't defeat the Teamsters. I returned home to California. This was a huge blow to me because it was at that moment that I realized that the bad guys can really win—no matter how much everything that is right is on your side. I went back to California, and decided, okay, I'll be poet and a labor lawyer. I also applied and got into a very prestigious math PhD program, but ultimately I chickened out. They let me in thinking that I was a man because I used to go by the name Dru. So I might have been a mathematician, but instead I took the labor lawyer/poet route.

HACKNEY: Was UCLA School of Law an intellectually vibrant community? Was there much in the way of theoretical debate?

CORNELL: The first year there was a hunger strike to defend an affirmative action program for Latino, Latina, and black students, and I became very active in the Lawyers Guild. I went to law school from 1978 to 1981. It was the heyday of critical legal studies so I began studying with Richard Abel, Steven Shiffrin, and Leon Letwin, all of whom were my professors. We formed a critical legal studies group. For me, my law school life was bound up with the critical legal studies group and the Lawyers Guild, where professors and students worked together on many interesting projects. I stayed in touch with many of the professors and students who were involved in that group. It was a very intellectually vibrant time for me.

HACKNEY: Was there any particular connection between what you had learned in philosophy and what the crits were talking about at that time? I know when I talk with Duncan Kennedy he is much more interested in French intellectual thought than German intellectual thought.

CORNELL: French and German intellectual thought are not as different as some thinkers take them to be. In *Moral Images of Freedom* I try to make that very clear. However, the key idea here is I'm a critical idealist. I never stopped being a critical idealist, even though I have of course revised my ideas through a lifetime engagement with French intellectual thought. Duncan and the crits are actually very close to the U.S. legal realist tradition. I wouldn't say they are as close to French radical thought. To emphasize the connection between French and German thought, Edmund Husserl is very close to Martin Heidegger, and Husserl is German and the main interlocutor for the early Derrida, who is an Algerian French-speaking thinker. So in that way certain crits who interpret the French tradition as separate from the German tradition are in a basic sense making a historical mistake. The two traditions are integrally connected. You don't understand Heidegger without understanding Husserl, you don't understand Derrida without understanding them both, and you don't understand Foucault without understanding Nietzsche, who is German. One of my regrets, which I have said throughout my work, is that the rich history of philosophy gets lost in the United States since we're not a reading culture. People don't take the time to learn German, and thus learn the interconnectedness of these two traditions. I was politically very involved with the crits, but intellectually I came from a very different understanding of critical theory. So I have a very different view of the word "critical" from many writers associated with critical legal studies. It didn't mean critique; it meant critical in a Foucauldian sense. Critical idealism in Kant means that limits must be placed on reason and space opened up for the imagination so that you and I can imagine ourselves and our world differently together, and think about what that re-symbolization has to do with how we might change our material circumstances.

HACKNEY: Did you go immediately from UCLA School of Law to Cardozo, or was there a transition?

CORNELL: No. I clerked for a wonderful judge, Justice Warren Ferguson, on the Ninth Circuit Court of Appeals, and I owe him a great deal for teaching me about the best way to bring theory to bear on any actual legal situation. He was a truly open-minded, committed judge, who would listen to arguments about what would be the just thing to do in a decision, even if all the law seemed to be against you. After clerking I went to the University of Pennsylvania where I taught from 1982 to 1987, and then I went to Cardozo.

HACKNEY: At Cardozo there were a series of famous conferences on deconstruction and justice with Jacques Derrida. Can you tell me how those came about? They obviously marked an important moment in American intellectual history. So how did that all work itself out, and what was the environment?

CORNELL: You asked me earlier what's the relationship between German idealism and French intellectual traditions, and how these traditions came to be viewed as antithetical—Kant here, Derrida there, which I think is a complete mistake. In my second book I renamed deconstruction "the philosophy of the limit," which echoes Kant's understanding of the limits of reason. I was working on this book when I met Jacques Derrida. I thought that his work had been received in this country so as to completely reject the notion of the possibility of justice. So I wanted to change what I felt was a rather linear and simple view of this intellectual history by having a conference not called "Deconstruction and the *Impossibility* of Justice," but "Deconstruction and the *Possibility* of Justice," and to bring together strands of critical theory. The conference was rooted in the question of what critical legal studies was within the academy of the United States, and how we could begin to look at the German and French traditions in a richer and more complex way. We not only had the two well-known conferences with Derrida, we also had a conference on Jürgen Habermas's work, and on Niklas Luhmann's work. Habermas obviously comes out of

German idealism, but Luhmann comes out of French phenomenology—even though he's a German sociologist. And then I also did a mini-conference on John Rawls's work. The whole point of these conferences was that we had tended in critical legal studies to say Rawls is *X* (a simple designator), Derrida is *Y* (a simple designator). We had not looked at the vibrancy of these thinkers as they might open up new spaces for critical thinking. So the conferences sought to put together people who would never be in the same room, discussing these topics together to develop a more complex notion of our ideas of what the words "critical" and "critique" meant.

HACKNEY: Okay, let's begin with deconstruction. What I hear you saying is that in order to have a theory that "works," you really need to take into account strands that have previously been cordoned off as separate, even if it's historically not true and theoretically false, but each of which brings to the table different pieces of the puzzle. Now deconstruction, in your mind, brings what to the theoretical table?

CORNELL: The way that I read Derrida, when I renamed deconstruction the philosophy of the limit, was that he brings two things to the table. The first is that I interpreted Derrida against the grain in that I did not understand deconstruction as a set of philosophical moves within language that shows what is impossible. The more conventional reading of Derrida had led someone like Duncan Kennedy to argue that there is something called the "fundamental contradiction." That's an ontological statement, or a view of human nature. But how do you know that? How do you get to the point where you say that human beings have this fundamental contradiction? In a certain sense, the entire oeuvre of Derrida points us to why it is impossible to make a statement like that. So I read Derrida to be making the exact opposite set of philosophical claims than some of his readers interpreted him to be making. He certainly would not support the claim that there is a fundamental contradiction in human nature, because that's an ontological claim. Ontological claims that in effect get you "off the ethical hook" are deconstructed in Derrida. At the end of the day, many crits used Derrida to argue against ideals such as justice, and in a certain sense promote a sense of paralysis in politics and certainly in law. The second important aspect of Derrida's work, at least for me at the early nineties, was his endless obsession with the role of the feminine as other, which is what I wrote about in my first book, *Beyond Accommodation*. What Derrida opened up for me was a radical feminist politics that focuses on the feminine other and the other as feminized, and the battle against that kind of othering becomes the key to a feminist politics that isn't just about women's equality—as important as that is in every walk of life. So in a sense feminism is radicalized, and made in a way more philosophically coherent. To show you what I mean by this, I have been involved in a lot of support work, in alliance with the Muslim community of North America, to support the Muslim men who were being forced to reregister in 2003, even though they were legal residents. For me, it was a kind of feminist politics because these men were being turned into an other who had been stereotyped and obliterated as a point of view.

HACKNEY: Now, if we can look at the phrase "deconstruction and justice" to go back to the beginning of our conversation. The justice component is really the moral center that's in each individual, because there is never any definition of "justice" in your work, as opposed to let's say Rawls, who has this idea of what an ideal theory of justice would be, once we can separate everyone out. Rawls derives principles of justice—you never do that. You have concrete exemplars of what justice would mean in a particular moment, but never an idealized set of justice rules—aside from the ideals of individual autonomy, imaginary dominion, etcetera.

CORNELL: I would have to disagree with you somewhat on that reading of my work. I do have an ideal of justice: "from each according to her ability, to each according to her needs." I am proudly a socialist. And I think socialism begins as an ethical ideal; it's defended that way in the work of the great German philosopher Ernst Bloch, and it's defended that way at times by the thinkers of the Frankfurt school. I have also argued, in *Defending Ideals*, that this ideal underlies the economic theory by Amartya Sen. In that book I also write a great deal about why I think Sen, more than Rawls, comes closer to that ideal, again, "from each according to her ability, to each according to her needs." Now, the imaginary domain was meant as an aesthetic idea to intervene in a field that was very contested at the time: How can you say that women are equal to men, or that gays and lesbians are equal to heterosexual men, and defend an ideal that actually says that to some degree or another there is a way of thinking about equality or freedom that doesn't pit freedom and equality against each other, or sexual choice and freedom against equality? These conflicts come out in the feminist contests with the issues of pornography and sexual harassment. In response to the seemingly inevitable conflict in feminist theory, I developed an aesthetic idea in Kant's sense of the word—an aesthetic idea is an idea that tries to configure, if imperfectly, the great ideas of reason. I also argue that this is the philosophical status of Rawls's representation of the veil of ignorance. If you understand socialism as an ethical idea, you can't reduce it to a slogan like Lenin did—nationalize, modernize, and industrialize—because it's an ethical ideal. But that doesn't get you off the institutional hook.

HACKNEY: Now, when you think about Rawls, it's interesting that a lot of feminist theorists are very critical of Rawls, and his idea of the veil of ignorance and everything that leaves behind. But you either reorient or reinterpret Rawls and his idea of tolerance, and make it really core, in conjunction with feminist theory, to your theoretical approach. When did you begin looking at Rawls seriously, and develop that connection?

CORNELL: In some ways Rawls was the greatest Kantian thinker in the 20th century living in the United States—no one even comes close to him. He brought Kant alive in the United States. I was naturally attracted to him because I started to read Rawls in his most Kantian period—the 1980s. I was struggling to think through *A Theory of Justice* via Kant. I also had joined Ronald Dworkin and Thomas Nagel in their seminar at NYU, and I had a chance to meet Rawls and engage with him. That was one of the most important intellectual honors that I have been given in my life. He came to speak at Cardozo because we did a mini-conference on his work. Rawls was truly a thinker, and one of the amazing things about participating in a seminar with him was also participating with him in thinking about the great ideas: Does *A Theory of Justice* aspire to give a representation of us as moral beings through the veil of ignorance? Is the veil of ignorance trying to embody the noumenal self? We know from Kant, and this is a very important point, that you cannot directly embody the noumenal self; nor is the noumenal self separated at the level of the ideal from an engagement with ideal others. So the veil of ignorance not only represents the noumenal self, but also represents us as ideal members of the legislatures in the Kingdom of Ends. Rawls wanted to think deeply about what this noumenal self might mean. One question that comes up when you think on that level is do you concede too much to rationality as opposed to the reasonable behind the veil of ignorance, because that introduces a moment of calculated self-interest that doesn't rest easily with the idea of what is being represented as the noumenal self in engagement with others, who are also noumenal selves, who are also members or legislatures in the Kingdom of Ends. So my engagement with Rawls was involved in a series of questions as to how committed his theory of justice was to Kant's idealism; to what degree could we imagine human beings actually able to rise above or transcend their self-interest as reasonable noumenal selves?

HACKNEY: How do you think or view Rawls' development from *A Theory of Justice* to *Political Liberalism*?

CORNELL: Extraordinary. I think, again because he was such an honest man and a man of deep integrity, he didn't give up on Kantian constructivism—that's lecture 3 in *Political Liberalism*. But one thing he was concerned with, long before others were concerned with it, was an ontologically based liberalism that had a hidden Hegelian agenda behind it—"We're all going to become liberal." Who's this "we"? I remember once being in the Nagel/Dworkin seminar and thinking, "I'm not part of this 'we.'" So Rawls tried to examine one of the big paradoxes: liberalism has at its heart a deeper respect for the path that you choose and people can lay down the laws for themselves, yet people are laying down laws for themselves that don't look like liberal laws. Also, they're saying this is my exercise of my autonomy. Do you, as someone who is a liberal, simply say you're just confused? This is part of the Rawls/Habermas debate—Rawls says we cannot simply write off other peoples who seem to choose non-liberal ways of life. So he begins to rethink the commitment of liberalism to pluralism—and not just pluralism as factions à la political science in the 1950s, but a pluralism in which people can have different general and comprehensive views, and can agree to be in conflict with one another. Therefore, there is no historical, ontological base underlying liberalism that can ground us. It has to be generated from a political or, I would argue, an ethical understanding of what liberalism is.

HACKNEY: That's the whole idea of constitutionalism. You talked earlier about how Derrida really motivates, or generates, a feminist ideal. Can you talk a bit about your views on feminist politics, versus the equality view, and the ways in which, and again you alluded to this earlier, "equality feminism" limits the discussion based on gender? What you're talking about with the imaginary domain, the sexuate being, etcetera, really expands the idea of freedom so that, although it might be centered in feminism, it also extends to sexual freedom for gays and lesbians, and also has implications for issues of race and class. So it has a broader scope, and doesn't get as trapped in the old, worn dichotomies (for example, black versus white, straight versus gay)—the whole litany of divisions and dichotomies.

CORNELL: Again I want to highlight these two points. The first is that I use Derrida, but also Lacan and Simone de Beauvoir, to deepen this discussion. What is feminist politics? Feminist politics in a certain sense is the struggle against all forms of othering that turns the other into someone who doesn't have a point of view, as I mentioned earlier. And so, by definition, you can say that it's a feminist struggle to stand behind the Muslim man who has been obliterated under stereotypes because he happens to be from Pakistan and doesn't have a green card. For me, that's feminist politics. You are not just fighting for women. You are fighting for someone who has himself been positioned as that other without a point of view. It's a responsibility to others who have been obliterated in the same way. Feminism on this understanding becomes integrally connected to antiracist struggles, and other working-class struggles, to the struggles of Muslim men who are being subjected to horrible levels of subjugation because they are identified with some fantasy of what being a Muslim is. This becomes a new kind of feminist politics. You also have a certain kind of liberal feminism, which simply seems to endorse the notion of freedom as lack of restraint, including in the area of sexuality. I have argued strongly that that absence of restraint is a disaster for feminism, and indeed for women. Instead of thinking of freedom as whatever you want to do, we should think of freedom differently, as through the imaginary domain, as the right to represent your sexuate being as long as it doesn't demand anyone's degradation. The difference between a heterosexual person who is offended by a gay or lesbian person but who can still work, and the gay or lesbian person who isn't afforded those freedoms, is that one is degraded in the Kantian sense and the other one isn't, because one is no longer being viewed as a source of value, which takes me back to Derrida and Lacan. To be degraded in Kant's sense is to be denied the status of a person with equal dignity. But I've also argued that there are psychic and symbolic laws that submerge the feminine as precisely that which cannot be configured through the ideals of personhood and equal dignity. Thus I've always felt that feminism must always return to Derrida and Lacan.

If you look at what we think of as the public realm, and say it interfaces symbols of who we are sexually, such as a Lacanian would argue—you never can get away from it—then Catharine MacKinnon is certainly right and the liberal feminists are certainly wrong in that we don't simply choose our sexuality. Symbols of sexuality have something to do with the way in which the "mother other" has been repressed, and that is my analysis of pornography. I mean, why do men watch a movie where women are cut up into little pieces and hung from the ceiling? I use Lacan to explain why pornography seems so integrally connected to masculine heterosexual sexuality. But I also argue that even if you don't like my Lacanian analysis of pornography, you can still accept the imaginary domain as a political ideal. Yet I also wanted to say we need to have a discourse where we can talk about things that we think of as unspeakable. Why do we have statistics where young women are marrying much older men, but older women almost never marry younger men? Is that just the way of the world? No. I think it's time to give an explanation for it, and Lacanianism can help us do that. The mother's body is the most terrifying body, precisely because it gives life and can therefore also give death. The more powerful the woman becomes, the scarier she becomes. So you need to have a discourse of desire that feminists in the late sixties and early seventies insisted on. But you do not want this discourse to lead to sexual repression. So it's complicated. Why don't men make their child-care payments in such large numbers? What makes a man think he has the right to do this—have a baby and then walk away from his responsibilities? Because that's his right? Maybe it's *not* his "right." Is it an exercise of freedom to walk away from your children? It is certainly not Kantian freedom. Kantian freedom always talks about obligation and responsibility. I thought we needed to both have an idea, an aesthetic idea, which could allow us to claim what was right in liberal feminism, and at the same time use psychoanalysis to show that there is no pure public realm. The public realm is infested with phallic images of what it means to have power, what it means to be a man, and those images have everything to do with how the public realm symbolizes itself.

HACKNEY: When you think about MacKinnon, one of the policy debates that you weigh in on is prostitution. The way that she views prostitution is that it's part of a continuum, which includes pornography, and you take a very different view with regard to prostitution. You discuss prostitution through the prisms of the imaginary domain and sexuate being. Please talk about that difference between you and MacKinnon, and how you get to the place where you end up versus where she is.

CORNELL: The MacKinnon/liberal feminist debate was raging ferociously when I was a young law professor, and I refused to support either side. When I decided to write about pornography—you asked me how does my philosophy and my activism interact, and here is an example. My first thought was to get in touch with the union organizer in the porn industry. I was determined to get to the ground. And indeed I did get to the ground. I developed a relationship with Ona Zee, who had been organizing the porn industry. I wanted to hear her story. I wanted to hear how she viewed the organizing efforts. And that's so important. If you're a feminist and believe that the other shouldn't be obliterated, and you're going to talk about porn, you've got to go down and talk to those in the porn industry. So I looked for the union organizer and I found her and interviewed her. From 1974 on I have been a supporter of unionized prostitution. In that year, there was this huge debate and a huge fight between feminists about whether prostitutes should be unionized. That debate returned in the feminist discussions about pornography. Ona Zee was going in with union members and rescuing young girls and boys being forced to have sex on porn sets without condoms. That's where I argued feminists should be or should have been, since the union had been broken by the time I met Ona Zee. We should have been supporting them. So let me get some things straight: Do I accept that Ona Zee, who was horribly traumatized and sexually abused, made her choice to become a porn worker because it was something she had to go through to work out her trauma? She had huge success as a porn star, and then went on to do sex education and then finally got out of pornography altogether to become a sex therapist. Meanwhile, she went through the whole union movement. So the union movement was about representing herself and representing workers in pornography. What she resented about MacKinnon was that MacKinnon didn't respect her trajectory through her trauma. MacKinnon would say that "you have lost your dignity, you are behaving in an undignified way"—so that dignity and dignified were and are conflated. What Ona Zee wanted was for feminists to recognize her point of view and side with her—have some courage, and not just moral courage but a little bit of physical courage. When you get a phone call that says, "I want you to come down and join me to organize the porn industry and we're going up against the Mafia," you have to have some physical courage. Of course, in some sense the porn industry doesn't really exist anymore because everyone does it on the Internet. So you might say that a whole group of sex workers, whom she is very interested in as a sex therapist now, has been displaced in terms of employment. What I meant to say about MacKinnon was that we need to respect sex workers. Like I said, the first thing I wanted to find out when I started writing about pornography was whether or not there was a union organizing the industry. Some feminist friends told me that I would not find a union organizing effort in the porn industry, and I argued on the contrary, that there will be an organizing effort.

HACKNEY: In *Moral Images*, you return to the same themes with respect to Kant, Derrida, Rawls, and Heidegger, the whole grouping, and then you introduce Ernst Cassirer. I think it's very fascinating imagery with the symbolism, and then the connection with black existentialist thought. Can you blend that all together, and how it all works for you?

CORNELL: Yes, I'll try. I'm actually working on a book with Ken Panfilio on the significance of Cassirer's view of language as symbolic form, and what that means for conceptions of reason, conceptions of the aesthetic, and even conceptions of race. What makes Cassirer so interesting is that he argues that we are not marked as humans as rational creatures, but rather as symbolizing creatures. This can be a very radical idea because animals are also symbolizing creatures. Because we are symbolizing creatures, language always carries the metaphoric power of transference in it. He's close to Paul Ricoeur in his insistence on metaphor as integral to language, but he digs deeper than Ricoeur because of his connection between metaphor and myth. For Cassirer, myth is not a secondary form of knowledge, it's actually part of the metaphoric properties of symbolizing itself. And why this is so important is that we can have some self-reflexivity about what our myths are, but we can never simply do away with myths in some kind of transparent inner rational dialogue such as the one that Habermas proposes. Thinking with Cassirer has also been important to my work in South Africa. And why? It is dangerous to say that particular forms of life in South Africa that include "traditional" practices and beliefs are just outdated ways of living that will be destroyed by modernity. For Cassirer, in myth and other "traditional" forms of life, it is just a different kind of reason at work, not one that is in any way necessarily lesser. Cassirer is a pluralist, in that sense, all the way down. Following Cassirer, this means that we have to understand that there are not just general comprehensive worldviews that might be reasonable, but that different people actually live in different ontological realities. That doesn't mean we can't reach each other. There is always the possibility of translation. However, we're not going to reach each other through translation if we argue, "Your symbolic reality is outdated and you must get in touch with modernity," because then you are obliterating the other as a point of view.

That gets to the second part of the question—relating this back to black existentialism. There is so much to say about Cassirer's notion of language, and Ken and I hope to bring out the connection between Cassirer, black existentialism, and race that deepens my own work in *Moral Images of Freedom*. Part of self-reflexivity, interestingly enough for Cassirer, is a recognition of pluralism—not that one is more rational and the other is less rational, but rather each are operating within a deep reasonableness. To do that is to recognize that there are other points of view, completely different than your own. You must learn and listen. Now, Frantz Fanon believed that colonialism simply obliterated the colonized as a point of view. So this is how the two ideas fit together.

HACKNEY: Fanon's analysis regarding what it means to exist as a black person is that you have two basic existential choices. One is self-hatred, internalization. The other is armed revolt—a forced change in the system, which given political reality, according to Fanon, can only be done through armed revolt. How do you think, with that observation (the observation of the necessity to recognize the other), how does that lead to liberation? What's the process, how do we get those who are in the position of oppressing to really take that message seriously?

CORNELL: I am going to say that Fanon has three positions, even though you are certainly right that he is often associated with two. And the third is the one that is most clearly associated with Ernst Cassirer—that blackness has to be re-symbolized. And one of the thinkers most associated with that call for the re-symbolization of blackness politically is Stephen Biko from South Africa. Blackness ceases to be a skin color. It becomes an assertion of an ethical relationship that has been pushed under and foregone in the colonial relationship. So people often ask, can a white person be black, and the answer is absolutely yes if you refuse the political privilege of whiteness in any given society. According to Fanon, the ethical relationship has been destroyed in colonial relations because there is no other. A first step in the struggle then is you have to assert the otherness. But the assertion of the otherness is for the purpose of the ethical relationship. So it's a symbolic struggle to re-symbolize the meaning of blackness, and it unites—or it did in South Africa—Coloureds[1] as well as whites. Black consciousness is a radical concept and it still remains very radical. My daughter is a Biko black consciousness person in South Africa—even though she is Latina. Under Biko, then, blackness is a political and ethical movement to re-symbolize all of those who are racially oppressed as worthy of their humanity. As Biko said, it's the only state in which the ethical relationship exists.

HACKNEY: Is this politics and set of ideals located in South Africa one of the reasons that you have been attracted to South Africa as a location, versus the United States? Do you see any ways in which those ideals could be manifested in the United States? It seems to be related to, for example, some of the moral teachings of Martin Luther King and the civil rights movement. Can you locate the distinctions in the political and cultural locations?

CORNELL: I went to South Africa in 2001, and at that time South Africa was still a beacon of hope in terms of two things: the possibility that there might be a real alternative to neoliberal capitalism, and that there might be ways for people to live up to their moral responsibility without having to go through a bloody civil war. Now, the truth is there *was* a bloody civil war in South Africa for about twenty years. There was no miracle transition. Like many people of my generation—I grew up with Gil Scott-Heron's song "(What's the Word?) Johannesburg"—the struggle to free Mandela and the fight for freedom in South Africa were very much a part of my life. When I began the uBuntu project, I began in part to understand why the majority black population, a highly organized and mobilized population, had agreed to these negotiations—although whites took almost all of their land. The 1913 Land Grant Act took 87 percent of the black population's land, conservatively estimated. I believe the actual figure is much higher—maybe 93.8 percent of their land. And what is the major reason for this expropriation? There was an urgent demand for workers in the newly discovered gold mines. Gold was discovered in South Africa in 1886. The expropriation of land was crucial to the creation of a proletariat that could be super-exploited in Marx's sense of the word "super-exploitation." You can at least understand from one view of justice that this was unjust enrichment and theft, and that all the land should be given back. But whites were not kicked out of South Africa at the time of the negotiation. Certainly some kind of reparations would seem to be necessary if the new South Africa were actually to bring about a new society. Thus I disagree with Jeremy Waldron's notions about reparations. Waldron argues against reparations because he contends that reparations might take away land from the innocents that was rightfully theirs. It would be very difficult in South Africa that anyone could actually defend the position of innocence. Secondly, Waldron argues that reparations are wrong because we can never know whether or not those who had their land taken away from them would have made effective use of it. And this brings me to my second disagreement with Waldron. It must be remembered that in the 19th century the Africans in the Eastern Cape and Western Cape were so effective as farmers that they needed the Land Grant Act and the entire British army to break them—portrayed famously in the movie *Zulu*. They had been working as farmers before they were taken up into the gold mines, so we historically can say that there wouldn't have been any need for the British army to be so ruthless if they had not been so successful as farmers. Given the history of 354 years of racialized capitalism, and even when recognizing the violence of the transition, we still have to ask why the majority of blacks have accepted the new constitutional dispensation. For me, one possible answer was the ethic of uBuntu, and that was what led me to begin the uBuntu project.

HACKNEY: One area in which there is a general juxtaposition between the localized perspective versus the "universal," whatever that means, is in the human rights arena. There's been tension with respect to feminist ideals coming from the West. I know you talk in your work—it's related to your discussion about recognizing the other and dialogue—about the relationship between feminism and the lives of folks in different localities throughout the world.

CORNELL: That is another important question. These are great questions. I think that the most important thing is humility. I think oftentimes Western feminists, as I've discussed in *At the Heart of Freedom*, take themselves to be in a position of freedom, and no woman is in a position of freedom who is living today. I mean, I have hope for my daughter, and her generation. But for now, all women are living in states of unfreedom. That's where you begin. It's easy to make certain assumptions, that someone who, for example, is rebelling against certain notions of what freedom is, is somehow or other unfree. I think that Saba Mahmood's book on the Piety movement in Egypt wonderfully demonstrates this. For Mahmood, she quotes this wonderful woman—any woman who is in the Piety movement is struggling with these huge questions that plague all of us, even if their answer to those questions may be very different from ours. So we take this very limited neoliberal notion of freedom as doing what you want to do, and women all over the world are saying it sucks—to use that word somewhat humorously. Feminism must operate on two levels. First we must acknowledge our own unfreedom, and acknowledge it on the deepest possible level. This often involves intergenerational relations between women. I want my daughter to be free in ways that I can't even imagine. Secondly, Western feminists have to realize that we make assumptions about other women's symbolic universes. Again, we have to get back to the question of listening and hearing. But then there's the danger—don't go in assuming that you know what the symbolic universe is that they're living in, and how they're in shame, when you don't know anything about it. You have to first really find out. Now, I have no problem saying that I'm against genital mutilation, and I think it should be universally condemned. That is one statement. Now what does that mean? Who is going to do it, and how's it going to be done? In Mali, the Sharia lawyers, some of whom are women, have played a major role in seeing to it that genital mutilation is abolished—it's unconstitutional, and it's seen as against the Muslim religion. Now, they did that. They accomplished that within the bounds of Sharia law, which was then the basis for its unconstitutionality. So what you oftentimes find—it's just like with the porn workers movement—if you go to the ground, find out what's going on, and see what you can do in a respectful way, there will be ways for women to unite. It's not that you can't say that things are universally condemnable, they are, but once you've said that, then how you actually work with others on the ground so that you don't obliterate others as human beings becomes a crucial question. If you obliterate them as human beings, that's not about human rights, that's just about colonialism. You should be able to separate the two. Sometimes it's going to take a lot of time, a lot of care, and a lot of attention.

HACKNEY: And that really seems to be a particular application of the earlier discussion of the moral imperative that everyone recognizes the other. It's not just women who are subjugated throughout the globe, but "white men" who are underprivileged because there are different levels and gradations of whiteness—class, sexuality, etcetera.

CORNELL: Exactly. Whiteness is no more real than blackness, right? It's simply a relationship that becomes imposed by hierarchical power. And so a white person who chooses to be ethical, say in the state of apartheid in South Africa, will be "blackened." So it's not about skin color, it's about this endless series of relationships between people. What colonialism does is obliterate the other as a point of view. If the other has a point of view, how can you possibly treat that other as less than a human being?

HACKNEY: Well also, it's a precondition to dialogue, which you talk about in *The Philosophy of the Limit*. There you articulate a vision of coming together, and the only way that we can come together and genuinely dialogue is we have to, in essence, not be attached to our individual beliefs, in order to actually engage with difference. That's an important piece in human interaction. It also comes into play with respect to—and you talk about this in *Moral Images*—academic disciplines. I was reading an interview with you, I'm pretty sure it was a German periodical but I can't be positive, in which you have a long discussion about rational choice theory, and the ultimate policy and social implications of rational choice theory—that is, privatization. You use New York as an example of public spaces being shrunk, and everything being privatized or the proliferation of multinational corporations—Starbucks is on every corner, the proliferation of fast-food chains, etcetera. So I know that you would have had to come to grips in the 1980s with the law and economics movement because it was the most powerful policy generator in the United States, by far. Did you ever engage those folks?

CORNELL: I had a debate with Richard Posner, and that debate is actually published in *Just Cause*. That's my main engagement in print with rational choice theory, although in the sexual harassment chapter in *The Imaginary Domain* I also talk about rational choice. In a long footnote in *At the Heart of Freedom*, I cite a book by my brother [Brad Cornell], which was never published, making the following argument. Rational choice theory says that the market will cure racism because at the end of the day it's irrational to discriminate. You want the worker who is going to give you the most marginal utility, period. So if you just let the market handle the problem and deregulate Title VII, then you will actually have a nonracial marketplace. Gary Becker argues this point. My brother, using some recent cognitive psychology arguments, argued that the market will not clear racism. One of the things he argued in this book, using cognitive psychology sources that I wouldn't have used but I think his point is valid, is that—I'm going to use my language and not his—people are so locked in their ontological universes, and their ways of familiarity, which Charles Peirce called habituation. When someone comes in who is not of your race and your dialect, and of your clothing style and your manners, you get very uneasy and in fact people will behave irrationally in terms of the market in order to facilitate their own pleasure. My brother's conclusion was that the only way that people can change is for people to learn many languages, and therefore to become at ease with many different symbolic universes because they know how to move in and out of many. I know that one of the women working on the uBuntu project speaks thirteen languages; she speaks all of the official languages in South Africa, and German and French. So in a way my brother's point is well taken. She would be at ease in the United States, and at ease in a shantytown. Now, rational choice theory is quite simple, which is why I never had that much to say about it. The central idea behind rational choice theory is that human beings will always choose to optimize their own self-interest and utility, and game theory says that there are certain problems that develop because that is how human beings behave. Now, anyone who is intelligent knows that that is just a theoretical projection. Any theoretical projection can be translated into mathematical language. Rational choice theory articulates a theory of human nature that it oftentimes does not defend; and it is a simple idea, yet one that needs defense.

HACKNEY: I agree. But the interesting political dimension is that that ideal of self-interest, which actually can work against group interest, was so powerful in the eighties that it drove an already-capitalist society, the United States, to even more privatization. It also globally—when we look at international economic policy—drove other nations, if we think about the eighties going forward, to become more decentralized. There is something about the power of the myth of self-interest—and here I think you're right—the myth that Reagan and Thatcher really utilized to construct a "brilliant politics." It blows the mind.

CORNELL: Yes. How could such a simple-minded idea come to have such ideological weight? It's such a simple idea—we are only self-interested, utility maximizing. And I think an interesting part of it, to come back to follow up with the idea of masculinity, is it's an appeal to a kind of masculine ideal, right? "I'm a man—I don't need anyone!" I think that without the appeal to some underlying, unconscious, fantasized projections of masculinity, it would not have that appeal or ideological hold. I've actually written a book about Clint Eastwood and the movies he directed (not the movies he acted in). I think that Clint Eastwood has grappled with the phallic fantasy of masculinity more than anyone in Hollywood. In movie after movie, he shows that it ends in horrific loneliness, destruction, and despair.

HACKNEY: So let's discuss contemporary politics. There were some pundits out there who analogized Obama to Reagan. They were saying that Obama was the type of figure who could articulate, given his force of personality, a different vision. Now, if you look at the eighties, in terms of what they brought (particularly in the United States, but also globally), there is hyper-economic segregation. You have, within industries and within corporations, these levels of disparity with respect to those on top and those on bottom. Is this a moment in which there can be an ideological shift, in which we can unveil the myth of independence? The obvious upshot is that the free market is not working. Do you think we're there or someplace else? I'm interested in your view of the contemporary situation, particularly in the United States but also globally.

CORNELL: I don't think that we have any real option, given that nothing takes us away from our ethical responsibility. We have to work as hard as we can for that shift in ideological vision. Do I think that Obama has coherently articulated that vision? I don't see a coherent ideological vision. In terms of myth making, you're right, Ronald Reagan seemed great to many because he was consistent. Obama is more complicated, and that makes the ideological shift different. And you cannot have that ideological shift without confronting head-on the continuing reality of racism in this country. Why is it that discrimination has not gotten better? I appealed to my brother's work earlier for one possible explanation. Can you just pretend that we can move forward to a non-racialized world without thc struggle against racism? I don't think so. So the interesting question is, is Obama black, in the Biko sense? And the answer is no. Now, I think that for a real ideological shift, Obama's white mother and biracial heritage aside, he would need to be black in the Biko sense, and proudly so. Part of the ideological shift is away from the unconscious racism, and implicit identification of power with what is white. And part of the struggle against racism is against the obliteration of black people as a point of view, as well as what that means economically for them. A German writer who has been in New Orleans after Katrina and was utterly devastated by what she saw there posed the question—What does it mean that nothing was done about the devastation Katrina caused, so as to significantly alleviate the destruction of the hurricane? How could we allow the black population of an entire city to suffer, and continue to suffer? How could that go so unnoticed?

HACKNEY: It obviously calls for social transformation. Is that politically viable? If Obama is anything, he is a political animal.

CORNELL: I'm afraid that's right. And if we were to have significant change in our ideological vision, we would also need a profound antiracist politics.

HACKNEY: Interestingly, although he doesn't articulate a full-throated vision the way that Reagan did, and I think for some real contextual reasons, there is a way in which Obama could represent the first step. His being voted in as president, while not reparations, does represent recognition. Also, what he does articulate is a vision of recognizing the other. In fact, in his convention speech when he declared that there is no red America, no blue America, no black America, no white America, there is just the United States of America, there is this way in which he articulated an ideal of recognizing all of our humanity from this cultural identity perspective. It doesn't go that second step to a socialist economic, justice ethic. But, as you just articulated, it might be that first initial step in which people begin to look at economic disparity in the same way, and believe that there is an ethical and moral obligation to pursue social justice.

CORNELL: Can you really say there is no red America, there is no blue America? Can we really take the bloody history of the United States and say, well, we're just going to go forward? Part of me says that what South Africa did right, although partially, was actually calling for truth and reconciliation, to recognize that you can't just go forward without facing the bloody and tragic past. There is way too much of this cheeriness in the United States, and the very violent imagery of the melting pot. There are differences in this country, and there is discrimination that is real. So I have been skeptical of Obama's rhetoric that there is no blue, no red, etcetera. I feel that the only way to get to a nonracist world is by fighting against racism—not by pretending that we are all alike already. He is skipping a step, and he's skipping a big step.

NOTE

1. Coloureds is the term commonly used for mixed-race peoples in South Africa.

Bruce Ackerman is the Sterling Professor of Law and Political Science at Yale University. He is best known for his work in political philosophy, constitutional law, and public policy. His major works include *Social Justice in the Liberal State* (1980) and a multivolume constitutional history, *We the People* (1993, 2000). His more recent books include *The Stakeholder Society* (1999, with Anne Alstott), *The Failure of the Founding Fathers* (2005), *Before the Next Attack* (2006), and *The Decline and Fall of the American Republic* (2010). Ackerman is a preeminent liberal theorist. His work comes out of the tradition of John Rawls, one of his tutors at Harvard. Ackerman also has a deep interest in "real-world" political problems and has developed concrete proposals to enhance democratic processes. He is a member of the American Academy of Arts and Sciences, a Commander of the French Order of Merit, and the recipient of the American Philosophical Society's Henry Phillips Prize for lifetime achievement in jurisprudence.

8

Contemporary Liberal Constitutional Theory

BRUCE ACKERMAN

HACKNEY: First I want to begin with some preliminary background questions. Can you just give me a brief description of your undergraduate training?

ACKERMAN: I was in government and philosophy at Harvard. My tutors were John Rawls, Judith Shklar, and William Yandell Elliott. I read about five hundred pages and wrote a twenty-page paper every week. So I really got a pretty good education in political philosophy at Harvard, and then I came to Yale Law School at one of its best moments. It was full of people with ideas, like Alex Bickel, Ronald Dworkin, Charlie Reich, Bob Bork, and Guido Calabresi. I'm sure I am forgetting quite a few. So this was a great moment at Yale Law School. And I was much taken by it.

HACKNEY: With the political philosophy background, what ideas did you gravitate toward at Yale Law School? Was it more toward Dworkin, or others?

ACKERMAN: Really I just had a great time. But the thing that was new to me was law and economics, in the form of Guido and Bob Bork, but Dworkin, Alex Bickel, Charlie Reich were also quite important people for me. And all of them were, in their own ways, taking some kind of middle distance from what the law was, and they were attempting some largish view. That inspired me a lot because my training in political philosophy was in the history of political philosophy. During the early sixties, there was a real academic debate on whether political philosophy was dead. Of course, I was lucky. Rawls came in the middle of my time at Harvard, and he was trying to say something significant about the here and now. But this was a rare thing at the time. The end of ideology was the large theme.

HACKNEY: What did you do between law school and coming back to Yale Law School?

ACKERMAN: I was a law clerk for two years with Henry Friendly and John Harlan. And then Susan and I started to teach at the University of Pennsylvania for five years. We got married right at the time that I was leaving Yale Law School in 1967. I met Susan in the Yale Law School dining hall. Both of us got jobs at the University of Pennsylvania, and we've coordinated our lives ever since. That was important to us. In those five years I started to do work on both the theoretical and policy side, because I've always tried to do a couple of things at once—some more practical than others. On the policy side I was working on slum housing and environmental policy. That really is what I got promoted on, which was a great plus because I don't think that I could have written *Social Justice in the Liberal State* while going through the tenure process. That's not a tenure book. It's much too risky to be a tenure book. You would get your head cut off for that one. But I was teaching a course on social justice from the beginning at Penn. I taught social justice, property, and environmental law. Those were the things that I taught for quite a number of years—not constitutional law. I started to teach constitutional law when I was about forty years old.

HACKNEY: So your focus was on the policy component and you got promoted on it. But you always had the philosophy piece of it.

ACKERMAN: That's right. From 1970 on I was writing *Social Justice in the Liberal State*. It took me about ten years to write that. But I didn't publish any of it until I actually published the book.

HACKNEY: That's an interesting strategy. Most people try to space it out based on articles. Before we get to *Social Justice*, during this continuum of time, there are obvious historical events that manifest themselves—the Vietnam War, the civil rights era, the women's movement, etcetera. Did any of those make an impact on you?

ACKERMAN: Sure. I was moderately engaged at Yale Law School both in civil rights and antiwar activities—moderately engaged. I certainly wasn't a leader. And, of course, I worked for these two conservative judges—Henry Friendly and John Harlan. I left Yale in 1967, just at the time when progressivism was being radicalized.

HACKNEY: Was Duncan Kennedy there then?

ACKERMAN: He and I went to Harvard College together. He went to Europe after college, and then he came to Yale. I think that he was maybe two years after me. And there was very much more of a radicalization as I left. I left and went into this ivory tower, more of an ivory tower, where I couldn't demonstrate or engage in anything really as a law clerk to Henry Friendly or John Harlan. When I came back, of course, I went to the University of Pennsylvania, where everything was alive with activity. That really was the motivation for *Social Justice in the Liberal State*, because I couldn't figure out what a serious project of social justice was in all of this. There was a lot of talk, but I couldn't really figure out what the new left, or the old left for that matter, was about. That, undoubtedly, was the motivator for *Social Justice in the Liberal State*, as well as the example of Rawls and to some extent Dworkin, and the milieu of Yale Law School in the middle 1960s. At the same time, it was always clear to me that I wanted not merely to engage in philosophical reflection, but to consider the actual practical, mid-level interventions guided by the theory of the activist liberal state. That's the one-line motif.

HACKNEY: When one reads *Social Justice*, or at least the way that you frame it out, it is clearly a project embedded within contemporary political theory—particularly Rawlsian framing. But it's also a reaction against a purely theoretical approach, a kind of middle theorizing. Perhaps you were a neopragmatist before it became fashionable. So was it a moment of decided confrontation or building on your undergraduate training, which featured the abstract liberal notion of contractarianism?

ACKERMAN: Well, sure. I mean, I was lucky. I was well educated. I am very grateful for my education, which was demanding and comprehensive so far as the history of ideas is concerned. I had to decide at the beginning whether to go to the University of Pennsylvania Law School or go to Princeton in the political science and philosophy departments. And my decision to go to the law school was precisely not to write little articles and be another person in the Rawls-Nozick debate. While writing *Social Justice* over the ten-year period, I think that it's fairer to say that I understood that my protagonist was Rawls and to a more limited degree Nozick. *Social Justice* was also written amid the emerging debates in the legal academy, most notably the lawyer-economists on the one hand (whose normative vision was trivial) and the crits on the other hand. With regard to the crits, Roberto Unger is in my opinion a giant among a group that never really delivered on the promise of political philosophy. Roberto Unger did deliver. *Knowledge and Politics*, which denied the very possibility of a coherent liberal political philosophy, was quite important to me. Because you are right in thinking that I am very much like Rawls in his latter-day political evolution (*Social Justice in the Liberal State* is indeed one of the things that Rawls himself cites as a precursor to *Political Liberalism*).

My book is very much an effort to create a space in which people with very different views can nonetheless have a dialogue with one another. That's the crucial thought. The idea that the liberal state was just a dream can be confronted once and for all by considering whether it is even possible to imagine a world regulated by liberal dialogue. Roberto Unger denied this. And the lawyer-economists trivialized the foundational values of liberalism by all their talk of "efficiency." These two groups really deserved one another with their skepticism about the aim of creating a world in which we could talk to one another. I was trying to situate liberalism as a coherent philosophy, in contrast to the lawyer-economists and the critical legal studies group.

I was not engaging directly with Rawls and Nozick. The person to whom I am most similar is Habermas. They were writing book reviews of my book in German, saying that I was an Anglo-Saxon Habermas, which they did not intend as a compliment! My emphasis was on the possibility of liberal dialogue—to establish that you can deeply disagree about ideals and yet engage in a conversation about power. That's the central thought organizing *Social Justice in the Liberal State*.

HACKNEY: Regarding law and economics, there is obviously in *Social Justice* a relatively frontal assault on utilitarianism as a norm, and I see that as connected to Dworkin and the liberal critique of utilitarianism. But the less-obvious and interesting component of it, which I didn't grasp in my reading, is Unger. That explains your confrontation with power. That's the core of the crit assault on dialogue and liberal theory—there is no accountability for power.

ACKERMAN: The shallow liberalism of a Nozick or a Posner prioritizes market trades among adults. I'm for markets. But let's put the market in its place in a more comprehensive understanding of the sources of power from the moment you were conceived to the moment you die. There needs to be some accounting for power from the moment you're born—do your genes give you an unfair handicap through the period you are educated, to the time when you inherit wealth (if you do)? Only then can we address the justice of a market system.

HACKNEY: Regarding dialogue, did you read Habermas directly?

ACKERMAN: Well, I did read *Knowledge and Human Interests.* He hadn't written all that much, *Legitimation Crisis* came probably in the 1970s and *Knowledge and Human Interests* is in the late 1960s. Between 1970 and 1980, Bruce "the kid" was basically being shaped by law and economics on the one hand, and Rawls and Dworkin, not so much Nozick, on the other hand. I became a little bit more grown up. *Social Justice and the Liberal State* came out in 1980. I was born in 1943, so I was thirty-seven. I was writing it between the ages of twenty-seven and thirty-seven, so I was only slowly actually getting to understand the shape of the legal academy, which was, as you suggested, being constituted by law and economics on the one hand and critical legal theory on the other hand—with traditionalist liberals not really knowing what hit them.

HACKNEY: Let me just pick up the dialogue piece. *Social Justice* is written at a very high theoretical level, and as you said, it's an exercise in determining whether we can even imagine a liberal state in which dialogue actually occurs. In contemporary politics there is not a lot of respect for dialogue. George Bush, who was not a fan of dialogue, was considered a "true leader." He was the "decider." His administration actually refused to engage in dialogue on any level. Do you see this as a short-term cycle, or do you see this as a general phenomenon in terms of contemporary culture? For example, political "debates" are framed on CNN and Fox News as always *A* versus *B*—as long as we have *A* and *B*, we have a representative sample. They each scream at each other and the ratings go up.

ACKERMAN: Before we get to George Bush, I think that we should get to a really substantial change in my approach, which I haven't really sat back and reckoned with. First, liberalism for me is a form of culture. Is this culture even in principle coherent? Or is it as Isaiah Berlin and Michael Walzer, who are liberals too, believe, basically not coherent? They say it's really the totalitarian impulse that even strives to make liberalism coherent. Well, I am much more a child of the Enlightenment than they are.

Social Justice in the Liberal State is an effort to establish, by presenting an example that is intelligible, hopefully, that in principle liberal dialogue is capable of organizing a political culture.

HACKNEY: You moved on from the ideal theory of *Social Justice* to think more concretely about constitutionalism in the United States.

ACKERMAN: Yes. I didn't spend the rest of my life, as some of the people I greatly admire did, simply exploring the one big idea. So I shifted, and here's where I got into constitutionalism, really with the rise of Reagan, and my question was no longer whether liberalism makes sense in principle. It was, rather, what were the organizing principles of our American political culture. My basic thought here is that American constitutionalism is not merely a platform for projecting one's favored political philosophy, in my case *Social Justice in the Liberal State*. Our tradition is more republican, more decisionistic, and less just than the ideal society described in *Social Justice*. So my next challenge, really, was to articulate the distinctive grammar of the American political dialogue without supposing that that grammar was the same as that elaborated in *Social Justice*. I suppose one basic continuity between the two enterprises is my continuing interest in grammars of legitimation, and whether we can identify, with relative clarity, the distinctive grammar of American constitutional legitimacy. But, of course, my book *We the People* is an American project. *Social Justice and the Liberal State* is cosmopolitan: it is, in principle, just as intelligible to a person reading it in China as it is to somebody reading it in America. There is a great deal of abstraction, and I've gotten a lot of criticism about the metaphor of discovering a planet, and considering the problem of distributive justice from the ground up. But this is a result of my effort to reach beyond the provincialism of my particular time and place.

We the People, in contrast, is about the distinctive historical development of constitutional culture in the United States over the last 220 years. Is there continuity? It's easy for an originalist to imagine that a piece of paper called the Constitution, amended after the Civil War and a few times since, has a claim on Americans of the 21st century. Is there anything to this claim at all? What binds together a small bunch of rich white slaveholders on the periphery of 18th-century Europe to a polyglot hegemon of the 21st century?

My own answer is our revolutionary tradition. This notion verges on the oxymoronic. Is a "revolutionary tradition" a term like "hot coldness"? Or does it have a distinctive structure? My aim has been to present our history as a series of revolutionary movements that sometimes succeed and sometimes fail to transform our tradition. American constitutional principles of today are a product of generational cycles of movement success and failure.

Understanding this revolutionary pattern is key to understanding George W. Bush's presidency. It was not by any means the only time Americans had seen a movement try to gain control of a political party and use the presidency as an ideological battering ram. This pattern has played itself out during the eras of Thomas Jefferson, Andrew Jackson, Abraham Lincoln, William Jennings Bryan, Franklin Roosevelt, Lyndon Johnson, and Ronald Reagan. That's why I conclude my Holmes lectures, which I wrote just before the 2006 congressional election, by saying that we are in the middle of a constitutional moment. A constitutional moment is characteristically marked by a movement—Martin Luther King—and a presidency—Lyndon Johnson—joining together to create new landmark statutes or constitutional amendments of enduring significance. What we saw during the Bush presidency was a right-wing movement, led by a president, trying to pass statutes like the Military Commissions Act and other things related to the so-called war on terror. There was also an attempt to transform the Supreme Court in the manner of Franklin Roosevelt—not as successfully, because the movement wasn't as successful.

I was opposed to this movement—that's the point of my book *Before the Next Attack*, which begins with a chapter arguing that the very idea that we can make "war" on terror is a mistake. But my constitutional work isn't an effort to argue for the superiority of my own political vision. It aims instead to present our constitutional development as generating a "grammar" that permits you to understand the meaning of our present struggles, even if you happen to be opposed to their general tendency.

HACKNEY: So as you move into constitutional law theory, there is a shift to a historicist viewpoint. You invite others in the constitutional dialogue, professors, lawyers, citizens, etcetera, to take a look at it historically, as opposed to the dominant rights theme.

ACKERMAN: Well, that is certainly right. The central object for me is to characterize the larger constitutional regime—consisting of parties, Congress, the presidency—and then put the Supreme Court within the regime, as it evolves over time. So we've basically had the federalist regime of 1787, which fails in 1860, and which between 1787 and 1860 is importantly modified both by Thomas Jefferson and Andrew Jackson and their "revolutions." Then we have the second republic, from 1868 to the

1930s, of laissez-faire, free market individualism, which was challenged in 1896 and 1900 by Williams Jennings Bryan. Bryan's failure produced a generation of stuttering—there were important but not overwhelming changes in the presidencies of Teddy Roosevelt and Woodrow Wilson. Nevertheless, the second republic retains its coherence until the Great Depression, when we see the legitimation of the activist welfare/regulatory state, and the increasing prominence of the presidency. This sets the stage for Martin Luther King and his movement that engages a bipartisan Republican/Democratic coalition in the 1960s. The conclusions of this revolution are codified by the landmark statutes in the 1960s as well as a series of Supreme Court opinions. This frames the current era, which begins with the movement-party-presidency of Ronald Reagan. George W. Bush stands to Ronald Reagan in roughly the same relationship as Lyndon Johnson stands to Franklin Roosevelt. Once we locate this great arc of constitutional struggle and development of meaning, we can begin to assess the constitutional accomplishments of the present era. Speaking broadly, the New Deal and civil rights revolutions managed to sustain broad-based majority support in a way that Ronald Reagan and George W. Bush have not quite accomplished—not yet, at least.

HACKNEY: Part of your discussion is the way checks and balances, electoral staggering, and other structural obstacles make it very difficult for a revolution to happen.

ACKERMAN: That is absolutely right. This machinery changes over time. The division of power between the states and the center was a very important part of the original design of the American constitution. But over time the separation of powers between the president, Congress, and the Court has increasingly become the central forum within which Americans debate and decide their constitutional future.

My aim, first and foremost, is diagnostic. My emphasis on popular sovereignty contrasts with a Court-centered tradition of scholarship that imagines that the central tool is philosophical reflection on judicial opinions. This tradition is represented by thinkers like Ronnie Dworkin, Owen Fiss, and Richard Epstein. On my view, philosophy is important, but it isn't as important as understanding how the American people have decided, from generation to generation, whether they have something importantly new to say about their constitutional principles.

HACKNEY: That is really the distinction between originalists and progressive rights theorists, neither of which really has any theory of popular intervention.

ACKERMAN: Well, the originalists have a theory of popular sovereignty. It's just that, miraculously enough, the people haven't said anything much for the last 140 years or so. On the other hand, the critical legal studies/legal realist proponents (oddly Dick Posner is now a card-carrying crit) say everything is just politics. What I would say is no, everything isn't normal politics. Constitutional politics is very difficult to sustain, but the American people have managed to give new marching orders to their government from time to time. For example, today the question is whether we should dramatically grant new powers to the presidency and reduce the powers of individual freedom in the name of the war on terror. That's the question before us.

HACKNEY: Now it's interesting, because that debate is going to revolve around a theory of originalism. Conservatives will say that they want judges who interpret the text, not who make up the law.

ACKERMAN: That's what Franklin Roosevelt said, too. And then they'll appoint someone who will, with a straight face, tell you that the founders wanted to give the president war-making powers greater than the king of England. But perhaps this revolution will not make it; maybe it will fail like the Reagan revolution or the William Jennings Bryan revolution. This isn't to say that it won't have significant consequences, but it won't lead to a radical reorganization of the system on the model of the New Deal or the civil rights revolution.

The formalists think that really important change occurs with article 5 amendments. Feminists thought that, too, and worked hard to pass their ERA through article 5. But as Reva Siegel has shown, their defeat didn't stop the Court from giving them most of what they wanted. Since the ERA went down, nobody is putting lots of energy into formal amendments. Despite their rhetoric, the revolutionaries on the right don't take article 5 seriously. They are revolutionizing the Constitution in just the same way that Franklin Roosevelt did, by passing statutes and by appointing justices. But because they don't have the support of the country, they have to engage in stealth tactics: since they can't pass a ringing pro-life statute, they are trying to win stealth appointments to the Supreme Court.

HACKNEY: Now, getting back to your point about the originalists, and how FDR had an originalist argument. That sounds a bit crit-like—the text is really meaningless, what is happening here is a set of power dynamics. So how do you draw the line?

ACKERMAN: That's very interesting, but there are big differences. The first point is that I actually believe in the possibility of popular sovereignty.

And that the American legal system, in one way or another, is responsive to the broad will of the American people when elaborated in this characteristic mix of Enlightenment revolution and Protestant born-again-ness. This has been the mark of American constitutional development since John Winthrop got to this country. One form of constitutional transformation that we have hit on in the 20th century is the myth of rediscovery. From the 1930s there's the elevation of John Marshall as the great jurist of national power, and then there was the reinterpretation of the true meaning of the 14th Amendment from *Brown v. Board* to the present. These myths of rediscovery enabled the judiciary to accommodate the New Deal revolution and the civil rights revolution. But they should not blind legal scholars, or ordinary citizens, to the larger constitutional dynamics through which Americans have exercised their popular sovereignty during the 20th century.

The modern system, as it has evolved, certainly could be improved. It would be better, as I suggest in the last chapter of volume 2 of *We the People*, if we actually had a new form of constitutional amendment. Under my suggested reform, a president would have the authority to propose a constitutional amendment during his second term of office. If his proposal were then approved by both houses of Congress, it would then be placed on the ballot during the next two presidential elections. If a supermajority of the American people vote for it, then it should be recognized as a constitutional amendment.

There is a fundamental mismatch between article 5 and the political identity of modern Americans. In 1787 the federalist forms accurately described the very weak sense of national identity prevailing in the late 18th century. But today's Americans don't think that the way to determine our destiny as a people is to focus our political energies on state legislatures, and convince them to ratify proposals by the Congress of the United States. We focus instead on the drama in Washington, D.C., and we understand that choosing a president and Congress is the way we are going to decide whether to change our fundamental principles. That's how we decide, not by electing people to the state legislature on the off chance that they are going to ratify an amendment. Speaking broadly, my work invites Americans to confront this basic change in our political identity—and move beyond the endless recreation of myths of rediscovery, which suppose that the Supreme Court miraculously discovers that "what the founding fathers really intended was what George W. Bush just happened to think." We should instead confront the new grammar of *national* will formation that has evolved in the 20th century, through which the president, Congress, and the Supreme Court manage to express, at rare moments, broad popular commitment to fundamental constitutional changes. While presidents and their political parties endlessly claim a "mandate" from the people, they rarely are in a position to pass the institutional tests that the New Deal and civil rights movement managed to satisfy. And when they fail, we ignore their efforts at constitutional revision. For example, we ignore Bill Clinton's constitutional philosophy. What was it anyway?

So my view is different from of the crits in two respects. One, I think that popular sovereignty is alive, if not so well, in America—though it isn't something that's easy to pull off. I also differ from the cynicism of the Duncan Kennedys and the Dick Posners of the world in a second way. I actually want to create and revive a better legal culture—and neither politicize the culture (Kennedy) or economize it (Posner). I also want to encourage lawyers of the next generation to develop legal categories that will help them understand the living Constitution as it actually exists so that they can play a constructive role in organizing future efforts to speak in the name of the people.

HACKNEY: With regard to the crits, you believe that the constitutional canon, with the addition of the historically significant exemplars you acknowledge, actually matters.

ACKERMAN: Absolutely. I don't want to be melodramatic, because our constitutional principles do not measure up to the ideals I present in *Social Justice in the Liberal State*, or those articulated by John Rawls or Jürgen Habermas. No country reaches that. But as things go, the American people have managed to govern themselves for a couple of centuries—poorly sometimes, better sometimes, very well a few times. We've managed to solve a few of our big problems. A lot of other political cultures have done a lot worse. And law and legal self-consciousness has been an important resource in permitting Americans to use dialogue, and not merely force, in attempting social change. I want to maintain this evolving constitutional-institutional matrix to permit the next generation to do better than ours in the art of self-government. I want to encourage more self-consciousness concerning the resources of our constitutional culture. The key point here is that we should be more aware of the deeper implications of our two-hundred-year transition from a federation to a nation. We are Americans first, and Georgians second, while in 1787 we were Georgians first, and Americans maybe not at all. Of course, the Civil

War was important in this transformation, but we have managed to generate a constitutional vocabulary for conducting a national conversation, confronting our differences—and sometimes resolving some of them. If lawyers, politicians, and American citizens are more self-conscious about this evolving system, we can have a foundation for continuing the conversation in a civilized way in the next fifty years. In saying this, I speak as a representative of the Enlightenment, not as a representative of critical legal studies or a reductionist law and economics.

HACKNEY: It continues the strand of thought from *Social Justice.*

ACKERMAN: Totally.

HACKNEY: How do we educate and train lawyers given your framework? In the Holmes lectures you make this appeal to the audience, which consisted of incoming law students, but the way we train lawyers is very much not the way you are suggesting. So the classic constitutional law paradigm, I assume you do it differently, is case analysis, interpretation, and then some theory. There is some acknowledgement that there is something going on out there in the "political" world, but it's not really discussed. Does it require a paradigm shift in the way we think about constitutional law and law in general? The Langdellian view of legal education really is called into question given its ahistorical focus.

ACKERMAN: I couldn't agree with you more, but it isn't only me. There are a whole bunch of people, including Jack Balkin, Reva Siegel, Bob Post, Mark Tushnet, and Larry Sager, talking about the Constitution outside the Court. So it isn't as if I am the only person around who is calling for this reorientation in constitutional law. Casebooks and the legal materials will take these views more seriously over time.

HACKNEY: You made reference to the prominence of law and economics at Yale while you studied there. Can you discuss your current views on law and economics?

ACKERMAN: I am very much in favor of law and economics as a set of techniques for confronting the central questions in the liberal activist regulatory state, which is (until the next constitutional revolution) the structure of our polity. I am opposed to the normative impoverishment generated by much law and economics—its single-minded emphasis on "efficiency"—which is generally poorly defined. But I am very much in favor of the tools of law and economics in a richer normative construct. This is the theme of my book *Reconstructing American Law.* What the tools of law and economics permit American lawyers to do is talk about the concept of market failure, and analyze the real-world implications of redistributive justice in a disciplined way. If we look around at where the intellectual action is in the legal academy right now, law and economics offers some valuable tools. But while the technical modeling has gone far beyond Guido Calabresi, for example, its normative analysis is today much more impoverished than it was when he wrote *The Costs of Accidents*. Today people talk about efficiency as if it were an unproblematic idea. I think that is a mistake.

HACKNEY: Is there a relationship between your vision of constitutionalism and economics?

ACKERMAN: I don't want to be seen as a guy shouting in the wilderness. I think that there is a lot going on in American legal education that's focusing on the structure of our constitutional regime (its relationship of popular sovereignty and American constitutionalism), and the structure of economic life (theory of market failure and the regulatory state). I've been trying to develop these structural concerns by writing a series of pragmatic proposals that make sense for America—*The Stakeholder Society*, *Voting with Dollars*, *Deliberation Day*, *Before the Next Attack*. These books carry on the themes developed in *Social Justice and the Liberal State* and *We the People* in a practical fashion—here's how liberal concerns with justice and constitutionalism can actually inspire real change in the structure of political and economic life. *The Stakeholder Society* helped inspire Tony Blair's baby bonds. Every Briton born since 2002 is born with a bank account of 250 or 500 pounds, depending on how rich his parents are. Further grants are planned as the kids get older. Hillary Clinton in her presidential campaign proposed that every child get $5,000. We'll see—this is an idea whose time may or may not be coming. Similarly, there are people thinking about Deliberation Day around the world. There is also my proposal for patriot dollars—every voter gets fifty patriot dollars that he can put onto his credit card and then go to any ATM machine to give to any campaign. These things have a future. I very much hope that we will have thirty other books written by other people in the same spirit. So I am not pessimistic about the potential of American lawyers thinking about values and actually proposing practical solutions to serious problems.

HACKNEY: I want to talk more about *Stakeholder Society*, but before we do that I just want to revisit some of your thoughts with regard to American legal theory generally. There is a post–Posner and Calabresi second generation of lawyer-economists who are more teched up and sophisticated. They are more likely to think about market failure. Of course, the principle contribution of Calabresi was his insight regarding market failure.

Is that the group from which you believe that the policy proposals will come? And one reading of that group is that they are so teched up, and in a sense insular, that they don't engage in a conversation with a larger legal community to the same degree as the prior generation. Whatever their shortcomings were, Posner and Calabresi engaged in a very broad conversation.

ACKERMAN: I think that's a problem. That's what Yale Law School is about, according to me at least. The school should aim to marry sophistication about values to technical model building—computer-analyzable, empirically based understandings of social problems—so that we can then talk much more thoughtfully about their solutions. But scholars who are normatively sophisticated are often condescending to the super-crunchers (who can manipulate computers), and the super-crunchers are condescending to those who talk about values (which they think is reducible to "personal preferences"). So we have a two-culture problem, no question about it. The challenge for legal education is to integrate the two. Of course, real-world judges and political leaders will neither be teched up or avid readers of Habermas. But a thoughtful practitioner can be both a skilled user of techno-fact-finding and a thoughtful participant in normative debate. My crystal ball is a little foggy: twenty-five years from now, the techies may have crushed the humanists, or vice versa, but that would be a very bad thing. Of course I am a historical relic of a different era. I never got a PhD in anything. I try to do political philosophy; I try to do history; I try to do policy stuff. All I have is a law degree; that's basically true of Dick Posner and Guido Calabresi as well.

HACKNEY: In an interesting historical twist, it would be difficult for either of them to get an appointment to Chicago or Yale as lawyer-economists today.

ACKERMAN: Yes. It would be difficult for them to get an appointment at Yale or Chicago because increasingly getting a PhD in one thing or another, whether it is comparative literature or statistics, is an entry requirement. So this thought of yours that we will have two warring subcultures, each promoting its own specialty but not actually contributing the distinctive merger of facts and values that we depend on the law to contribute, I think that's not an unrealistic fear.

HACKNEY: Other groups building off of critical legal studies are the critical race theorists, feminist theorists, and queer theorists. You can look at it as the balkanization of American legal theory—all of these strata of expertise and theories. How do you situate those groups in relationship to what you are trying to accomplish, which is, in some ways, not a universal citizenship but a U.S. citizenship?

ACKERMAN: Well, you are quite right. I, too, am an identitarian, but the identity that I am interested in is the cultivation of citizenship in the United States—and ultimately a sense of world citizenship. My aim is to construct a thin public discourse, which is mutually intelligible to people whose thicker self-identities are widely disparate, to permit them to speak and act as citizens. The crits initially, and then the later critical race theorists and gender theorists, would argue that I am barking up the wrong tree. And so, too, do Christians, who see me as advocating for an empty public square. So the thing that is really important to me, and is part of the problem for the crits and the Christians, is that I think there is a difference between public discourse and private life. Citizenship, and liberal political culture more generally, is partial and universal. And the point of it is to liberate us to be complicated and particular in more private spheres of our own devising. This vision of the public and the private has been and will forever be controversial.

HACKNEY: Do private, thick associations (race, sex, sexual orientation, etcetera) act as obstacles to even a thin dialogue among citizens? We see this at particular moments—a quintessential example is the way the Republican right played the race card during the Reagan era to break off "white voters" away from a larger vision in terms of the social good.

ACKERMAN: One of the key projects for the next generation should be—which is not to say that it will be—the construction of institutions in which we encounter one another as citizens. The 20th century bequeathed us a set of contexts in which citizen encounters took place—the public school, the political party, the army. All of these are under attack. We now have a professional army, proliferating private and voucher schools, and traditional political parties have been displaced by political consultants who engage in media manipulation. For millions of Americans, the most significant act of citizenship is the moment they return from a foreign vacation and hand their passport over to the border patrol so that they can get into the country. That is the only time, really, that their citizenship is important to them. Voting is a minor inconvenience. And that is why my proposal, with my friend Jim Fishkin, for a Deliberation Day is pretty important. The idea: Two weeks before each major election, citizens are invited to spend a day at their neighborhood community center talking to one another in small groups of fifteen and in plenary sessions about the debate between the leading candidates. This begins the day. Then local representatives of the leading candidates answer questions that are framed by these little groups of fifteen. Jim Fishkin's work with deliberative polls shows, throughout the world, that at the end of one such day people know a lot more, and they change their minds. People actually can engage in public conversation.

HACKNEY: Like the Iowa caucus?

ACKERMAN: Well, the Iowa caucus actually isn't very much of a deliberative assembly. Putting aside the fact that you have to show up on a cold winter's night during the workweek, participants spend most of the two hours calling to one another things like, "Whoever wants to vote for Mitt Romney, please come over to this corner of the room." There is very little in the way of conversation. Fishkin and I are building more on the American experience with the jury than Iowa's experience with the caucus. Like the jury, participants on Deliberation Day will actually talk to one another about important issues. We have the following paradox. The average white American has fourteen years of formal education. The average black has thirteen or something like that. We have never been better educated. In 1939 the average white had nine years of public education, and the average black four. At work we increasingly use our symbolic competences in complex ways. And yet politics is getting more irrational because of media management and other factors. I do not believe in a Schumpeterian vision of democracy in which people just go to the polls, flip a lever, and once in a while the "ins" beat the "outs" and we avoid the worst forms of tyranny. I think that a democratic republic is more than that. But it can't be more than that without citizens. Old-fashioned political parties, for all their many vices, actually promoted citizenship, Americans marched through the streets of New Haven, Connecticut, before every election under Republican and Democratic banners.

It was not very rational, but it was at least active citizenship. The challenge is to rebuild contexts for citizenship in the twenty-first century—social contexts in which we deal with one another as citizens and not only as fellow members of a church, fellow employees, fellow Yankees fans, or whatever.

HACKNEY: When I talk to fellow citizens they seem perfectly rational and it's plausible to engage in conversation. But we consistently see American politics being driven by cultural wedge issues such as gay marriage. Part of the lesson of critical race theory, queer theory, and feminist theory are the ways in which these divisions get inserted in the body politic and break down conversation.

ACKERMAN: I certainly agree with that. And you're quite right that in my uncomfortably centrist position, between critical theories and law and economics, for me the central concept is culture. For the crits of various kinds, the central concept is also culture. So that's a common theme. While for the lawyer-economists, they don't know what culture is about: "People have preferences, but we can't figure out why they have the preferences they have; we don't have any tools for that, so let's not talk about it." I disagree; for me, legitimacy is generated by the way we talk to one another. I am more optimistic than the crits regarding the prospect of generating a respectful culture of citizenship. But my real antagonists are Madison Avenue types: Karl Rove, Mark Penn. Every presidential candidate hires a media guru who is constantly designing sound bites and pushing the hot buttons that will generate emotional responses from smallish groups. We have better and better technology so that politicians can locate the soccer moms between the ages of eighteen and twenty-one and figure out which hot buttons to press in their media campaigns. Deliberation Day tries to create an alternative structure—in which ordinary Americans confront and discuss the leading issues. Candidates have to frame those issues, recognizing that millions of very different people are going to discuss them together: some will be soccer moms; others retirees; but all of them citizens—talking and listening to one another. In 2004, Fishkin and I conducted Deliberation Days in seventeen cities throughout the United States in collaboration with MacNeil-Lehrer and PBS. The subject: the Bush-Kerry election. Not by accident, one of them was held at Yale Law School; 220 people showed up. We made great efforts to get a random sample of the New Haven community and it was really great. When I was leaving my house, I asked Susan, my wife, do you think I should wear a suit? She said definitely. I showed up and everybody was dressed up—carpenters, bus drivers, they all had suits and ties on, and things were taken very seriously. Before Deliberation Day began, a pollster had gone to each invitee's house and interviewed him or her with a standardized questionnaire on the issues. Afterward a professional interviewer gave each participant the same questionnaire—so we could actually judge how things had changed in the participant's mind. Deliberation made a big difference. At the end of the day people wanted to come back and participate again. It was very touching to see how many of these people took their citizenship seriously when they were given a chance.

HACKNEY: I think your analogy to the jury is perfect because people do take that moment very seriously.

ACKERMAN: Yes. I listened to those conversations during Deliberation Day at Yale very carefully. Here is the basic D Day format: There is a TV show at the beginning of the proceedings, which allows representatives of both candidates to present their views on the leading issues. This is followed by small group discussions. Then everybody goes to the auditorium to confront representatives from both sides. Each little group has chosen a question to ask: "Okay, Hackney from group six," and then Hackney gets up and says here's our question. Each candidate's representative has five minutes to answer, and then another group gets the chance to ask its question. After the plenary session, participants go back to their small groups, and they talk about what they learned or didn't learn from the first round of questions and answers. They then formulate more questions, and return to the auditorium. And so forth. The results were impressive: participants were making very good points in their small group discussions, and lots of people learned, and even changed their minds, about the basic issues. I am not invested in my particular proposal. My key aim is to get people to take citizenship seriously—you cannot have a liberal republic without citizens.

HACKNEY: I think that's a good segue into your and Anne Alstott's idea of the stakeholder society. First, just briefly sketch it out, and then discuss the ways that it relates to this idea of citizenship.

ACKERMAN: Sure. Well, the proposal comes directly out of *Social Justice in the Liberal State*—though I think John Rawls, and similar activist liberals, would also support stakeholding. My key claim here is that the family inheritance of property lacks powerful foundations in liberal theories of justice. After all, the kids didn't work for their inheritance. If your father was a stockbroker and my father was a schoolteacher, both of them contributed to build America during their time on earth. The fact that your dad-broker made $4 million and my dad-schoolteacher made $50K a year shouldn't define our relative starting points as we set out on our own life journeys as young adults. Some limited form of intra-family inheritance can be justified on incentive grounds, but nothing like what we have today. So the central idea, coming out of *Social Justice in the Liberal State*, is that each citizen should inherit some property when starting out as a young adult. In my book with Anne Alstott, we propose that every American citizen should start out adult life with the equivalent of four years' college tuition, which was more or less $80K in 1999, when we wrote the book. (We are going to be writing a second edition with newer numbers.) This should be funded by a wealth tax, an inheritance tax, or a mix of the two. If we taxed wealth at a flat rate of 2 percent, with an exemption, on more recent numbers, of $600,000 or $700,000 on a family's wealth, there would be enough money to fund an $80,000 stake for every American. There are a million design issues: I would give the stake out in four annual payments, between the ages of twenty-one and twenty-five if you don't go to college. If you do go to college, then you get a chunk of money to pay for each semester. In short, the idea is that everyone should have an economic stake that will give them some kind of buffer, and the capacity to shape their lives as young adults when they need it most. It's a birthright of citizenship. Now, nothing this big has been adopted, but a much smaller version has been adopted in the United Kingdom. Stakeholding was developed in a very nice pamphlet with a very nice English title called *A Capital Idea*. It was written by an economist, Julian Le Grand, and an editor of the *Financial Times*, David Nissan, and served as the basis for Tony Blair's second reelection campaign. Under the Blair plan, every English person gets a bond at birth that matures at the age of eighteen, providing him or her with the initial grant of 500 pounds, plus interest. As time moves on, Blair hopes to provide additional grants when the kids turn seven, and maybe twelve. The whole sum might add up to seven or eight thousand dollars by the time the bonds mature at eighteen—not quite the $80,000 or more that Anne Alstott and I envision, but it's a start. Under our proposal, a very large proportion of the wealth tax would be paid by the superrich. So this is a pro-market, pro–private property way of expressing our common citizenship. All Americans have helped build America over the generations, all citizens are worthy inheritors of the labor of past generations, and all should therefore start out with a substantial stake as an adult. Stakeholding would make the Declaration of Independence a living reality for an overwhelming majority of people. Our proposal refutes the surprisingly common idea that you can't tax the wealthy and generate something substantial—you can. What is more, our proposal is perfectly compatible with the liberal premises of a market economy. It's our present system of family inheritance that is really a feudal, racist idea—it supposes that the only decisive feature in your economic starting point should be that you are 50 percent genetically related to your mom or dad. More fundamentally, stakeholding is motivated by a vision of a property-owning, citizenship democracy. Citizenship is also core to the idea of my proposal, with Ian Ayres, of patriot dollars to finance election campaigns. In addition to voting on a one-person, one-vote basis, each citizen is granted fifty patriot dollars to make campaign contributions during presidential election years (with smaller amounts available during off-year congressional elections). If 120 million Americans voted with their patriot dollars, $6 billion would flow into the coffers of candidates, which would overwhelm the $3 to $4 billion of private money spent for all federal elections in a presidential election cycle. So here, once again, you have the use of private property mechanisms to improve the character of citizenship, rather than to undermine it.

HACKNEY: And the patriot dollars are allocated in what way?

ACKERMAN: Each citizen can give his patriots to any party or candidate of his or her choice. Now that's voting with dollars. Anne Alstott and Ian Ayres (who collaborated on stakeholding and patriot dollars, respectively) are both pro–law and economics. But what we've done is to put it in a much richer normative context than mere "efficiency," whatever that might mean.

HACKNEY: One of the premises behind your stakeholder society is that you criticize the left for being overly focused on identity distribution—in the form of workers, in the form of the poor, in the form of race, etcetera. A big issue now is the idea of reparations—African American reparations. There are some theoretical and historical justifications for reparations, but the politics of it don't seem to work—particularly when maybe 10 percent of whites believe that this should actually take place. It's a nonstarter. I'm interested in your thoughts on identity politics versus citizenship and how they play out in your proposals.

ACKERMAN: Well, citizenship is a form of identity. And what I am interested in is creating a much more vivid sense of American citizenship. Now stakeholding will obviously have the consequence of making poorer communities a lot richer. The beneficiaries of a universal $80,000 stakeholder grant are people in the bottom 50 percent of the wealth distribution. The bottom third of the wealth distribution in the United States has negative wealth. The proportion of African Americans, Mexican Americans, and other Hispanics that are in that bottom 50 percent is larger than whites; those populations will benefit the most. My son would get $80,000, but I would be taxed a lot more because the wealth tax would hit me. So the Ackerman family would be a lot poorer, although my children will have a greater degree of independence if they disagree with what their dad thinks they should do with their money. So there are clear winners, and the winners are the traditional minority groups. I quite agree with you that I am not arguing for redistribution to minority groups through the concept of reparations for past injustices (even though they did in fact occur). Stakeholding is instead a future-looking enterprise. It is an intergenerational project through which all Americans can recommit themselves to freedom, justice, and a common sense of citizenship.

Charles Fried is the Beneficial Professor of Law at the Harvard Law School. He served terms as Solicitor General of the United States during the Reagan presidency and as an Associate Justice of the Supreme Judicial Court of Massachusetts. Professor Fried is considered to be a leading conservative constitutionalist and libertarian theorist. His major works include *Anatomy of Values* (1970), *Right and Wrong* (1978), and *Modern Liberty* (2006), which develops themes in moral and political philosophy with applications to law. *Contract as Promise* (1980), *Making Tort Law* (2003, with David Rosenberg), and *Saying What the Law Is* (2004) are fundamental inquiries into broad legal institutions. *Order and Law* (1991) discusses major themes developed in Fried's time as Solicitor General.

9

Classical Liberal Constitutional Theory

CHARLES FRIED

HACKNEY: I'm going to begin first with some general background. You're originally from Prague. Can you tell me a bit about your family migration to the United States and what impact that experience had on you?

FRIED: I was very young when it happened. The impact is obviously conjecture and retrospective analysis. My parents were what I would describe as typical assimilated Jews from the Austro-Hungarian Empire. My mother was born in 1904; my father was born in 1899. Their adolescence and childhood was in the Austro-Hungarian Empire and then Czechoslovakia in their youth. My father was an engineer by education and he was obviously a very brilliant man because in the late twenties he became a very important figure in the export/import world, traveling all over the world. Bohemia, and then Czechoslovakia before the end of the First World War, was the most prosperous and the most industrialized part of the Austro-Hungarian Empire. In fact, Bohemia was probably as prosperous as any part of Europe, so this was a very developed commercial world and my father became very prominent at an early age. My mother's parents had a wholesale electric supply company in Prague. So my family was very *haute bourgeoisie*, and I gather we lived in very comfortable circumstances—beautiful apartment in Prague, house in the countryside designed by a modern architect (which was taken over first by the Germans and then by the Communists). They were very well-off. We left in a hurry in 1939 when the Nazis came. As a matter of fact, my father was already out of the country when they arrived, and we somehow got permission to leave. It was ostensibly just to visit with the idea that we'd come back, but, of course, we didn't. My mother could not persuade her parents to join us. They died in Auschwitz, as did all of my immediate relatives. My father had three sisters—one of whom survived—but beyond that they were wiped out. We went first to England, where my father continued to make some use of his prior connections, and continued in his business as a metals trader. In 1940, when it looked like the Germans would prevail, we decided to leave and we went to the United States, where we arrived in the late winter of 1941. My parents had a hard time of it, but my father by virtue of his ingenuity, energy, and contacts was able to start a business in trading (export and import). His English was not very good; it improved. My mother's English was very good. She was a linguist and had been brought up learning about languages. So, in a way, it was an isolated, hard life for them—not too hard, but always something of a struggle. It got better, and after the war my father's business prospered. That's the family background. I went to public school in New York, and to boarding school in New Jersey, the Lawrenceville School, starting in the ninth grade. From there I went five miles down the road to Princeton.

HACKNEY: What was your major at Princeton?

FRIED: My major at Princeton was French and English literature. I was interested in literature, and I sort of created this major. I was also interested in philosophy. Princeton went on to have the premier philosophy department in the country, but not so when I was there. I was a literary sort of person. I read a lot; I played a lot (a lot of poker). It was very intellectual, but more in a literary vein. So much so that as I moved toward graduation I realized I needed to figure out what I was going to do. I got a Fulbright to study in France, and my project was to work on Bergson, Proust, and the concept of time. My father, who didn't think this was a great idea, said, "I'll offer you a scholarship to Oxford to do law, and if you don't like it then you can do literature." I didn't have enough conviction in literature to resist the offer, and I got into Oxford and did law. For a time I thought that

I might switch to literature, but I stayed with law and discovered that law and philosophy mixed rather well. This was the time of the rise of analytic philosophy—particularly at Oxford. I did rather well, and got what they call a "congratulatory first." However, my real interest was philosophy. I attended all of the philosophy lectures I could, and read. So I thought, "Well, what I'll do is teach law and philosophy." H. L. A. Hart was the presiding genius of that time. It was analytic philosophy, but it was already moving in a normative direction. Hart was not a pure linguistic analyst by any means. He wrote *The Concept of Law*, which is rather analytic. However, he also did *Causation in the Law* with Tony Honoré, which is analytic but also has a normative strand to it. He wrote about Bentham. I'd say he was a utilitarian. So the intellectual environment was not oppressively analytic, and the normative strand was coming to the fore. You had people like Elizabeth Anscombe and Philippa Foot. They were just starting at that point to become dominant.

HACKNEY: Did you attend any lectures with any of them in particular?

FRIED: All of them. That's what you did. Your curriculum consisted of doing tutorials in your various legal subjects, but the lectures you attended the way you read books. It was a couple of years after Ronald Dworkin was there. I'd say that Dworkin and I had much the same formation. From Oxford I went to Columbia Law School. I could have gone to Harvard, but I was attracted to Columbia by two things. First, the people at Columbia to whom I talked were very welcoming. I spoke to Harry Jones, who was teaching jurisprudence at that time there, and he was very encouraging and enthusiastic. Harvard was just very bureaucratic about it—recommendations and so on. And the other thing is that Harvard had at that time an almost totally compulsory curriculum, while Columbia had more flexibility. I had to take criminal law and civil procedure in the first year, but after that I could do what I wanted. I did a lot of legal philosophy, and I did some Roman law with Arthur Schiller. But the main influence at Columbia on me was Herbert Wechsler. I had him for criminal law at the time he was doing the model penal code. I also had him for constitutional law and one-half of my federal courts course. I did very well in those courses, and he was amazing. I still try to teach like him. He was my ideal of the law teacher, a man who was involved in his own work. As I said, he was at that time writing the model penal code, but he was also doing work on neutral principles and the Hart and Wechsler text. This work was illuminated through his teaching, which had a strong bent to it. In criminal it was utilitarian, emphasized codification, and had an analytic bent. In constitutional law it was the neutral principles. But it was also informed by his experience practicing in the Justice Department during the Second World War. He had a powerful analytic mind, intolerant of any sloppiness or lack of rigor, but with the sense that law mattered. I'm sure it was on his recommendation that I got the clerkship with Justice Harlan. That was a wonderful year. The high point of it was *Poe v. Ullman* because my philosophical interests came out in the work I did for Harlan drafting the preliminary drafts of his dissent. You could see there that this was Wechsler on the constitutional law but also the normative side, and that there were such things as intrinsic values present in the law. They are expressed in it at its best, which most people would call natural law. That experience made me realize that there could be a wonderful combination of philosophy and law. I mean philosophy in the practical sense that there is no compromise in your practical pursuit by doing law. I was then fortunate enough to be asked to come to Harvard. I remember when I first came, Erwin Griswold, the dean, had the motto that if you're junior you teach what needed to be taught. The school needed two sections of trusts. I couldn't stand that, so I suggested one section of commercial law and one section of criminal law. I liked the intricacies of the UCC. The criminal law was Wechsler's course. I used Wechsler's book and it was basically his course. That's when my own intellectual and ethical notions about intrinsic right and wrong and the categories of causation, which I'd studied with Hart, came together in criminal law. It was a wonderful experience. I remember my first class. I had this fabulous group of students, the most outstanding of which was Steve Breyer, who was three years younger than me, and he became my friend. He's remained one of my closest friends ever since. There were Bert Rein, Paul Dodyk, and others. There was a friendly debate going on because they were trying to irritate this young guy and trying to rough me up. However, I wouldn't allow it and we had a good time. In those days criminal procedure was part of criminal law and we were just getting into the habeas corpus stuff, which was just beginning to be constitutionalized, and that was part of the course. So I could do both—part of the federal courts as well as some of the Hart and Wechsler criminal law. That was fun. I did those three things, and then I was allowed to do Roman law and jurisprudence. Because of my interest in philosophy I'd met John Rawls, who in '61 was a visiting professor here from MIT and eventually a full professor. We became very good friends, and I read everything he wrote. He got me more interested in Kant, whom

I'd already had some interest in. I would say the normative side of my thought, the Kantian normative side and rights liberty side, began to become more and more prominent. I wrote a little piece called "Natural Law and the Concept of Justice" in the *Natural Law Forum* about how liberty and natural law came together.

HACKNEY: How do you think they come together?

FRIED: It's the same idea articulated in my most recent book, *Modern Liberty and the Limits of Government*. It's the Rawlsian idea, which by the way I mean the Rawls of *Theory of Justice* rather than *Political Liberalism*, in which he lost his romantic push and became too sensitive to the people who objected to *Theory of Justice*. His work became much more modest and professional. *Theory of Justice* is a very romantic book, particularly if you look at the last part. That's the Rawls that's always stayed with me. I think the whole overlapping consensus idea from *Political Liberalism* is winding down.

HACKNEY: Had you read Hayek at that point?

FRIED: I didn't read Hayek until quite a bit later. My work was Kantian, with an attempt to see concrete implications for law. So the metaphysical elements of justice that I taught regularly in the seventies are full of concrete implications for contract law, tort law, property law, etcetera. That's the way I taught contract law. It was very successful. The rule of law remained. The assault on law by critical legal studies was an assault on liberty and natural rights, because you can't have rights without a firm legal system, and one that has structure to it.

HACKNEY: Can you talk about what you hoped to accomplish in *Modern Liberty* and contrast it to what Hayek tried to accomplish in *Road to Serfdom*, which is an incredibly significant book historically? The two books, although they have at their core the concept of liberty, read radically differently. There is almost a sense of anger when you read Hayek, and immediacy with regard to the posed threat. Hayek was writing amid World War II; there was the specter of Stalin and Hitler. Hayek set up this jarring choice of two paths: liberty or totalitarianism. *Modern Liberty* is written at a different historical moment.

FRIED: I think I say that. In a way we won. There are all sorts of nuances to it. It's a different moment, because in Hayek's time it was not clear who was going to win. He was writing in a country that was about to be taken over by socialism. The threats today are different. They are insidious, they're intellectual, and they're self-doubt. They are the threats that come with success.

HACKNEY: This is highlighted by the three examples you use throughout *Modern Liberty*. They are somewhat underneath the surface. Health care is obviously front and center, but the examples of the Quebec Charter and Walmart in Vermont are more subtle.

FRIED: They involve people with good hearts. Of course, nice people with good hearts can turn nasty. The debate around the Quebec Charter is an example of the language turning nasty, and there's always the threat of that. However, the fact that they are nice people is what makes it attractive and therefore dangerous. With Lenin and Stalin you didn't have that problem.

HACKNEY: What about the three examples stuck out for you so that you decided to build your book around them?

FRIED: Just the things that we've been talking about. They pose a challenge, which is an intellectual challenge rather than a kind of military challenge. They pose a challenge to what I call liberalism—19th-century liberalism. They pose a challenge where it is vulnerable, rather than direct confrontation—where decent liberal people feel that there is something to this. My idea is to acknowledge that there is something to the appeal and see that it doesn't undermine liberalism. Returning to your original question, I picked the three examples because they were the strongest challenges—not the challenges you could easily use rhetorical weapons against. I wanted to make it tough for myself rather than easy.

HACKNEY: Another piece of *Modern Liberty* is your engagement with the idea and concept of equality—particularly substantive equality. You discuss it very carefully and ultimately reject it as rubbing up against liberty.

FRIED: Yes, but again I was trying to give this its due by noting, for instance, that people I have great respect for, such as Jeremy Waldron, take this seriously. The idea is that there are aspects of substantive equality that I reject. They undermine liberty. However, we do need to be very careful in the way we think about disparities. Liberty requires what Rawls called the well-ordered society. I have a passage to say how if the disparities are too great, and you have people whose material circumstances are so demeaning that they don't seem to be part of the same moral community, you're going to fail. You're going to fail for two reasons. First, because they don't have an investment in the community and you can't convince them to have one. Second, the notion of human respect, which undergirds liberty and equality, is undermined. You cannot look people in the eyes and pass them by when they are in a situation of distress. That's denying them the respect, which is the basis of liberty. Now when I say I don't like disparities, that may suggest that somehow equality is more important than the actual situation of the least well-off (to use another Rawlsian phrase). I resist that. The fact that someone is prospering is not itself ever a bad thing, and to make it a bad thing is to justify pulling that person down without necessarily even helping anybody. That's the wrong disparity notion. My notion is that what equality gets right is that nobody should be in the situation, for long or in large numbers, that makes it impossible to view them as part of the same community. Now that does not mean pulling anybody down. It means building some people up or building a foundation underneath them. However, you have to admit that what counts as not being in such a situation that you aren't considered in the same community is in part a function of what everybody else enjoys. You can't ignore that. But is the motivation equality as such, or is the motivation to assure that you don't have people who are not part of your community?

HACKNEY: That actually resonates with C. B. Macpherson's distinction between positive and negative liberty in *Democratic Theory*. He argues that you do have to have a certain amount of what Isaiah Berlin referred as positive liberty in order to exercise negative liberty. But Macpherson's critique of Berlin is that he takes the notion of positive liberty too far. Positive liberty has to be tied to negative liberty.

FRIED: Yes, and Rawls talks about rights and the value of rights. But I think that's an abstract notion. That's where distributive justice comes in to make the rights tolerable. Rawls actually places liberty first in priority in *A Theory of Justice*. I think he retreated from that. I think where I am is that there is no easy formula to figure out when you have the balance right. The question is why you are doing it. Are you doing it because the inequalities rankle, or are you doing it because the situation of the less well-off rankles? I'm not sure you can do a lot better than that. How does that relate to law? It's very clear to me how that relates to law. Law has got to be the framework for the exercise of liberty. If law is infected by excessive egalitarianism, then you lose confidence in its functioning as underwriting liberty. Liberty is functioning if it is underwriting free men's and women's projects. If those projects are subject to invasion for nationalistic, cultural, or egalitarian reasons, then liberty is insecure. But how do you take care of those people whom I think we have to take care of, and provide for public goods? You take care of them in a way that respects liberty as much as possible through the most neutral tax system—a redistributive tax system.

HACKNEY: That seems like a departure from Nozick who attacks the income tax system in *Anarchy, State, and Utopia*.

FRIED: Well, he eventually backed off of that. My idea is that you try to do it causing the least amount of harm to liberty. You don't use the tax system as an excuse for promoting other values. You use it for the underwriting of human respect. And that means, which is why I continue and love to teach contract law, that contract, torts, property, bankruptcy, antitrust (the private law subjects) have got to maintain their integrity and neutrality (their Wechslerian neutrality). Of course, this is the exact opposite of the position taken by critical legal studies.

HACKNEY: I want to get back to critical legal studies in a moment. It's obvious that *Contract as Promise* is a direct assault on critical legal studies as well as law and economics.

FRIED: Yes, and I pick that theme up again in *Modern Liberty*.

HACKNEY: Let's continue to flesh out your thoughts from *Modern Liberty*. You articulate the notion of a state in which there is redistribution based on the concept of community. The way you attempt to cabin off the impulse to take redistribution too far is the restriction with regard to what you believe are legitimate motivations for redistribution. You also have a principle of liberty of the mind that you take as untouchable. Can you discuss the way you view the mind as the quintessential element in the exercise of liberty and the implications of that?

FRIED: It's Kantian. The mind is the locus of judgment and choice. You may not be able to do what you want. You may be constrained by the laws of gravity, by circumstance, law, or whatever. But you recognize what's constraining you. That preserves within the pressure of the constraints, which are all of these necessary things we talked about, an indestructible core of liberty, because at least you can judge those constraints. And you are the judge of how you will adjust to them—whether you rebel against them, seek to change them, how you will adjust your own project to them, and so forth. But if the constraints enter into that judgment . . .

HACKNEY: It's totalitarianism.

FRIED: It's totalitarianism of a sort, yes. It's not political; it's a moral totalitarianism.

HACKNEY: Of course, in totalitarian regimes one of the first goals it to constrain thought.

FRIED: Right, that was Mussolini's motto. That's where he wanted to go.

HACKNEY: There's an interesting next step when we think about contemporary politics. You move from liberty of mind to liberty of sex. You begin to play around with ways in which the two are very much related. Liberty of sex constitutes another core value and constraint.

FRIED: Well, it's not the same. Some constraints are more pressing. There should be no constraints on the mind. You have to be free to think. As soon as you move to the body, there have to be limitations because other people are implicated in a way that's not present with respect to the mind. Of course, even with the mind we must recognize the social nature of language and its implications for thinking. You can transcend that, and you have the experience of transcending it. However, there are constraints. Even with liberty of the mind there are social constraints such as language, as Michael Sandel would point out. But you can transcend them. You can think even if you have to think in the language you are trying to transcend. Someone whose thinking parallels mine on this in many ways is Thomas Nagel. I have the highest regard for him. When you deal with the body—and sex is just a graphic manifestation there are others—the constraints are much more difficult. And the question is what you make of them. How do you account for them, accommodate them, and build them into things? Do you account for them in the way that leads to the greatest possible equal liberty for all? That's what Kant stands for, and Rawls too in a different way. That's a theory of law; that's what law is. It is a system that seeks to create the greatest equal liberty of all. You look at Kant's *Metaphysical Elements of Justice*—that's the system he tries to create. The rule of law and certainty of law are indispensable elements in that, because you've got be constrained in what you do but at least you know what those constraints are. Then you can plan within them and around them. But if at every turn they can switch, then that's no longer true.

HACKNEY: In terms of constraints with regard to sex, you talk about two concrete examples. One is people's property right with regard to gay sex, and the second is prostitution.

FRIED: Those are two examples where people think there ought to be constraints, and those constraints challenge the ideas I'm putting forward. When it comes to gay sex, the answer is that they are wrong. That's fact. With respect to prostitution, the answer is they're wrong and they're not wrong. There's something second-rate about prostitution. But is it enough to justify prohibition? There's something second-rate about playing video games in your free time, too. There's something second-rate about many lawful occupations that people choose instead of other ones. There's something second-rate, maybe I shouldn't talk about this, about being a hedge fund manager rather than an entrepreneur—but not enough for us to interfere. On the other hand, there are aspects of prostitution, such as the exploitation of the unwilling, which are intolerable from any moral perspective. It may be that you need prophylactic measures, which impinge on what liberty might otherwise teach in order to guard against an even greater infringement of liberty that might occur in an imperfect world.

HACKNEY: I had an interesting moment in reading through those passages on sex. I did an interview with Drucilla Cornell for this book. I don't know if you're familiar with her work.

FRIED: Not recently—maybe twenty years ago.

HACKNEY: Her position actually comes close to yours with respect to the issue of sex.

FRIED: No surprise.

HACKNEY: She talks about the idea of the sexuate being, and has had an ongoing debate with feminists who want to make prostitution illegal. Cornell takes the position that there can be free expression in prostitution. Her remedy with regard to coercion in prostitution is union organization. I thought that the juxtaposition of your views was interesting. But let's talk about constitutional law for a moment—the way in which the U.S. Constitution and constitutional jurisprudence comes close to your idea of what the law should be.

FRIED: Absolutely.

HACKNEY: The basic framework is a strong commitment to freedom of the mind, freedom of sex (with some notable exceptions with regard to gay sex), protection of private property, and allowing for but not requiring the protection of the disadvantaged. Your essential structure of liberty matches very well with contemporary constitutional interpretations.

FRIED: I think so. One should always be suspicious when that happens, but there it is.

HACKNEY: The basic premise of law is the Burkean idea of precedent. There is conservatism with respect to adherence to precedent, as opposed to a different strand of conservatism, such as originalism or natural law. Let's say that the radical left had taken over the U.S. Supreme Court, the basic outcome of which would be what you think of as anti-liberty jurisprudence.

FRIED: You're talking about judges who "look after the little guy." They believe that their job is not to keep the legal system in repair. They're not legal plumbers or engineers but architects, even further, they are stage directors of a musical production. If that's their position, then liberty is out the window.

HACKNEY: Given that situation, you would not be a proponent of adherence to precedent.

FRIED: That's a real dilemma, because you are adhering to a precedent that itself did not adhere to precedent. *Roe v. Wade* is a perfect example. I have testified for Justice Roberts and Justice Alito that, although I argued against *Roe v. Wade* on grounds of precedent, overruling it would be too violent and abrupt a departure from precedent. I testified in 2005 that it's over thirty years later and precedent requires holding on to *Roe*, and I strongly believe that. I believe that in part because the substantive outcome is to my mind favorable to liberty.

HACKNEY: It doesn't go to a core liberty interest. What if there was a precedent that did undermine a core liberty interest?

FRIED: That's the way people might feel about the gun case. The gun cases, *Heller* and *McDonald*, were a huge offense to precedent. I suppose that what they thought was that there was a core liberty principle and therefore precedent has to yield. The trouble is that it isn't a core principle, and it's not worth it.

HACKNEY: But you do think precedent would have to yield to liberty.

FRIED: Yes, but it would be very unfortunate if one had to make that choice, because liberty is protected by stability in law.

HACKNEY: You are very dismissive of originalism. What are its principle faults?

FRIED: It can't be right. The gun case is a perfect example. We do not know and it is a total fantasy to think that what the framers said in the 2nd Amendment, and their intention in respect to our present situation, is a knowable thing or that it is a thing at all. When I teach this I like to tell the story about the historian Michael Bellesiles, who used to teach at Emory and won the Bancroft Prize for *Arming America*. He claimed to prove that owning guns was not a big deal in the founding generation by going through all types of records. And then the guns guys got after him and discredited his research. They took the Bancroft Prize away from him. The comedy in that is that before Bellesiles the original intent was this, after Bellesiles the original intent was that, after Bellesiles was discredited it's something else. That can't be right. Law is law. Historians have been and will be free to do their research and come to their conclusions, which will be contestable, but the law (whether people can have guns in their houses) shouldn't be something that changes depending on what the historians come up with. That's crazy.

HACKNEY: What about the liberal side of the ledger. We can take Bruce Ackerman as the example.

FRIED: I think he is where I am on this in a way.

HACKNEY: Of course he is, with respect to his view of originalism.

FRIED: I mean in terms of the use of precedent.

HACKNEY: He believes in precedent except for what he describes as "transformative moments."

FRIED: Transformative moments operate, if there are such things, by offering and producing new precedent. One could dispute whether, for instance on the Commerce Clause, those doctrines were good or bad, but there's no going back. There may have been a year or two afterward, but not sixty years after. So to that extent he's right.

HACKNEY: Let's think about transformative moments a bit more. Obviously the Reagan revolution was a real transformative moment in the United States as well as worldwide. You played a role in that in your position as solicitor general. What was that like in terms of the politics of the Justice Department?

FRIED: I wrote a book, *Saying What the Law Is,* about this. There were extremes—pushing toward a kind of Borkian view. After all, Bork was the nominee of these people. I never went that way. My concern was to maintain the integrity of law against the onslaught of William J. Brennan. He would either overturn or totally twist three precedents a day if he could. When Barack Obama said that he was going to appoint justices who would look out for the little guy, I said, "Uh oh, that violates the tradition of equal justice for the rich and the poor." The idea of law as manipulation struck me as incredibly threatening.

HACKNEY: There is a conservative version of failure to adhere to precedent as well.

FRIED: Again, there is *Roe v. Wade*. But the idea was that *Roe* was itself a break from precedent. When I worked on *Roe* it was a dozen years old. In fact, if you look at when I argued the issue as solicitor general, I didn't take an extreme view of "never any abortion." It had turned into a situation in which any type of regulation of abortion was suspect. That's what I argued against.

HACKNEY: So you didn't take the evangelical position.

FRIED: Not at all. There were people who were pressing the position that there's a constitutional protection against abortion, that the fetus is a person.

HACKNEY: Do you think that that type of religious fundamentalism undercuts liberty? On the one hand, the idea of liberty of mind argues that everyone should be free to worship in their own way. On the other hand, the extent to which it's interjected into law seems to undercut your vision.

FRIED: It's democracy, and people can come into politics with whatever visions they wish. However, in pursuing those visions they have to respect liberty. Obviously, some of the fundamentalist positions would not respect liberty. I think actually many of those people would be quite content if we implemented a voucher system for education. If you read John Stuart Mill's *On Liberty*, he thought idea of state school system was incredibly dangerous, and he said the way to deal with this is a voucher system.

HACKNEY: That goes all the way back to Milton Friedman in *Free to Choose*. There's a long tradition of that view in conservatism. This is actually a good point to segue and discuss your views on law and economics. You were critical of it in *Contract as Promise*.

FRIED: I'm troubled, and actually plan to do some writing on this, by the fact that my conclusions and the conclusions in law and economics in contracts tend to be very much the same. That may be true in other areas as well. I write about that a bit in *Modern Liberty*. In *Contract as Promise* I don't necessarily disagree with law and economics, because it really wasn't on the scene yet. They view the market in the Posnerian way, but I view the market as simply free people getting together.

HACKNEY: Is yours a view more akin to Friedrich Hayek?

FRIED: Yes. But I'm not sure that you don't come to the same outcomes irrespective of the difference in view with regard to the market. Law and economics often provides you with techniques, analysis, and all sorts of sophisticated methods to elucidate what a Hayekian market would lead to. So though the underlying motivation of law and economics seems to be different, I think it converges to a remarkable degree—a degree that actually makes me uncomfortable. I see very few examples of where law and economics leads to a different conclusion from a libertarian view. There is the Ian Ayres and Cass Sunstein version of law and economics.

HACKNEY: What about Guido Calabresi?

FRIED: Guido is a funny character. When Guido was really doing law and economics there probably wasn't a divergence in what he was doing.

HACKNEY: What about the loss-spreading concept? That's a big difference.

FRIED: You should take a look at the book I wrote with David Rosenberg, *Making Tort Law.* Insurance is the market form of loss spreading, so the loss-spreading concept doesn't diverge from the market perspective.

HACKNEY: But that assumes the capacity to purchase insurance.

FRIED: I am bothered. I am curious. I'm going to work on why these two are converging now. There is a recent brand of law and economics analysis that is used by my new colleague Cass Sunstein, Ian Ayres, and Christine Jolls that I would call left-wing law and economics with a heartbeat on the left. They make a great deal out of behavioral law and economics. Behavioral law and economics provides all kinds of accounts, I would say excuses, for paternalism.

HACKNEY: Market failure . . .

FRIED: It's not just market failure. It's irrationality. "They" don't know their own interest so we're going to do it for them. It's law and economics because economics itself has become much more behavioral and empirical. They do all of these empirical studies to show that economic actors are not rational and therefore we have to correct for the irrationality. That's where divergence with libertarianism will come.

HACKNEY: A lot of those themes are present in *Costs of Accidents*. I want to explore your observation regarding different strands of economics. One phenomenon I've thought about as an intellectual historian is the changing composition of the legal academy. If we compare the 1980s to the contemporary legal academy, there is a high premium on candidates walking through the door with a PhD in addition to a JD—particularly at elite law schools. There is a high premium on the level of technical proficiency.

FRIED: That's absolutely right.

HACKNEY: The implication is that while you have a lot more sophisticated drilling down into subjects, there is a lot less stress and bumping up against different approaches.

FRIED: Yes. They are doing what the economists are doing. The economists are doing the economics of art. They're becoming broad. I'm thinking of people like Ed Glaeser. They're becoming broad by spreading their techniques and mind-set to all kinds of areas. I think that it is the model that is taking over the academy. You can think of Tony Kronman's book *The Lost Lawyer*. You might say that it's the equivalent in the academy of what he sees in the profession. In the profession, instead of the humanist lawyer, it's the lawyer as businessman. Here, instead of the humanist law professor, it's the law professor as social scientist. Social science is what's taking over—no question.

HACKNEY: Yet there is a very narrow focus.

FRIED: It will broaden, but it will be social science.

HACKNEY: One question, for example, is whether the PhDs in literary criticism will ever engage the PhDs in economics to the same extent that Dworkin engaged Posner who is engaged by Duncan Kennedy, etcetera.

FRIED: Those conversations don't take place.

Jules Coleman is the Wesley Newcomb Hohfeld Professor of Jurisprudence, and Professor of Philosophy at Yale University. He is best known for his important contributions in legal philosophy and tort law theory. His most prominent works include *Markets, Morals, and the Law* (1988), *Risks and Wrongs* (1992), *The Practice of Principle* (2001), and *Hart's Postscript* (2001). Coleman has famously engaged in a debate with Ronald Dworkin regarding the nature of law and legal positivism. This has resulted in Coleman being associated with what has been referred to as inclusive legal positivism. Coleman's main substantive law area has been torts, and he has made several contributions to our philosophical understanding of tort law. Part of Coleman's engagement with tort law has involved critiquing the economic analysis of law generally, and in particular its application to tort law.

10

Law and Philosophy

JULES COLEMAN

HACKNEY: First I want to begin by asking, why did you make the choice to be situated in a law school as opposed to a philosophy department?

COLEMAN: Well, I view all these choices as somehow temporary, but that's probably not the point. Rather than temporary, let's say they are subject to revision, like my views generally in philosophy. My main area was always in philosophy of law, and I focused on the issues that I was interested in through the lens of philosophy—largely uneducated about how lawyers thought about the same subject and the context in which these issues were discussed in law schools. I had a very abstract sense that to learn more I would need to teach law. I wanted to learn more about the subject by teaching tort law. I felt that there were issues in the philosophy of law at law schools that were addressed at a much higher level of sophistication, but there was a much higher level of jurisprudential sophistication in philosophy departments than there was in American law schools. I thought both that I had something to learn and that I had something to give. I also thought law school would be a good life, would be a good place to pursue this. Of course, I had been teaching and working in philosophy before I went to law school. It's not like I chose at the very beginning to just go into law teaching. In addition, it wasn't just any law school. Before I came to Yale I had been offered a job at the University of Chicago, which would have been quite a distinguished place to be, but still that was not really a philosophically inclined law school at the time. Yale had the reputation of being an extraordinarily philosophically inclined law school. So it seemed like the best overall fit. There were personal issues beyond the intellectual and the academic. At the time I was teaching philosophy at the University of Arizona, but I felt isolated in the Southwest. The second thing was that I had reason to believe that I would be paid more, which turned out to be true. I also wanted to be nearer to my family—my parents, my brother—and others.

HACKNEY: You were a New Yorker. You went to CUNY–Brooklyn College. Did you study philosophy there? What was your major?

COLEMAN: I think that my major was hormones. I was young, immature, and naive. I lived at home with my parents while I went to college. I was the first person in my family ever to go to college. I didn't have much of an imagination about what schools were possible, so I went to Brooklyn College rather than going to Cornell, where a lot of my friends went. When I was there I didn't know what I wanted to major in. I grew up a semi-Orthodox Jew. My grandfather had picked me out to be a rabbi so I had a Talmudic education. From that I developed a whole set of issues about questioning authority and the nature of commitment. I majored in three things when I was at Brooklyn College—in part because I was in a program called the Scholars Program, which was a version of you make your own major, take smaller classes, and so on. So I did physics, philosophy, and political economy. The truth is that with physics I hit my wall, and I stopped because the math you needed to do physics was at such a high level. I was confident up until a certain point on differential equations, and then I realized that I had hit my wall and that physics was not really in my future. Political science and economics were very interesting, but at that point much of it was macroeconomics. It was more of a study about a macro-political economy. The quality of instruction was highest in philosophy at Brooklyn College. There was an outstanding faculty, and I just felt at home asking all sorts of bizarre questions—the sort of questions you ask when you are at college, like whether you have reason to know that you exist or whether others do. Solipsism that is not socially acceptable is philosophically acceptable. I went into philosophy when I probably should have just gone into therapy. That came later. It drove my parents crazy. We had a lot of very good philosophy majors at Brooklyn, many of whom went on to become professional philosophers. I graduated in 1968, and I went to the University of Michigan for graduate school.

HACKNEY: Were there any particular instructors who influenced you at Brooklyn?

COLEMAN: Absolutely. I was very lucky. There were a lot of very good teachers, but I think I fell under the influence primarily of three people. One was Paul Edwards, who was in fact the editor of the very first edition of *The Encyclopedia of Philosophy*. He was a very good teacher, a broadly engaged intellectual, and got me interested in philosophy. Then there was a fellow named Michael Bayles, who did philosophy of law and political philosophy. He was very young for a professor, and I developed a personal relationship with him. He was most influenced in philosophy by Joel Feinberg, who was later my thesis adviser when I went to graduate school. He eventually committed suicide later in his career and I have since then felt the loss. The third was Paul Taylor. He was very straightlaced, completely different than any guy I had ever grown up with, and wore tweed sports coats every day. This is during the late sixties, but he wore tweed sports coats and his hair was shortly cropped. He was very handsome and clean-cut. You couldn't tell his age; he was one of those people. He was a very careful thinker, precise, and had been a graduate student at Princeton. He took the train in every day from Princeton Junction, New Jersey, to Brooklyn. I would say that he was the most encouraging of all my teachers. I have the most respect for him. He was the most mature as a scholar, and he was the one who convinced me to continue in philosophy. I've actually kept the papers that I wrote in his class. Fortunately, I haven't tried to publish them!

HACKNEY: So when did you make the transition to Rockefeller University? That's where you got your PhD.

COLEMAN: Right. I started at the University of Michigan. They were very strong in ethics, and that was the field that I thought I would pursue. Ironically, it was the first time I had lived away from home, and I didn't do so well. I was in a terrible car accident and lots of personal things went wrong as well. There wasn't a thing that went right in my personal life when I was at Michigan. I don't think that I was emotionally mature enough, or psychologically able to be away from home. It's embarrassing but true. In addition, though there were these three famous people who were the ethics professors at the University of Michigan—Richard Brandt, William Frankena, and Charles Stevenson—none of them in fact taught ethics the year that I was there. I ended up taking courses in the philosophy of science with Jaegwon Kim and Larry Sklar. They became very influential on me. When I realized that I was not emotionally mature enough to be away on my own—again, which was ridiculously embarrassing—they encouraged me to apply to Rockefeller University for philosophy of science. So I applied to Rockefeller University. It was a very small program. I joked with people that I got in because they lowered the admissions requirement. Typically they would take only two students a year, but my year they admitted four. So they dropped their standards completely, and I snuck in under the wire. I went there to do philosophy of science, but as it happened they were very strong in ethics, and social and political philosophy. I did do philosophy of science and logic with a professor named John Earman, who is still around and was very young then. He taught a seminar I sat in on. It was filled with other professors who did philosophy of physics in the New York area. I realized that not only could I barely follow what was going on, but I had nothing to add on my own. While I had adequate technical skills—way beyond the norm for people studying ethics—I did not have technical skills required to excel in philosophy of science. This was very apparent to me as two of my entering classmates were David Malament and Scott Weinstein, both of whom have gone on to illustrious careers in the philosophy of science and logic. Fortunately for me, when I first came to Rockefeller, Robert Nozick was on the faculty. He was soon to leave to take a position at Harvard, but while he was at Rockefeller he worked closely with me and directed me ultimately to political and legal philosophy. Like me, Nozick had technical skills unusual for someone in political theory. We worked on Newcomb's problem, which I believe was the subject of his dissertation at Princeton, and we worked in game and decision theory more generally, and some political philosophy. Then he left to go to Harvard, and I fell under the influence primarily of Joel Feinberg. It really was Nozick who took the technical skills I had and got me to work on things in political philosophy employing them.

HACKNEY: I am trying to think about the combination of intellectual influences. There's the whole technical structure you had developed through studying physics, the encounter with Nozick, and philosophy of science. That's combined in a way with ideas that you had been thinking about through your youth, with the initial questioning of authority and studying to be a rabbi. You went on eventually to do a graduate degree at Yale Law School.

COLEMAN: Yes. Let me see if I can make some sense out of all of this. Some of it is intellectual and some of it is personal. So I will answer the question directly and then I will fill in the background. I ended up doing my dissertation at Rockefeller under Joel Feinberg and Donald Davidson, and the dissertation was called "Justice and the Distribution of Accident Costs." Here's what happened. Like everybody else working in philosophy of law at the time, I wanted to write a dissertation about the philosophy of punishment. I went to see Joel Feinberg with my prospectus. He didn't quite laugh, but he said something along the lines of, "No matter how smart you are, or how creative you are, you are not going to have anything new or interesting to say about the philosophy of punishment." I didn't know if he was saying something about me or about the subject matter at the time. He gave me a book—*The Costs of Accidents*. It had just been published. This was the turning point in my academic life. He said, "Here is this book; read it and see if you are interested in it." It was this fortuitous moment in which he gave me this book. He said, "Maybe the interests that you have in responsibility and liability can go to working in an area that philosophers have not worked on—tort law rather than criminal law." So I read the book. I have to say in all honesty that it was incredibly intellectually exciting for me, but the writing style drove me nuts. The syntax was almost unreadable, but the ideas were incredible. I had never before thought about any of these subjects. I was still very impressionable, and I said to Feinberg, "Okay, I would love to work on this. I mean, I don't know what I would work on, but I'd love to work on it." He arranged at the time for me to take a torts class at New York University Law School. So I went to take the torts class, with a professor named Gidon Gottlieb, who soon left NYU for the University of Chicago. I don't believe having me as a student led to his fleeing NYU. I got interested in torts from that. I wrote my dissertation. The fundamental question I asked in the dissertation was philosophical. Namely, are there any principles of justice that apply to tort law, and what do they have to say about the allocation of the costs of accidents? Much of my dissertation was useless. I had two chapters where the discussions were pretty good. Much of the rest of it synthesized the work of others, and some of it was frankly filler. It's not as if I didn't try. I was working under some real intellectual constraints. After all, I had moved from the field of philosophy of criminal law, in which everyone who was intelligent had already written something, and the chances that I would find something new to say were small. However, the field was so well developed and structured that you didn't have to get in there and figure things out.

HACKNEY: You knew what the right set of questions were.

COLEMAN: Yes. And then I went into the philosophy of tort law, in which there was no writing by anybody and I had to define the field. That sounds more important than it is. I just meant that there was no guidance. I had to think about what would be philosophically interesting about it. I had to pick something, and make a case that this is philosophically interesting and important, and work from there. That became my research project. That's been one of my research projects for my whole academic life. The project has been less about answering particular questions than trying to figure out what the important questions are. So I have been working on it for a long, long time, not in the way in which you have one idea and you just keep churning it out. I don't think that accurately describes what I have been doing. More it's that I have been trying to reformulate, recapture, and mold the field for the purposes of understanding what is philosophically interesting and important about it, and what does law have to contribute to our understanding of responsibility and the place of liability and accountability in our lives. I take a lot of pride in growing with the field, and trying to be significantly involved in defining what the field is. But when I first got started I had no clue. I mean I was making it up as I went along.

HACKNEY: I want to get back to tort law and your theory about tort law a bit later. There seem to be two emphases in your work. One is subject-specific—tort law and other issues that you have raised. The other is general jurisprudence. So there are a whole set of questions that come into play. I want to talk about that, but before we even get to that point, as a matter of intellectual history, how would you define the connection between analytic philosophy (which is the philosophy that originates in Vienna and then burst onto the Anglo-American scene, Great Britain and on to America, post–World War II) and analytic jurisprudence?

COLEMAN: Well, there are probably a million different ways. But let me try one or two that hopefully will be illuminating. I tend to think of analytic philosophy, which as you said, tends to reach back into the history of philosophy, such that everybody is an analytic philosopher or what they did could be called analytic philosophy. Maybe it helps to think of it as part of the overall Enlightenment project, rather than just associate it with

Vienna and the logical positivist movement. The idea is that the universe is rationally comprehensible and available to us by reflecting on it. No doubt many of those who pursued the Enlightenment project thought that by grasping the world rationally we could ultimately control it or exert some control over it. More modestly, if we can ultimately understand the natural world and determine its rational structure, we might hope to understand our place within it. Part of that project was also the project of demystification—so it had demystification, a scientific epistemology, and the idea that ultimately our experience is rationally reconstructible. So for me, analytic philosophy is part of this more general Enlightenment project. Even if it turned out that nature lacked a deep rational structure, at least one could uncover that fact by use of analytic tools of inquiry. If we will suffer the fate of irrationality, at least we had the benefit of discovering that rationally.

This doesn't connect yet to my interest in analytic jurisprudence. The link for me had a more personal point of origin. As a college student I was particularly drawn to Kafka, who was himself both a lawyer and a Jew, and whose characters seemed constantly to burden themselves with guilt—largely for wrongs they were certain they had committed but whose content had escaped them. Free-floating, undifferentiated guilt has been a large part of my personal psychological and emotional life. I spent a good deal of my life seeking out objects to which it might attach!

Well, the thing about Kafka that intrigued me beyond the guilt was the lawyering and the crippling sense of inadequacy before figures and institutions of authority: the sense that you feel you must defend your life as it were—like the Albert Brooks film—at the same time that you realize both that you are powerless to do so and that your life is indefensible. What matters about law is all this, and especially authority. The nature of authority was especially puzzling to me. If an authority commands that you do *X*, then the thought is that you must do *X*; if the authority commands that you do not-*X*, then you must do not-*X*. This is truly independent of what *X* is. How can that be? Yet that is the nature of law and all these notions of powerlessness before authority, guilt for failure to comply with its demands are central to it in a personal way for me. So I had a personal set of reasons that explained why I was drawn to law; at the same time, I had the tools of analytic philosophy as my instruments of investigation. For some this would seem like a mismatch between subject matter and tool. But this is what it means to be an analytic philosopher of law. The deepest, most pervasive aspects of one's personal emotional life are treated at a distance with the surgeon's knife and the scientist's microscope in the hopes that we can ultimately grasp them and perhaps understand ourselves better for having done so—even if we may be unable to free ourselves from their grasp.

HACKNEY: Kafka is often associated with existentialism. There are different ways that people have responded to the questions he posed. One is scientific—let's get underneath and take it apart. The other is existentialist—psychological reflection on the meaning of life.

COLEMAN: I have a theory that most of the people that I knew who got into analytic philosophy began with existentialism. You read the existentialist literature and it is filled with these ideas that you begin to think about, and then you feel that it is not that precise. You are drawn to the themes, and the literary way in which they are presented, but those are very unsatisfying discussions ultimately—depending on what kind of temperament you have. You then look for mechanisms, tools, and methods for getting at it that are familiar to you, whether they involve math, science, or philosophy. They all felt the same in terms of their concern about priorities of argumentation, infrastructure, and so on. It's also a matter of seeing yourself as part of the subject matter from a slightly third-person perspective.

HACKNEY: It sounds very Cartesian.

COLEMAN: Yes, sort of. You are part of the subject matter. Rather than just phenomenologically importing your experience of things, you generalize about them. Basically, that was the analytical approach. It isn't so much reduction—reduction is a certain kind of project—but getting to the bottom, getting to the deep structure, rather than trying to reduce everything.

HACKNEY: I want to talk more about the analytic jurisprudence project in a bit. But let's go back a little bit in terms of your personal biography. As you marched your way through and had this series of intellectual encounters, obviously the world was marching along and history is marching along, so we have Vietnam, we have the civil rights movement, and other critical social events. Did any of those impact you in terms of the questions you wanted to ask or direction you wanted to follow?

COLEMAN: Well, I think the answer is yes, different things in different ways. Sometimes you get influenced by things directly and sometimes indirectly. So first, there was my hatred for the Vietnam War, for example. When I was an undergraduate in philosophy, the main concerns in ethics and political philosophy were meta-ethical. Hare was big. Stevenson was big. The meaning of "good" was sadly way too big. Rawls had not yet come onto the scene. In an odd sense, the Vietnam War created an environment for speculative or substantive political philosophy. In a way, the Vietnam War saved political philosophy. There was also the civil rights period. It was based on the idea that the government can contribute to the good. The question is to find the right technology. This led to a view of the law as part of the technology and tool kit; the government had to do good. That was the big influence on me. Whatever interests I had in the law, they were interests that could be framed in terms of what the law is capable of with regard to its capacity to solve social problems.

This is all speculation on my part, of course, but soon after World War II, philosophy retreated from substantive to meta-issues. Substantive political and legal philosophy receded in favor of ordinary language philosophy and the place of language. We were all taught to learn about the world by exploring the ways in which we spoke and thought about it. The late sixties and especially the seventies were pivotal in philosophy. The Vietnam War made substantive political philosophy relevant, and the civil rights movement sparked the rehabilitation of the idea that the state could be an engine of reform and that law could be a tool or instrument of reform. Ironically, it was a period of great distrust of government at the same time that it was a period of great optimism about what government—acting through law—could do. Just look at the leading philosophical works of the time. They were reformist manifestos. There were social problems and the state cannot retreat from working on them. The state through law could be an instrument of change and reform. There probably wasn't a law school course in the seventies in which the central question wasn't "What would individuals behind a veil of ignorance choose to do about *X*?," as if answering that question was a way of determining what the law should be or do.

The social problem that I happened to be interested in at the time was the one about accidents and misfortune. Ultimately I realized my deep, abiding interest was in misfortune and responsibility, but at the time I didn't differentiate between my interest in misfortune and in accidents or simply bad luck. I just became totally interested in the question of how can we reduce life's misfortune. I was largely optimistic about the state's capacity. That was the key idea for me. If Rawls and Calabresi were the spokespersons for optimism and reform, Nozick was the spokesperson for skepticism. The same governments that could fight unjustified wars, after all, were far more likely to take from individuals what they were entitled to without justification. The government is best left to enforce the framework within which autonomous agents interact with one another, rather than to substitute its judgment for theirs.

The libertarian had a number of partners on the economic side: from public choice economists, who viewed political elites as rent seekers, to welfare economists, who had an intellectual preference for markets. So my concerns about the foundations of economics, while motivated by technical issues in economic theory—such as the nature of efficiency—were also motivated by issues in political philosophy. The irony, of course, is that many of efficiency theorists in economics were also great believers in the state's capacity for action that is in the collective good; they were just very careful about the conditions under which the state is in the best position to help. In contrast, the libertarians were anything but confident in the state's capacities to do good. And so it was obvious to me from the outset that this alliance between libertarian free market political theorists and economic analysis was fragile at best—a view I believe that has been vindicated by the evidence.

I was quite an optimist about law and the possibility of reform, and in this way I was tremendously influenced by Calabresi. I was less concerned with optimal deterrence than he was, of course. For me the problem was misfortune. It was about looking to principles of social justice for allocating the cost of this overall social problem.

HACKNEY: I want to go back to the tort component. But first let's fill out the matter of jurisprudence: the tension between Hart and analytic jurisprudence, the critique of Hart by Dworkin, and then the philosophical back and forth with respect to the two camps in legal positivism.

COLEMAN: I got interested in Hart through Feinberg, who told me that he was more influenced by Hart than he was by anybody else. Except for one thing—Hart wrote a lot about the nature of law and Feinberg never wrote anything about the nature of law. He wrote about the problems in criminal law, about the nature of responsibility, many of the same things that Hart wrote about, but Feinberg never wrote anything in analytic jurisprudence—nothing. So that was a void. When I was a graduate student at Rockefeller Ronald Dworkin came to give some lectures. He had just left Yale and gone to Oxford, and he gave a series of lectures at Rockefeller that I found very interesting. They were abstract questions, like whether you should think of law as a kind of game defined by closed rules that determine outcomes. He associated with Hart the view of law as basically a closed system of rules that specified its own success or validity conditions. Oddly enough, I had been studying philosophy of science with

Earman at the time and we were discussing the disputes between Quine and Carnap. Carnap thought that any domain of discourse is made possible by a set of meaning rules that make the domain of discourse possible. Those meaning rules had a distinctive status. Whereas everything within the domain is subject to revision, the meaning rules are not, since they make the discourse possible. The meaning rules or meaning postulates could be altered or changed, but only if the domain defined by them fail us pragmatically. That is, if this way of approaching the world does not help us ultimately to make our way successfully through it—if they provide inadequate explanations and predictions. The rule of recognition plays the same role in defining the domain of law for Hart that meaning postulates play for Carnap. The rule of recognition makes law possible, and the rule of recognition in a particular community makes its legal system possible. So while you could make changes and revisions in the law, the rule of recognition had a different status. It could be changed only if the legal system, taken as a whole, fails at its practical tasks. Quine rejected the Carnap picture. The meaning postulates are in the mix in the same way that the discourse it makes possible are. And Dworkin can be seen as making the same objection to Hart. There is nothing qualitatively different about the rule of recognition. It, too, is in the mix. Law does not depend on a rule of recognition that stands apart in character from the domain of discourse it makes possible. For me, this is the animating insight of all of Dworkin's objections to legal positivism. I only realized the similarity between Quine and Dworkin many years later, when the point was made to me by my friend, the very distinguished tort theorist Ben Zipursky.

To my mind, Dworkin is a Quinian with respect to methodology, with one major difference. Quine is skeptical of the normative and Dworkin is anything but. And it is this connection to Quinian holism and pragmatism that motivates his deepest criticisms of Hart. Nevertheless, the objection is never made explicit in this way, and his earliest criticisms of Hart were more specifically focused on the way in which moral principles can figure in law. His view was that the positivist conception of law had no place for a common feature of legal practice—namely, the role that moral principles played as binding legal standards. I did not find this objection persuasive, but I had not fully formulated a response even when I wrote a book review of Dworkin's *Taking Rights Seriously*. My preliminary thoughts were expressed in this review that was published in the *California Law Review*. I sent him a copy of my review of the book before I published it. In my previous experience with him we got along very well. I was not as confident of my views in jurisprudence as I would become, largely because I had done no work in the field, confining my research to that point to tort theory. And finally I just thought it was the right thing to do. I was very young and naive. If I had made mistakes or been unfair, who better to let me know than the author. So I thought the respectful thing to do was for me to send him this review, which I did. And he sent me back a telegram; this is long before e-mail. He sent me back a telegram, which basically had the following form: "Received your review, stop; don't publish, stop; filled with mistakes, stop; long letter to follow." As I said, I was very young and impressionable, and prone to feel bad about myself under the best of circumstances. This telegram threw me completely. I was scared shitless. I really was. I then got the letter a couple of days later. I don't remember if it came from the United Kingdom or from Cambridge, where Dworkin was visiting at Harvard. The letter devastated me. To this day, I can repeat the first paragraph verbatim—more or less. It went something like this:

> Dear Jules,
>
> Since the publication of my book, there have been many reviews. Most of them are by political scientists and lawyers who have no idea about what I am trying to do. I was so pleased to hear that you were doing a review of my book, someone who is actually a well-trained philosopher and would understand what the book is actually arguing for. Imagine my surprise to find that you too don't understand the argument . . .

It didn't get any better after that. The letter continued with five pages of criticisms of my review. I barely had the strength to read it through from beginning to end. It took a few days before I could—a commentary on my lack of confidence no doubt. There were several points. Fortunately for me, there were a couple of issues I took up in the review on which I was confident I was right with which Dworkin had taken exception—to put it mildly. These concerned efficiency, and I knew that this was an area in which I was more likely expert than most philosophers. That was the best thing for me because it gave me some confidence that I wasn't wrong about everything! More important, it made me think that maybe there was an effort at intimidation going on, and that the letter I received wasn't all on the merits so to speak. But believe me, I was a nervous wreck about publishing the review, so I sent my review along with his letter to

Richard Wasserstrom and David Lyons, distinguished legal philosophers who had mentored me once I entered the profession. I asked them for an honest, objective evaluation of my review in the light of Dworkin's comments. They were very helpful. They gave me some suggestions, and told me that on balance the review was very fair and there are no doubt substantive issues on which individuals might reasonably disagree. I made some changes in light of their suggestions and published the review. That was the first time but by no means the last time that Dworkin has questioned my philosophical competence.

I resolved then to work in a sustained way to see if I could develop in detail how Hart might actually respond to Dworkin's criticisms of his positivism. And a few years later I published "Negative and Positive Positivism," in which I offered what I took to be Hart's line of defense to Dworkin's earliest criticisms of his view. It turned out that this essay was widely identified—by Hart among others—as "creating" a particular form of legal positivism. This form of legal positivism has come to be called "inclusive legal positivism." Believe me, I didn't realize that I was inventing a "new" form of positivism. I just thought that I was developing the kind of theory that Hart always had in mind. At roughly the same time, Joseph Raz was responding to Dworkin's objections differently. And I didn't know Raz at all, which is funny. He came to visit Rockefeller for an entire semester (or perhaps a year) right after I graduated. I wish I had the opportunity to study with him then, as we have become good friends since and I probably would have avoided a number of mistakes in my work that he could have saved me from. I can try to explain the difference between Raz's response and my response.

HACKNEY: The exclusive/inclusive distinction?

COLEMAN: Yes. Okay, now I'll go on record saying a couple of things. My response to Dworkin's objections to Hart and to positivism more generally was to say that the key idea behind legal positivism is not whether moral principles should be legally binding; it's by virtue of their features that they are legally binding. If they are legally binding by virtue of them being practiced by officials treating them as legally binding, in contrast to their character or content, then that's all positivism requires. At the foundation of law is a certain practice among officials. As I would put it now, the important feature of this practice is that officials take a certain attitude toward their behavior. Hart called this attitude the internal point of view. The right way to see this is to understand officials as taking a certain point of view toward their behavior. That point of view is normative. They regard facts about what they are doing as having a kind of normative significance, reflected in what Hart called the internal point of view. If in their behavior they treat certain moral principles as binding legal standards and they adopt the "normative" attitude toward that behavior, then those moral principles are authoritative legal standards. The internal point of view is a way of regarding certain facts; it is to regard them as having a certain normative significance, which is itself spelled out in behavior—the behavior of justification and criticism. If judges have a practice of regarding certain moral principles in this way, then that is enough from the positivist point of view to count those principles as among the set of binding legal standards. That is exactly what makes other authoritative standards law according to the positivist, so why wouldn't it be good enough for moral principles as well. So Dworkin is, I argued, just wrong that positivism cannot account for the fact that moral principles can be legally binding. This is the position that is ultimately called inclusive legal positivism. I did not call it inclusive legal positivism. I called it incorporationism, because my thought was that the law can incorporate morality in certain kinds of ways. My response to Dworkin was, look, you say that moral principles can be legally binding, here is the way that they can be that is compatible with positivism.

Raz's response had two parts. First, you, Dworkin, say moral principles are binding, and you draw the inference that therefore they are part of the law and thus binding because they are law. Your mistake is in thinking that because something is legally binding on officials it is part of the law. The fact is that there are many things that can be binding that are not part of the law. The law of one jurisdiction can be binding in a case litigated in another jurisdiction without therefore becoming part of the law of that jurisdiction. The law of France can be binding in a dispute in the United States without therefore being part of U.S. law as a result. So Raz's distinction was between something being binding on officials and being binding because it is part of the law. This is an excellent point, and there is no way around it. On the other hand, it is not enough to show that moral principles are not binding as law. It shows only that one cannot infer from the fact that they are binding that they are law. Therefore Raz needed another argument for his strong conclusion that moral principles cannot be part of the law or criteria of legality. His argument rested on his claim that law purports to be a legitimate authority. I said moral principles can be law in a way that is compatible with positivism. He said they could not be law because their being law would be incompatible with law's claim to being a legitimate authority. His view ultimately came to be called exclusive legal positivism and my view became inclusive legal positivism.

Then there was this debate about which one of these is the correct form of positivism, which went on for far too long. I have to say, this has a scholastic feel about it. It's a very in-house debate. There is a part of it that is very useful and valuable, and that part is, what is the relationship between morality and law? That's a big question, and it was illuminated from a certain angle by this debate. But which one is the real legal positivism, I mean, to tell the truth, was of no interest whatsoever to me. And whatever interest it was to me, which was very little, it was of much less interest to Raz. I found out, maybe a few years ago, when I went to Europe to give a series of lectures, that in Spain and Italy this is the main debate, and that my side is winning. The irony is that when I went to give these lectures I had to tell them that I had no interest in this debate. I didn't care if my position was winning or not. All I was trying to do was to mark out a position that needed to be addressed. I have never defended it as the correct view of law or positivism about law. In fact, to be honest, whereas I never thought that the objections to it by exclusive legal positivists were telling, I always felt theirs was the more attractive view. I have had a wonderful relationship over the years with Raz. In my mind he is simply the best jurisprudent of our time. I am sure I kept the debate alive with him so I could guarantee being mentioned in the same sentence with him.

I think that Dworkin is the most creative and most imaginative legal philosopher of our time. I also think that he has drawn the deepest and most interesting and important connections between law and political philosophy. Ironically, perhaps Dworkin is more responsible than anyone for making Hart relevant because he kept him alive through his criticisms of him. I have the utmost intellectual respect for Dworkin as a brilliant and creative philosopher with wonderful ideas, and Raz has the highest intellectual integrity and the best quality of argument. I see myself as lucky to be named in the same group as the two of them. So Raz and I have had a very good relationship over the years, and Dworkin and I have had a much cooler relationship over the years, so much so that for years and years it was actually very disturbing to me personally.

HACKNEY: That makes it even harder, given the level of respect—makes it more difficult.

COLEMAN: I mean, he wrote a review of my book *The Practice of Principle* in which he was extremely disdainful of my views and my arguments. It was months before I could read the review from beginning to end. It hurt me tremendously, and what hurt me even more was the following. The review came out a couple of days before a conference in legal philosophy was to take place at Yale Law School. Along with a handful of others, I had been putting this conference together on a yearly basis to help mentor young people in the field. I think it was around the tenth year of the conference. A participant in the conference brought about thirty or so copies of the review to hand out to others. I couldn't imagine why anyone who had read the review would do that other than to try and hurt me. It certainly wasn't to display how mean-spirited and wrongheaded Dworkin was. This was an incredibly hostile act. In any case, it was doubly troubling because among the many things Dworkin accused me of in the review was organizing, along with Raz, a guild of young positivists by publishing the work in a journal and holding conferences for people in the field. I viewed that as mentoring and not poisoning the youth of Athens. And of course it was at one of these very conferences that the reviews of my book were being handed out. It should be obvious how hurtful the entire episode was. The fact is that I had invited Dworkin to give a talk to this conference for ten years and he never accepted our invitation. My belief was that along with Raz he was the most important person in the field, and I wanted the many young people in the field to have some exposure to him so that they might be as motivated by his brilliance as I had been. Unfortunately, he was never able to attend.

In the review, he also said that positivists don't really care about substantive issues in law. The irony here was that the first third of my book was devoted to tort law. This ironic fact was pointed out in a review of the book in the *Times Literary Supplement*, which chided Dworkin for making a claim about legal positivism's lack of interest in substantive law in a book a large part of which was devoted to substantive law. What can I say? To be honest, when I finally was able to read the review from beginning to end, I found the quality of his objections disappointing. I was given the opportunity to respond, but I just didn't know where to begin. More important, I figured that the field would sort it out—which it has.

HACKNEY: I'm glad to hear your discussion of the exclusive/inclusive debate, because in reading it as a non-insider to the philosophy of law it was a bit perplexing. You have broadened your view from this narrow philosophical issue. You've adopted the position of philosophical pragmatism. I am interested in the relationship between philosophical pragmatism and inclusive legal positivism—if there is any relationship, that's one question. The other is, having taken on the mantle of pragmatism, you say that you are not a faddish intellectual latching on to Richard Rorty as the font of pragmatism, and that you are specifically taking on the mantle of Quine. Can you just flesh that whole story out?

COLEMAN: Sure, I will do the best I can. Let's go back to the Quine/Carnap debate and the debate between Dworkin and Hart. For me, it has to do with how to think about the rule of recognition. There are two central claims of pragmatism that I am inclined to emphasize. One is holism, and the other is revisionism. The holism can be illustrated by the idea that we should take our beliefs as a whole and not so much individually. Everything is connected to everything else. It's really just that some connections are weaker or stronger than others. The revisionism can be illustrated by taking our beliefs as a whole, and then noticing that we come across some evidence that appears incompatible with the set of beliefs we have. The question is: Should we incorporate the evidence and thus give up or alter some of our beliefs, or do we refuse to accept the evidence—explain it away? If we incorporate it, then we have to alter our beliefs. We have to revise. But how do we revise; what do we alter or abandon? That is going to depend on which relationships among our beliefs have the strongest connections to one another. In other words, which can we give up to incorporate the new belief while holding on to the greatest number that fit together best. By that I mean which ones are most important to supporting or justifying the others? Which are more central from a justificatory and explanatory point of view to others? We revise by doing the least damage to the web of beliefs and the inferential and confirmational relationships among them.

The key idea is that none of our beliefs are in principle beyond revision in the light of new evidence. Everything is, so to speak, in the mix. Now I take it that Hart thought the rule of recognition was not in the mix. It was beyond revision because it was the claim that made the very idea of law possible. It was like Carnap's meaning postulates. For Hart, like Carnap, all the rules made possible by the rule of recognition were in the mix and subject to revision and change. With a rule of recognition in place, we can talk about what norms are valid law, but we can't talk about whether the rule of recognition is valid. That's why it's like the meaning postulate. It's what allows the rest of the game to go on.

Now, one way of understanding Dworkin is to see him as Quine in the Quine/Carnap debate. He is saying in effect that if you are a real holist and pragmatist in this sense of the term, then you are committed to the view that everything is in the mix. Nothing is beyond revision in the light of "new evidence." And so on. This is what I thought Dworkin and I shared;

a philosophical methodology that is holist and revisionist, in which nothing is immune to revision—including the rule of recognition. So if I were to believe in Hart's rule of recognition, which I don't, I would not think of it as a rule that makes law possible and thus beyond revision in the normal way. I would be more likely to view it as a core belief at the very center of the law—something that we would be reluctant to revise or alter because it is so central to so many other beliefs that we have by virtue of it. But it would not be beyond revision or change. And that I think is really what Dworkin is after when he rejects the positivist picture of the rule of recognition. And for me, this is something one sees most clearly within a pragmatist way of thinking about things. The rule of recognition is not a rule that is a convention that must be accepted in order for law to be possible. It is itself part of the mix.

HACKNEY: Subject to revision . . .

COLEMAN: Right. So, I thought that this is what Dworkin and I really shared. I'm a holist. I tend to think about the legal system as a whole. And I also believe that everything is in the mix and subject to revision. Some rules are more inferentially important than other rules. Nowadays in law schools especially, pragmatism stands for something else altogether that is foreign to what all sorts of philosophical pragmatists believe. It is now a largely skeptical or cynical view that embraces subjectivity over objectivity and resists the possibility of truth—and more. This is sadly the consequence of ignorance and unreflective absorption of the worst of Richard Rorty's work. Then there are others in law schools who claim the mantle of pragmatism who are influenced by Richard Posner's self-identification as a pragmatist. When Posner calls judges pragmatists he is emphasizing a view of them as exercising suitably nuanced common sense. Of course, on his view, common sense amounts to economic efficiency. The legal actor is best thought of as a pragmatist, not in the sense of a skeptic about truth and objectivity, but in the sense of someone exercising practical judgment, muddling through as best he can, keeping the boat afloat and steering it through hazards that threaten to sink it. Of course, in order to do this he must be something of an economist—without the math. The Rortyites in the legal academy are philosophical—just bad at it. The Posnerians don't even pretend to be philosophical. If anything they are anti-philosophical. I am trying to save pragmatism in the legal academy from both—with very little effect so far.

HACKNEY: I don't think Posner really views himself as a philosophical pragmatist. He thinks of himself as a pragmatic judge.

COLEMAN: Posner has a discussion in *Overcoming Law* questioning the value of contributions from professional philosophers, including me, to legal policy. Posner's criticism reflects the modern fixation among law professors. If your work doesn't have a policy recommendation or doesn't include ten pages on how the law should change or on how judges should decide cases, it is of no interest. It's not practical. So philosophical pragmatism is not practical in this sense and of no interest. Sorry, but all the policy recommendations that fill the pages of law review articles are by and large useless. They are in every paper and no decision maker anywhere is going to pay any attention to the vast majority of them. And, by the way, there is nothing wrong with trying to understand what we do, how we do it, and who we are as a result. Pragmatism as a theory is not supposed to be practical; it's theory.

HACKNEY: I just want to see if I can flesh out the distinction between your view of Rorty versus Quine. Is it really more of a sensibility? Because Rory says, essentially . . .

COLEMAN: It's about politics.

HACKNEY: Well, eventually he says it's about politics, but before he gets to that point he says that the truth is revisable; he's thinking about truth in a way that kind of sounds like what you said about the rule of recognition.

COLEMAN: I think that Rorty is not always serious. There is the Rorty for the public and there is the Rorty for serious investigation. I think he moves back and forth between philosophy as an activity of the mind engaged in by professionals, and philosophy as a form of democracy, a kind of politics. He was a public figure and entitled to present himself as he liked. The problem is that the adoring academic public of second-rate thinkers couldn't tell the difference between his serious and, let's just say, less serious work—and he was unwilling to sort it out for them. The result has not been especially good for many disciplines. He has not been as detrimental to various humanities departments as have been the French philosophical theorists, but there are times he gives them a run for their money.

HACKNEY: Now I want to talk a bit about tort law, which is obviously near and dear to both of our hearts. Can you lay out your view of corrective justice and tort law, and how you think it works within tort law?

COLEMAN: I've had so many different views about corrective justice; it's hard to say that I have just one view about it, because I have been thinking about it for so long. If your career spans a long enough time and you think about a subject for a considerable length of time, your views are more likely than not to have undergone some considerable revision. Speaking for myself, my views about corrective justice, the nature of tort law, and the relationship between the two have been and remain in constant flux. Whether I should allow myself the conceit that my views have merely evolved or instead admit that they have changed significantly is of no real interest to me. The reason is that I have spent most of my career trying to identify what the important problems are and looking for a way to formulate the right questions. To do that I have put a variety of positions out there. Hopefully, in doing so I exercised intellectual integrity, which is to say that I put out the best version of my current thinking. After that, I was anxious to see if the views presented could stand up to criticism and to see if they stimulated others to have a go at the same problems.

When I was in college I had an English teacher whose name I cannot recall just now. He was extremely influential on me. He used to say that the hardest thing to do was to ask the right questions. Those questions are good because the answers to them are genuinely illuminating. So if I had to choose between giving good answers and formulating good questions, I guess I would choose the latter. I knew an excellent philosopher who befriended me early in my career named Sidney Morgenbesser. When former students of his collected essays for a book in his honor, they titled it *How Many Questions?* I like that. Now, of course, Morgenbesser was also a rabbi I believe, so I hope that my fixation on questions is not the result simply of my being Jewish and having a religious upbringing. If you've seen the movie *A Serious Man*, you know that no one has the answers really. It is enough to aspire to ask the right questions. And to ask good questions you have to have a certain creativity in thinking about issues, and a willingness to attack a problem in a number of different ways and to remain open to rethinking your views.

If I go into your house and I carelessly break a vase, the question is what should I do now. One helpful way to think about the problem is this. I had a reason to be careful when I went into your house, or onto your property. I didn't comply with that reason when I broke the vase. So far, so good. Now what has happened to that reason that had counseled me to be careful not to break anything of yours? It would seem odd to say that the reason that should have guided me before no longer guides me now. That would imply that I could make a reason not apply to me simply by ignoring or acting contrary to its demands. I could eliminate its normative impact by not attending to its normative impact. That doesn't seem right. So instead we might say that whatever it was in morality that counseled me to take care not to break your vase, *ex ante*, persists and applies to me still. It just counsels or demands different actions now that I have broken the vase. Arguably, we might say that it now counsels that I do the next best thing, which, say, would be to make repair by replacing the vase, and so on. The duty to make matters right or to make amends is a part of ordinary morality. Our duties to make repair are in a sense part of our understanding of what our duties to take care amount to.

Now it would be seductive to think of tort law as just an institutional form of this feature of ordinary morality; and to see corrective justice as no more than calling attention to this feature of the connection in morality between our duties of care and our duties of repair. And many people have interpreted my view of corrective justice in just this way. But this is not my view. No doubt, it probably was among my views at some point, but it is not my considered view. For me, corrective justice is not a principle of ordinary interpersonal morality. It is a principle of social justice on a par with the principles of distributive and retributive justice. It is not about what we owe one another in morality. Instead it is about how we collectively (as a group) should respond to certain kinds of misfortune and bad luck—that owing to mischievous behavior. So when I say that tort law is justified by, and is an instance of, corrective justice, I mean to be saying something about what the state speaking in the name of all of us believes is an appropriate response to misfortunes owing to human agency. It is not a claim about what we have moral duties to one another to do. It is easy to miss this point, because in our tort system the way we think that misfortunes owing to human agency should be dealt with is by conferring a right on the victim to impose a duty of repair on his injurer—and this is very similar to the response that we think is called for by ordinary morality. Corrective justice tells us we must respond as a collective and that we must do so appropriately, but it does not tell us exactly what forms of response are appropriate. Tort law is our response and because it is, it is not only justified by corrective justice, but it also provides some of the content of corrective justice itself.

HACKNEY: Yes. It's interesting because I play a game with incoming students. We have an orientation day when prospective students come with their parents. Part of it is a mock-class. I hand out the *Palsgraf* case that was decided by Benjamin Cardozo.[1] It's a tough case. I'll just run through the facts, and ask the audience what their moral intuition is based on the facts. We then engage in a dialogue about what tort law says about it, and the ways in which basic intuition feeds into, if not the tort law rule, the kind of issues around which the judges in tort law have to grapple. There really is a close connection between moral intuition and legal rules even with people just "off the street." I get a lot of interesting responses from the parents, many of whom have no interest in law. However, they have experience with respect to the basic issues that we talk about in torts.

COLEMAN: Let's talk about Cardozo and *Palsgraf*. If you think Cardozo is on to something, if Cardozo is right, what is he saying about Mrs. Palsgraf? Can she successfully sue the Long Island Railroad? She is claiming, in effect, that the railroad acted wrongly and she was harmed. We all agree that the Long Island Railroad behaved badly. We all agree that she suffered a loss, or an injury, that is of some fundamental importance to her. And we all believe, no one earth rejects the idea, that she suffered the loss she suffered because of their misconduct. Cardozo says this is not enough. Now, what reason on earth could there be for why she can't prevail against them? Cardozo's answer to that is that in order for her to recover there must be some preexisting, normatively significant relationship between them that they failed to live up to the terms of. That preexisting relationship is that they had a duty of care to her—not that they behaved badly. If she is to have a claim that they owe her now, it must be by virtue of her having a claim that they owed her something before. It can only be the failure to meet that obligation that can ground any right she has against them now. A duty to her is the right kind of normative relationship; in contrast, causation is not. In other words, the fact that their bad behavior caused her harm is not the right kind of reason on which a claim to repair can be grounded. What Cardozo is saying is that only a breach of duty to Mrs. Palsgraf can ground her claim to repair. So when I say that tort law is a system of corrective justice, I am claiming among other things that tort law spells out a conception of corrective justice. And that means that the dispute between Cardozo and Andrews can be viewed as follows. Is it enough for corrective justice that a loss result causally from mischievous conduct that one has a duty not to engage in, or does corrective justice require more? Does it require that the losses that are the concern of justice are ones that involve the breach of a duty that category of persons owed to those whose security is put at risk by their undertaking? Arguably, Andrews holds the first view, Cardozo the second. There is at least a third view as well: that it is enough that there be loss, wrongdoing, and a causal relationship between the two. No duty to anyone in particular or to everyone in general is required. Just bad behavior, causation, and loss resulting from the bad behavior. This is the view of law and economics more generally. Let me explain.

Law and economics holds that externalities are the social costs of one's conduct, and that in order to get people to behave efficiently they must be made to internalize the externalities of their activities. They identify externalities with causal upshots, and so it is no surprise that economically inclined torts professors have argued in favor of getting rid of the duty requirement in tort law. On their view, if a victim cannot recover unless he is owed a duty, then some of the costs of the bad behavior will be borne by victims. This is what happened to Mrs. Palsgraf. Cardozo says the LIRR does not owe her a duty and so she has to bear the costs of their bad behavior. That means that some of the social costs of LIRR's behavior are not going to be internalized. They will be externalized onto Palsgraf. From a law and economics point of view, that is a problem.

But this is all wrong. In my view, the very idea of an externality presupposes the distinction between what is a cost of my activity and what is a cost of your activity. And what is a cost of which activity depends on what duties of care we owe to each other. So it is duty, not causation, that defines the notion of an externality. I am certain that Coase saw this, though he got there in strange ways and said a few foolish things along the way—for example, his view that causal relationships are reciprocal. This is idiotic. But he had the deep idea right. The problem is that many law and economics people who have followed him have missed the deep insight and have been drawn to the more infelicitous claims. You can't get rid of duty in torts, because without it there is no concept of an externality. They see it the opposite way. You have to get rid of the idea of duty in order to internalize externalities. Absolutely backward.

HACKNEY: That's a good segue into the distinction between corrective justice, and law and economics. *Palsgraf* is a good case, doctrinally, to sort it through. I had the opposite reaction to *Palsgraf*, but the reaction might have the same basic premise. My reaction to *Palsgraf* was that it could go either way doctrinally: duty, Cardozo's formulation, or proximate cause, Andrews's formulation. But it seems to me that Andrews makes a lot more sense when he talks about proximate cause, as opposed to the way Cardozo talks about duty. There is a kind of mystical quality to how Cardozo talks about duty and orbit. It really makes no sense. You read the case, and she's outside the orbit. What does that mean? Is it only twenty-five feet away from the scene of the initial incident? Now your point seems to be that the economists are wrong, and they should think about duty. They can take into account externalities, basically Andrews's facts and circumstances analysis, but duty is prior. Are you saying that you can take externalities into account in defining duty, or that duty defines externalities?

COLEMAN: The question is what duty do you have to another person, and what are the risks. When cows are next to corn, you can expect that they will trample corn. The question is whether the costs associated with cows trampling corn are costs of ranching or costs of farming. And that is going to be a function of whether the rancher has a duty to keep his cows from trampling corn, or whether the farmer has the duty to protect his corn from trampling cows. That issue is not resolved by the causal question of whether cows trample corn. They do, but now what. You need some normative notion to define what the externalities are. Coase drew the right conclusion from the wrong premise. He said that because the causal relationship is reciprocal we cannot conclude who should pay by citing the cause of the harm. But of course the causal relationship is not reciprocal. The reason we cannot decide who should pay has nothing to do with the causation question, because the issue is normative, not factual. We need to know who has which duties to whom. And when we figure out who owes what to whom, then we figure out what the costs are of each activity. So I think that the notion of externalities is a derivative notion. It's derivative from the notion of duty.

HACKNEY: How do we figure out the duty question?

COLEMAN: What we owe to one another is partially determined by our settled practices and developed through conventions and common law adjudication. We don't derive it a priori in all its full content from first principles. Of course first principles—and for me the first principles are those of fairness in the distribution of risk—provide guidance and constraint, but the particular duties we have are fleshed out by practice. That is a big part of what I mean in calling my most recent book on this topic *The Practice of Principle*. That is the key to my pragmatism.

HACKNEY: So do you think that Andrews had set the correct standard?

COLEMAN: I wish I could answer that question meaningfully, but I can't. It depends in part on how you read Andrews. If he thought that your liability was restricted by duties you owed, then he was half right because he may have been wrong about the scope of those to whom you owe a duty. On the other hand, it is possible to read him as saying that you are liable for the foreseeable consequences of your negligence where your negligence does not invoke the idea of a duty. Then in my mind he is all wrong. Was Cardozo right? Yes. Was he right about to whom you owe a duty exactly? I am a bit less sure of that.

HACKNEY: That actually might get back to your initial interest in criminal law, because there is a way in which when we look at even the tort law casebooks trespass gets shoved into property. I'm actually eliminating some trespass material in my torts class because the property people are talking about trespass. I don't really need to get into it. Battery—torts professors kind of talk about it, but they are not really interested in it. The core really is accidents and products liability law.

COLEMAN: This is one of the ways in which theorizing about a subject changes the subject. I am not here to offer resistance to changing the subject matter, because it may well be that the way I think about tort law will not accurately describe tort law ten years from now. Many of my critics (some of whom really don't understand the view) would argue that my theory of tort law does not apply to any actual tort practice ever. Or they will be more kind and say it applied to tort law 150 years ago; the less kind will say that my theories of tort law have never applied to any tort law other than the tort law that exists only in my mind. I think my view in fact applies to tort law today. But many believe that the core of tort law is accident law and the question is how did that happen? My tort law, they will say, is the tort law of *A* hits *B*; it is the tort law of battery and trespass. But modern tort law is the tort law of accidents. Are they right? To me they confuse the most common tort with the paradigm tort—the paradigm tort is the tort that most vividly illustrates what is distinctive of torts. The most common tort is an accident. How did tort law come to be accident law? The answer is in Calabresi then Shavell; *The Costs of Accidents* then *Economic Analysis of Accident Law*, respectively. The dominant law and economics theory identifies tort law with accident law and ultimately everyone else does as well—however confused doing so may be. The theory of the law helped to change what people take the law to be.

HACKNEY: There was an interesting moment, getting back to law and economics, in 1980. I think it's one of the most fascinating intellectual moments in legal theory: the *Hofstra Law Review* symposium on law and economics. It essentially constituted the demise of a certain standing for law and economics. That is the way that I read it historically. But it is also interesting in terms of the players aligning with each other versus Posner. In particular, there were the critical legal studies players—Duncan Kennedy, Mort Horwitz, and Edwin Baker. (Baker was not quite as ensconced in the critical legal studies camp but definitely a fellow traveler.) Then there were the non-crits: Ronald Dworkin, Guido Calabresi, and you. They were all in it together, and then there is Posner by himself.

COLEMAN: My criticism of law and economics has two parts: one entirely internal to law and economics, and one having to do with the value of efficiency and the justification of the state's using its coercive powers to enforce policies on the grounds that they are efficient. The more recent version of my objection is articulated in my criticism of the absolutely awful book by Shavell and Kaplow, *Fairness versus Welfare*. Actually, there are some very interesting discussions in the book within an economic point of view that anyone could benefit from reading and studying, but the overall argument that is designed to show why efficiency is the uniquely appropriate standard for evaluating the law is frankly abysmal.

HACKNEY: That's very interesting because Duncan Kennedy has a devastating critique of them as well.

COLEMAN: I won't repeat the argument of my review here. It is one of the few things I have written over the course of my career that I still believe stands up to the test of time, and I remain willing to encourage others to read it. But there is an objection I don't discuss much in the review that I would like to reinforce here. Kaplow and Shavell suggest that if there is an evolutionary argument in favor of our commitment to moral principles or ideals, that fact is enough to explain away the moral force of these principles. In their view the naturalistic or causal story deflates the normative one by showing that our moral principles have a naturalistic basis. To show the rationality of morality or to show that morality has a naturalistic foundation is to vindicate morality, not to undermine it. I much admire Kaplow and Shavell and their work more generally. They are very bright, and they are experts at what they do. This isn't what they do. There was a great deal of discussion when the book first came out, but it has proved to have no staying power. That seems right to me.

HACKNEY: What's your view of Posner's philosophical defense of law and economics?

COLEMAN: Some may think that my aim was to "defeat" law and economics, but that's not true. The fact is that concern for efficiency is part of justice. My aim has always been to improve law and economics. To the extent I had a more aggressive ambition, it was to stop the intellectual imperialism of law and economics. My problem with both Posner, and Kaplow and Shavell is their disdain for philosophy, which they express in different ways. Posner's disdain is expressed in his dismissal of it; Kaplow and Shavell's disdain is reflected in their efforts to do it. If any of them had taken half the time with philosophy that I have taken with economics, and law and economics in particular, I would not have to say these things about their work or their attitudes toward philosophy. But forget that and let me explain why I am committed to the importance of efficiency, and that is because in my view efficiency is an aspect of justice. I think that Dworkin has a somewhat similar view, though his reasons for thinking so are different than mine. So let me illustrate what I have in mind.

Take corrective justice. I think that corrective justice is the set of principles that specify appropriate responses to misfortunes owing to human agency. Surely among the appropriate responses to misfortune owing to human agency is to reduce the incidence of the behavior that causes it, another is rectifying the losses caused by it. So reduction in the incidence of the source of misfortune is part of an appropriate response in justice to misfortunes owing to human agency. So this effort by law and economics people to narrowly understand justice as "distribution" or as "equity" is misguided, and the disdain for justice more broadly is necessarily self-defeating—since insofar as efficiency is valuable, it is because of its connection to justice.

HACKNEY: What's your general opinion of critical theory, particularly critical legal studies and critical race theory?

COLEMAN: Now, I tend to think that critical theorists, by and large, have a nihilistic, anti-rationalistic, political-ideological account of things. So my problem with them is that we may be strange bedfellows when it comes to criticizing various people, but we part company methodologically in what we believe the aspirations of philosophy should be. I typically do not like projects that are just negative, because negative projects run out of energy. They have to turn into something positive. Critical legal studies died because nihilism only takes you so far. You have to have something that you stand for as opposed to all the things that you stand against. I think that the claim that it is all politics is too quick. I do think, of course, that there are political dimensions to legal problems. I am not naive. But it is just a mistake to reduce debates about the content of various proposals to political disputes about the interests of the relevant parties.

Critical theorists, as a general matter, have reduced questions about the way the world is to questions about why we say what we say about the way the world is; and they reject out of hand the view that the way the world is provides the best explanation of why I say that it is that way. They look to political or other interests I might have that would explain the views that I hold. There must be cultural reasons or self-interested reasons or the like. For me, belief is the sort of thing that aims at the truth; and for the vast majority of what I assert, I assert it because I believe that it is true.

Truth is the criterion of correctness for belief, whereas if you take critical theorists seriously, you would think that the criterion of correctness for belief must have something to do with interest, wealth, race, or what have you. More generally, critical theorists are prone to philosophical exaggeration and confusion, as when they say things like facts are socially constructed. Money is socially constructed. Facts in general are not. I don't have a strong view about critical race theory. My problems are with the philosophical methodology and philosophical theories that are thought to go hand in hand with these critical theories: relativism, agnosticism about truth and objectivity, and so on. I recommend that everyone read Paul Boghossian's book *Fear of Knowledge*. It's a primer that everyone drawn to the soft social sciences should read.

Here's the problem as I see it. The social sciences for the past two decades, at least, have been caught in a methodological dilemma. The successful disciplines adopt a rational choice perspective. Actually they adopt two methodological commitments that are different: methodological individualism and rational choice. The social sciences that don't adopt the rational choice approach have fallen out of favor and have been drawn to the hermeneutic and narrativist methodology of the literature departments. They view the rational choice method as dehumanizing in a way, and they carry the mantle of humanizing the social sciences—but at too high a cost, for at the least they have lost the "science" in social science. They reject the possibility of objectivity and truth, and to that extent have lost their claim to being a science at all. In contrast, the rational choice approach is largely "externalistic" and individualistic. They have lost their capacity to understand the "social" in social science. They would deny this, of course, but I would argue otherwise. I have taught in the philosophy of the social sciences and would be happy to expand on these claims at another time, but as someone committed to the social sciences all I can hope for is improvements in both methodologies that currently dominate the fields.

HACKNEY: Obviously you think that philosophy is a worthy field, but when you look at the landscape today it really looks like all of the flowers are blooming. When I attended Yale Law School between 1986 and 1989, it seemed to me, and perhaps it was a function of the fact that I was an economics major, that you could not have a conversation about certain aspects of law without going through law and economics. It was the central paradigm. Everyone, no matter where you came out, had to deal with law and economics. I don't think that's the case now. I think it's been demystified. So there are a lot of "law and" projects out there. What fields do you look at as being interesting?

COLEMAN: I think law schools have to plant some of the seeds, building better relationships with other parts of the university. I don't know what the promising fields are or will be. If I had to bet, I would bet on law and cognitive science. Law and philosophy will be strong again, and law and social science is the future. The near-term future of social science will be methodological individualism but with a more sophisticated view of human psychology. This will eventually find its way into the law. The legal academy in this way is a consumer of other fields, not a producer.

HACKNEY: I have this same conversation at the end of all the interviews; it's the same basic story. As part of the generation that is in their thirties and forties, I don't think that there is absolutely anyone in their thirties and forties that you have to encounter to say that you are conversant as a legal academic. There are schools of thought that you have to encounter, given particular subjects of expertise. If you are an expert in tort law you have to grapple with law and economics. But if you are doing something else, then you don't necessarily need to. We have experts within narrowly defined fields talking to one another. They are very teched up. So I'm sure it's very difficult for someone to get an appointment at Yale without having a PhD degree. They are very teched up, and they talk among themselves, but they don't have to listen, or be listened to, with regard to others. There is going to have to be something out there that forces the conversation among everyone. That's what law and economics did; it's what legal realism did.

COLEMAN: Nice point. But keep an eye on the Yale Law School. We have always been at the forefront of legal education and we mean to stay that way. Don't be surprised if we introduce a PhD in law. If law is to be an academic field worthy of the best work in the field, it will demand its own PhD. Not a JSD but an academic PhD. It will come and it will begin at Yale. The reason I love being at Yale is exactly that. It is all about changing and deepening the conversation. Thanks, James.

NOTE

1. *Palsgraf* is a famous case in which the victim was injured on a railroad platform by a falling scale. The scale fell as a result of a package exploding that was dislodged from the arms of a passenger as he was being assisted onto a train by railroad employees. Benjamin Cardozo, a much-revered common law judge, ruled that the railroad did not owe a duty to the victim. *Palsgraf v. Long Island Railroad Co.*, 248 N.Y. 339 (N.Y. 1928).

INDEX

About the Author

James R. Hackney, Jr., is Professor of Law at the Northeastern University School of Law and author of *Under Cover of Science: American Legal-Economic Theory and the Quest for Objectivity*.